Wildflowers

The TIME LIFE
Complete ☀ Gardener

Wildflowers

By the Editors of Time-Life Books
ALEXANDRIA, VIRGINIA

The Consultants

Robert S. Hebb is a horticultural consultant, garden designer, author, and frequent lecturer on gardening. He received a diploma of horticulture from the Royal Botanic Gardens in Kew, then became assistant horticulturist for the Arnold Arboretum of Harvard University, where he wrote the pioneering book *Low Maintenance Perennials.* Hebb has been director of horticulture for the Mary Flagler Cary Arboretum of the New York Botanical Garden and executive director of the Lewis Ginter Botanical Garden in Richmond, Virginia. The recipient of the Massachusetts Horticultural Society Silver Medal for leadership in American horticulture, Hebb is the author of numerous works on low-maintenance gardening and oversees several estate gardens in the Richmond area.

F. M. Oxley is senior botanist and education programs manager at the National Wildflower Research Center in Austin, Texas, a nonprofit educational and research organization devoted to the preservation and use of native wildflowers, grasses, trees, and shrubs in the American landscape. Ms. Oxley oversees public outreach programs, organizes and leads ecological tours in the United States and abroad, lectures frequently, and writes for the newsletter *Wildflower* and other National Wildflower Research Center publications.

Time-Life Books is a division of **TIME LIFE INC.**

PRESIDENT and CEO: John M. Fahey Jr.

TIME-LIFE BOOKS

Managing Editor: Roberta Conlan

Director of Design: Michael Hentges
Director of Editorial Operations: Ellen Robling
Director of Photography and Research: John Conrad Weiser
Senior Editors: Russell B. Adams Jr., Dale M. Brown, Janet Cave, Lee Hassig, Robert Somerville, Henry Woodhead
Special Projects Editor: Rita Thievon Mullin
Director of Technology: Eileen Bradley
Library: Louise D. Forstall

PRESIDENT: John D. Hall

Vice President, Director of Marketing: Nancy K. Jones
Vice President, Director of New Product Development: Neil Kagan
Associate Director, New Product Development: Quentin S. McAndrew
Marketing Director, New Product Development: Wendy A. Foster
Vice President, Book Production: Marjann Caldwell
Production Manager: Marlene Zack
Quality Assurance Manager: Miriam Newton

THE TIME-LIFE COMPLETE GARDENER

Editorial Staff for *Wildflowers*

SERIES EDITOR: Janet Cave
Deputy Editors: Sarah Brash, Jane Jordan
Administrative Editor: Roxie France-Nuriddin
Art Directors: Kathleen Mallow, Cindy Morgan-Jaffe
Picture Editor: Jane A. Martin
Text Editors: Sarah Brash (principal), Darcie Conner Johnston
Associate Editors/Research-Writing: Katya Sharpe, Robert Speziale
Technical Art Assistant: Sue Pratt
Senior Copyeditors: Anne Farr (principal), Colette Stockum
Picture Coordinator: David A. Herod
Editorial Assistant: Donna Fountain
Special Contributors: Linda Bellamy, Jennifer Clark, Carole Ottesen, Rita Pelczar, Marianna Tait-Durbin (research-writing); Marfé Ferguson-Delano (writing); Marge duMond (editing); John Drummond (design); Lina B. Burton (index).

Correspondents: Christine Hinze (London), Christina Lieberman (New York). Valuable assistance was also provided by Liz Brown (New York).

Library of Congress Cataloging in Publication Data
Wildflowers / by the editors of Time-Life Books.
p. cm.
Includes bibliographical references (p.) and index.
ISBN 0-7835-4104-X
1. Wild flower gardening—United States. 2. Wild flowers—United States. 3. Wild flower gardening—Canada.
4. Wild flowers—Canada. I. Time-Life Books.
SB439.W54 1995   635.9'676'097—dc20   95-24057
                                                  CIP

First printing. Printed in U.S.A.

Published simultaneously in Canada.
School and library distribution by Time-Life Education, P.O. Box 85026, Richmond, Virginia 23285-5026.

TIME-LIFE is a trademark of Time Warner Inc. U.S.A.

This volume is one of a series of comprehensive gardening books that cover garden design, choosing plants for the garden, planting and propagating, and planting diagrams.

Cover: *Three West Coast natives—orange California poppy, lavender-blue Douglas iris, and white Iris macrosiphon—paint a California garden in spring.* **End papers:** *Golden ragwort, which grows wild from Newfoundland to Florida to Texas, illuminates the dappled shade of this Delaware garden. In the foreground are the pale blue flowers of Jacob's-ladder.* **Title page:** *Rose pink Lewis monkey flower, scarlet Indian paintbrush, and blue lupine put on a gorgeous summer show in a mountain garden in Washington.*

CONTENTS

CHAPTER ONE

Our Native Plant Heritage

Wildflowers in your garden create a living link with the natural landscape that no other plant can duplicate. Cultivating some of these lovely natives, which have evolved and flourished in North America, reaffirms a basic principle of good gardening: It is always better—and easier—to work with nature than against it. In the New Jersey garden at left, for example, New York ironweed and Canada goldenrod, natives of eastern North America's meadows, are so perfectly adapted that they have formed a self-perpetuating colony.

Native perennials, annuals, bulbs, and grasses are easy to weave into existing landscapes. Another approach is to dedicate a portion of your garden—or even all of it—solely to wildflowers. Whichever approach fits your vision, this chapter and those that follow will help you select appropriate plants, design the spaces they'll occupy, and care for them at every stage, from planting to propagation.

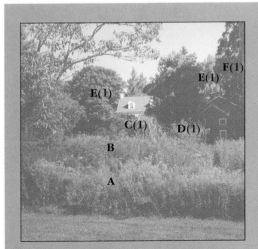

A. *Solidago canadensis (goldenrod) (many)* **B.** *Vernonia noveboracensis (New York ironweed) (many)* **C.** *Miscanthus floridulus (giant miscanthus) (1)* **D.** *Salix caprea (goat willow) (1)* **E.** *Acer saccharum (sugar maple) (2)* **F.** *Salix x sepulcralis 'Chrysocoma' (weeping willow) (1)*

The key lists each plant type and the total quantity needed to replicate the garden shown. The diagram's letters and numbers refer to the type of plant and the number sited in an area.

Bringing Natural Charm into the Garden

Wildflowers have a unique power to charm and delight the gardener. Theirs is an artless beauty that owes everything to Mother Nature and nothing to human intervention—no careful breeding accounts for the size and proportions of the flower, its fragrance, color, or season, or for the line and texture of foliage, fruit, and seed pods.

Besides their visual appeal, wildflowers have an innate ruggedness. In their native environments, wildflowers thrive and reproduce entirely on their own. In a garden where conditions resemble those of the habitat in which the plants evolved, chances are they will reach their full glory with little care. In fact, species like *Lilium canadense* (wild yellow lily) and *Phlox paniculata* (summer phlox) may sometimes look drab in the wild because of competition but grow vigorously and produce spectacular blossoms when given ample space and ideal soil. Moreover, many wildflowers are far more resistant to insect pests and diseases than the hybrids and nonnative plants—also called exotics—that are ubiquitous in North

American gardens. For the low-maintenance gardener, a judicious selection of native grasses, perennials, annuals, and bulbs will help balance the constraints of time and the desire for outdoor beauty.

Links to Nature

Beauty and ease of care are not, of course, the exclusive province of wildflowers; these are also attributes of many exotics and hybrids—peonies, daffodils, daylilies, Japanese anemones, lavender, hosta, and astilbes, to name a handful. As desirable as these plants are, however, they lack the sense of place and primeval American landscape that Kansas gayfeather, Rocky Mountain bee plant, prairie smoke, and Virginia bluebells convey.

A WELCOME MAT OF COLORFUL NATIVES
Cushions of dainty white Mexican fleabane, violet moss verbena, fiery Indian blanket, and a smattering of yellow desert marigolds flank the driveway crossing this Phoenix, Arizona, courtyard.

WIDE OPEN SPACES
In the fertile soil of a virgin tallgrass prairie in central Iowa's Store County, a bountiful expanse of rose pink prairie blazing star, yellow compass plant, and milky white prairie hyssop stretches toward the tree-lined horizon.

A NATURAL FOR WETLANDS
Common cattails rise from the shallow water at the edge of a Massachusetts pond. To keep the plants' potentially invasive roots in check in a small water garden, plant cattails in submerged containers.

THRIVING IN THE THINNEST OF SOILS
The coral blooms of hardy desert mallow and a trio of brilliantly flowering brittlebushes spring forth even from a dry, gravelly crevice in a rocky outcrop in Phoenix.

Even in the most formal and manicured of gardens, wildflowers evoke the natural history of the regions where they originated, many thousands of years before Europeans—and their plants—began arriving in North America. It can be intellectually and emotionally rewarding to establish a connection with the environment as it once was by making your garden hospitable to wildflowers. They reinforce the garden's role as a place of repose that offers escape from the modern world.

The Adaptable and the Fastidious

With a realistic assessment of your garden's environment—the composition of its soil, the light, temperature range, humidity, and the amount and distribution of rainfall and snow—you'll be able to choose wildflowers that will readily take up residence in your garden. No matter where you live, you will have many options; North America is home to at

least 6,000 species of attractive, garden-worthy wildflowers.

Some natives are far easier to grow than others. *Coreopsis verticillata* (threadleaf coreopsis), for example, is highly adaptable, flourishing in sunny woodland clearings and on south-facing hillsides and prairies in virtually any kind of soil from Zones 3 to 10. The New England aster is not solely the Yankee its name suggests, for it ranges westward to North Dakota and south to Alabama. Such wanderlust in nature makes for reliability in cultivation. A list of these and other accommodating wildflowers appears on page 15.

For gardeners new to wildflowers, it's wise to begin with plants that are easily grown. In fact, it's possible to create a richly varied garden with these species alone. However, thinking of your property as a habitat—or a group of habitats—to manage rather than a plot to decorate may lead you naturally to make room for some of the more fastidious, less commonly grown species. The result can be a highly personal garden whose plants look as much at home as do drifts of *Helianthus annuus* (common sunflower), *Linum perenne* var. *lewisii* (prairie flax), and *Amorpha canescens* (lead plant) on an Iowa prairie.

Native Ferns

Ferns and wildflowers, which grow side by side in many natural settings, are just as companionable in the garden. They are very different kinds of plants, however. Ferns are more primitive, reproducing themselves by spores instead of by seeds, as the flowering plants do.

Many of the fern species native to North America are more than 300 million years old, making them some of the most ancient plants on earth. They are found in a variety of habitats but are most numerous at the edge of woodlands. In the garden, most ferns thrive in moist but well-drained, slightly acid soil enriched with humus. Given these conditions, they demand little care beyond occasional thinning. Except for slugs and snails, they have few pests.

Their many shades of green, varied frond outlines, and distinctive growth habits make ferns ideal garden companions for showy wildflowers, with their less intricate foliage. In cool northern climates, some ferns can be grown in partial sun. Elsewhere, most ferns prefer partial shade; the dappled shade under trees is ideal. Avoid planting ferns in dense shade, since they need some sunlight to develop fully.

Matteuccia struthiopteris (ostrich fern) and *Onoclea sensibilis* (sensitive fern) are found in abundance in moist sites in the East and as far south and west as the Carolinas and Missouri. The plumelike fronds of the handsome, vase-shaped ostrich fern reach 6 feet in height, while the broad fronds of sensitive fern are under 3 feet but share the ostrich fern's erect habit. Both ferns offer a vertical accent to ground covers such as *Pachysandra procumbens* (Allegheny spurge), *Podophyllum peltatum* (May apple), and *Asarum canadense* (wild ginger). For wet locations, pair the bright green fiddleheads of *Osmunda cinnamomea* (cinnamon fern) with the sunny yellow blooms of *Caltha palustris* (marsh marigold) for a striking early spring display.

In limy, slightly alkaline soil, plant *Cystopteris bulbifera* (bladder fern) or *C. fragilis* (fragile fern), both of which have brittle, light green fronds with a delicate, feathery appearance. *Adiantum pedatum* (northern maidenhair fern) also appreciates limy soil. Its graceful, palmate foliage held almost horizontal on wiry, purple-black stalks combines elegantly with the deeply cut leaves and nodding pink or white flowers of *Dicentra eximia* (fringed bleeding heart).

Two hardy native ferns, *Dryopteris marginalis* (marginal wood fern) and *D. intermedia* (fancy fern), have gray-green fronds that remain attractive through most of the winter. Found in moist woodlands and on rocky slopes, they are pretty companions for shade plants like *Arisaema triphyllum* (jack-in-the-pulpit), *Geranium maculatum* (wild geranium), and *Gillenia trifoliata* (bowman's root). For gardens in the humid warmth of the Southeast, *Thelypteris kunthii* (river fern) quickly colonizes shady areas; it also tolerates full sun in damp or wet soil. Its large, hairy fronds complement the blue petals and heart-shaped leaves of *Viola papilionacea* (meadow violet) and the frothy white flower spikes of *Tiarella cordifolia* (foamflower).

FOLIAGE TEXTURES IN A SHADY NOOK
A sweep of northern lady ferns makes a delicate backdrop for the coarse foliage of blue flag iris (far left), false Solomon's-seal (center), and May apple (right) in a Connecticut woodland garden.

Where Wildflowers Live

A MOUNTAIN COLONY OF SNOWY BLOOMS
The clublike flower heads of bear grass crown a high-elevation clearing in a forest of alpine firs in Idaho. A member of the lily family, bear grass tolerates dry conditions but blooms more reliably in moist soil. Its foliage is easily mistaken for coarse blades of grass.

The United States can be divided into three basic habitats—woodland, grassland, and desert *(opposite)*. Within each habitat, features like steep slopes and flood plains shape the local environmental conditions that give rise to different plant communities. Within a community, species do not simply exist side by side but influence one another and the environment they share. Tall prairie grasses, for instance, screen wildflowers from intense, daylong sunlight, and the combination of thatch and densely intertwined grass roots keeps shrubs and trees from getting a toehold.

Eastern Woodlands

Forests once covered much of the United States, and where they remain, trees define the landscape. In the Northeast and in the highest, coolest parts of the eastern mountain ranges, needled evergreens keep the forest floor shaded, humusy, and moist, but the brighter light of clearings and gaps in the canopy made by falling trees favors such wildflowers as *Clintonia borealis* (bluebead) and *Cornus canadensis* (bunchberry).

In the warmer, more humid climates prevailing farther south and at lower elevations, conifers yield to deciduous trees, and the absence of a leaf canopy in winter and early spring allows wildflowers such as *Allium tricoccum* (wild leek), *Erythronium americanum* (trout lily), and *Sanguinaria canadensis* (bloodroot) sufficient light to bloom. In open, sunny areas with drier soil, *Monarda fistulosa* (wild bergamot) and New England aster thrive, whereas in wetlands flooded with sunlight other showy wildflowers proliferate—*Lobelia cardinalis* (cardinal flower), *Iris versicolor* (blue flag), *Hibiscus moscheutos* (swamp rose mallow), and *Gentiana andrewsii* (closed gentian).

Forests of the West

The evergreen forests of both the Rocky Mountains and the Sierra-Cascade ranges are more extensive on the western slopes because more rain and snow fall there than to the east. The wildflowers also grow in greater profusion there. Bunchberry, a high-altitude native in the Rockies as it is in the East, blooms with heart-leaved arnica, mule-ears, and *Tellima grandiflora* (fringe cups). At lower elevations, blue columbine and rose pink western bleeding heart flower in groves of deciduous white-barked aspens, while balsamroot, blue-pod lupine, *Veratrum californicum* (corn lily), and many other splashy wildflowers color meadows surrounded by the dark green of firs and pines. In the Sierra-Cascades, the purple spikes of monkshood and orange leopard lily bloom in forest clearings, and skyrocket and red-violet fireweed are widely distributed throughout the region.

Prairie Wildflowers

Grasses shape the character of the prairie habitat. The once vast grasslands of North America—the tallgrass, mixed-grass, and shortgrass prairies—blend into one another along a decreasing moisture gradient from east to west. Easternmost and wettest is the tallgrass prairie, dominated by three grasses that grow to a height of 5 feet or more: big bluestem, Indian grass, and switch grass.

Grasses between 2 and 5 feet in height characterize the drier mixed-grass prairie, particularly little bluestem, June grass, and western wheatgrass. In the shortgrass prairie, the driest of the three areas, clumps of buffalo grass and blue grama less than 15 inches in height are interspersed with rugged, drought-resistant bloomers like Rocky Mountain primrose, whose 4-inch-wide yellow flowers glow amid rosettes of dark green leaves.

Some wildflowers are common to the mixed-grass and shortgrass prairies and the drier parts of the tallgrass prairie. Spring yields a sea of yellow and red blossoms beginning with pasqueflower and prairie smoke. Soon after, *Viola pedata* (birdfoot violet)

Plant Habitats of the United States

The three maps below, developed by the National Wildflower Research Center, delineate three broad plant habitats—woodland, grassland, and desert. Distinguished from one another by climatic factors and soil, the habitats overlap and blend into each other gradually as environmental conditions change.

The three basic habitats are broken down into smaller regions whose conditions give rise to unique plant communities.

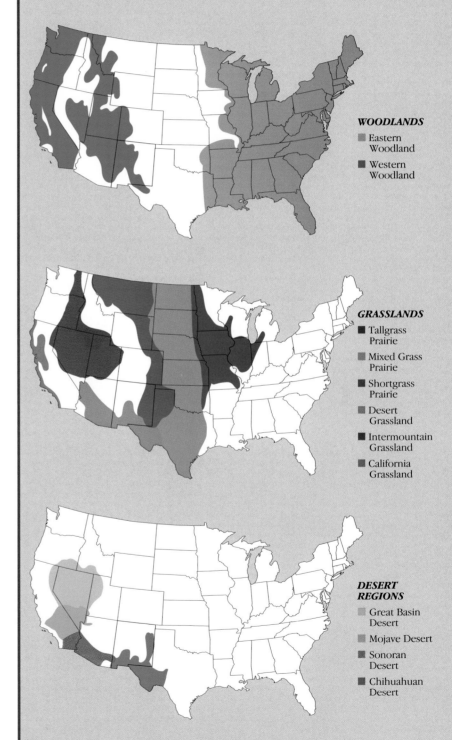

WOODLANDS
- Eastern Woodland
- Western Woodland

GRASSLANDS
- Tallgrass Prairie
- Mixed Grass Prairie
- Shortgrass Prairie
- Desert Grassland
- Intermountain Grassland
- California Grassland

DESERT REGIONS
- Great Basin Desert
- Mojave Desert
- Sonoran Desert
- Chihuahuan Desert

13

and *Phlox pilosa* (downy phlox), the yellow-orange flowers of *Lithospermum canescens* (hoary puccoon) and yellow plains coreopsis intermingle with the fresh new leaves of grass. Summer sun encourages even more variety as the blooms of tall wildflowers over-top the grasses: purple coneflower, blazing star, greenish white rattlesnake master, golden yellow black-eyed Susan, and, toward fall, the long-stemmed lemon yellow flowers of *Silphium laciniatum* (compass plant). Wild-flowers such as evening primrose, Indian paintbrush, and lupine also are common to the desert grasslands that border the warm southwestern deserts of New Mexico and Arizona and to the intermountain grasslands between the Rockies and the Sierra Nevada.

California's Grasslands

Lying between the Sierra Nevada to the east and the Coast Range 50 miles or so to the west, California's Central Valley was a grass-land until it was almost entirely overtaken by agriculture. A place of hot summers and low

WHERE FIELD AND WOOD MEET
Drifts of coarse-leaved corn lily, blue-violet larkspur, yellow cutleaf coneflower, and pink daisy fleabane end abruptly where the sun of a Colorado meadow gives way to the shade of a stand of quaking aspen.

rainfall, it once supported perennial bunch grasses such as purple needle grass, Indian rice grass, and tufted hair grass together with the beautiful orange annual California poppy, brilliant yellow *Lasthenia chrysostoma* (gold-fields), pink and yellow owl's clover, pink or lavender farewell-to-spring, and *Layia platyglossa,* or tidytips, so named for the white tips of its yellow daisylike flowers.

Running the length of the state on the other side of the Coast Range, the California coastal grassland enjoys cool, wet winters and warm, dry summers. Native drought-tolerant perennials such as *Penstemon centranthifolius* (scarlet bugler), *P. heterophyllus* (blue foothill penstemon), *Erysimum capitatum* (coast wallflower), *Eriophyllum confertiflorum* (golden yarrow), and *Yucca whipplei* (our Lord's candle) populate the coastal zone.

Desert Habitats

In the arc of four different deserts that sweeps from southwest Texas through Utah, the precipitation averages no more than 10 inches a year. Plants there must adapt themselves not only to the lack of moisture but also to poor saline soils, intense sunlight, desiccating winds, and ground surface temperatures as high as 190° F. The most abundant wildflowers in the deserts are annuals, which survive the dry periods as seed, then with the return of rain rapidly germinate and bloom.

Great Basin and Mojave

Unlike the other three deserts, the Great Basin experiences severe winter cold, with temperatures plummeting to -20° F. This harsh region is characterized by aromatic sagebrush, saltbush, and, in its less arid reaches, grasses such as wild rye and bottlebrush squirrel-tail, but it also has some beautiful wildflowers—white and lavender *Calochortus nuttallii* (sego lily) and bright red-orange *Castilleja chromosa* (desert paintbrush).

The Great Basin blends into southeastern California's Mojave Desert, which gets only 6 inches of rain per year, most of it in winter. In early spring, more than 250 species of annual wildflowers dot the desert floor, including the lovely *Eremalche rotundifolia* (desert five-spot), whose cup-shaped pink flowers are boldly brushed inside with crimson.

BROOKSIDE IN SPRING
The damp, humusy bank of a mountain stream in Georgia hosts a Trillium sessile (red trillium) with mottled leaves, a bright green clump of Christmas fern (right), and cinnamon fern, whose tall fronds are just unfurling.

Sonoran and Chihuahuan

By contrast, the Sonoran Desert has rainy periods in both summer and winter and consequently supports more diverse plant communities. Green-barked palo verde trees grow in the gravelly soils of the arroyos carved by rushing rainwater, and the candelabra-like trademark saguaro and other cacti dominate the eastern Sonora. *Hesperocallis undulata* (ajo lily), whose white trumpet-shaped flowers arise from a bulb that lies as deep as 2 feet beneath the desert floor to escape desiccation, livens up the scene in spring, and the coppery flowers of *Zephyranthes longifolia* (rain lily) appear after both winter and summer rains.

The summer rain and cool winters of the high-elevation Chihuahuan Desert of New Mexico and Texas foster a profusion of perennial wildflowers. Yellow *Baileya multiradiata* (desert marigold) is especially common, as are the diminutive cousins of garden zinnias—desert zinnia (*Zinnia acerosa*) and the 10-inch little golden zinnia (*Zinnia grandiflora*).

Adaptable Wildflowers

Allium cernuum
(nodding onion)
Amsonia tabernaemontana
(bluestar)
Aquilegia canadensis
(wild columbine)
Baptisia australis
(wild blue indigo)
Camassia scilloides
(wild hyacinth)
Chrysopsis mariana
(Maryland golden aster)
Cimicifuga racemosa
(bugbane)
Coreopsis verticillata
(threadleaf coreopsis)
Erigeron speciosus
(showy fleabane)
Eupatorium coelestinum
(hardy ageratum)
Filipendula rubra
(meadowsweet)
Gaillardia aristata
(Indian blanket)
Helenium autumnale
(common sneezeweed)
Helianthus maximiliani
(Maximilian's sunflower)
Heuchera micrantha
(common alumroot)
Iris prismatica
(slender blue flag)
Lilium canadense
(Canada lily)
Lysimachia ciliata
(fringed loosestrife)
Monarda fistulosa
(wild bergamot)
Oenothera fruticosa
(sundrops)
Penstemon digitalis
(beardtongue)
Phlox divaricata
(blue phlox)
Ratibida columnifera
(Mexican hat)
Rudbeckia hirta
(black-eyed Susan)
Salvia farinacea
(mealy-cup sage)
Solidago canadensis
(Canada goldenrod)
Tiarella cordifolia
(foamflower)
Verbena stricta
(woolly verbena)
Vernonia noveboracensis
(New York ironweed)
Viola papilionaceae
(common blue violet)
Yucca filamentosa
(Adam's-needle)

From the Wilds to the Garden

The beauty of wildflowers in their natural setting makes bringing them into the confines of the garden irresistible. But before you start planting, take a close look at your garden environment. Although the hardiness of a wildflower species should be taken into account *(map, page 100),* other important factors to identify are summer heat, levels of humidity and moisture, exposure to sunlight and wind, and soil composition and pH.

Familiarize yourself with the native species that will excel in your garden's particular conditions or, if you are willing to spend the time and effort, change the environment to suit the plants you want to grow. The more their environment resembles the conditions they experience in the wild, the less coddling your native plants will need to flourish. And, whether the style of your garden is formal or casual, you'll also want to take special note of how native plants group themselves naturally and apply that knowledge to your own planting schemes.

TAKING CUES FROM NATURE
Western wildflowers adapted to the fast-draining soil of the Claremont, California, rock garden shown above include a cascade of yellow meadow foam between drifts of light blue Douglas iris, orange California poppy, and deep blue Ithuriel's spear at the top of the slope. In the moist, humusy soil of a Connecticut woodland (right), native ferns create a lush framework for merry-bells (center foreground) and white crested iris at the path's left edge. The nonnative primroses growing among these natives provide a flush of spring color.

16

Choosing Your Plants

First decide on what scale you wish to introduce wildflowers into your garden. If gardening with native plants is something you haven't tried before, a simple start would be to plant some of the most adaptable and widely available wildflowers. The red-flowered *Monarda didyma* (bee balm), the gold-petaled annual *Coreopsis tinctoria* (tickseed), with wine red centers, and the deep pink late summer spikes of *Physostegia virginiana* (false dragonhead) would be superb additions to an established sunny border.

You can also press wildflowers into service as problem solvers. The dry, bulldozer-compacted soil on the sunny side of a new house, for example, which would need a great deal of amending to grow such popular exotics as peonies and dahlias, would be perfectly adequate as is for such wildflowers as *Lupinus perennis* (wild lupine), *Sisyrinchium angustifolium* (blue-eyed grass), *Asclepias tuberosa* (butterfly weed), and *Baptisia tinctoria* (yellow wild indigo). And, if the gardener were to work a small amount of coarse sand and compost into the impov-

THE HUMID AND THE DRY
A border in a sultry Virginia Beach garden (above, right) is dominated in late summer by the billowy mauve flower heads of Joe-Pye weed and yellow-gold rudbeckia. At the front of the border are three white coneflower blossoms (Echinacea purpurea 'Alba') and a clump of orange butterfly weed (Asclepias tuberosa). Nonnative roses give height to the planting. In the northern California hillside garden at right, rose pink sea thrift and white and pale blue Douglas irises bloom luxuriantly during the dry season. Also native to the West Coast is bearberry, or kinnikinnick, the small, shiny-leaved shrub massed behind the sea thrift.

Native versus Alien

Mingling with the wildflowers of North America's forests, prairies, and deserts are colorful nonnatives that were first brought over to the continent by Europeans and have since become as firmly entrenched as any native plant. Like wildflowers, these naturalized species grow and reproduce without human help wherever they find a congenial combination of climate, light, and soil.

It often comes as a surprise to learn that plants as familiar as *Daucus carota* (Queen Anne's lace), whose delicate umbels of white flowers dot sunny meadows and roadsides, originated elsewhere—in this case, Eurasia. Such aliens are often improperly included in books about American wildflowers or are found in what purport to be wildflower seed mixtures. Among the nonnatives frequently encountered in these mixtures are oxeye daisy, cornflower, and corn poppy. If you want a truly all-American planting, read labels carefully.

Naturalized plants compete with wildflowers for food, water, light, and space, and sometimes overwhelm them. A particularly destructive alien is purple loosestrife, which has invaded wetlands from Nova Scotia to California, displacing native plants and depriving animals of food and habitat.

Naturalized Plants

Achillea millefolium
(yarrow)
Bidens aristosa
(tickseed sunflower)
Centaurea cyanus
(cornflower)
Chrysanthemum leucanthemum
(oxeye daisy)
Cichorium intybus
(chicory)
Daucus carota
(Queen Anne's lace)
Digitalis purpurea
(foxglove)
Hemerocallis fulva
(tawny daylily)
Hesperis matronalis
(dame's rocket)
Lathyrus latifolius
(sweet pea)
Linaria vulgaris
(butter-and-eggs)
Lobularia maritima
(sweet alyssum)
Lythrum salicaria
(purple loosestrife)
Mirabilis jalapa
(common four-o'clock)
Papaver rhoeas
(corn poppy)
Saponaria officinalis
(bouncing Bet)
Tussilago farfara
(coltsfoot)
Verbascum thapsus
(flannel mullein)
Verbena bonariensis
(purple vervain)

erished soil to a depth of 6 inches, these natives would thrive.

For more ambitious planting schemes, survey your garden's physical characteristics with a critical eye. Chances are your property contains more than one set of environmental conditions, each of which constitutes a microhabitat. Trees, shrubs, and buildings, for instance, slow air movement and reduce sunlight, creating a hospitable spot for plants adapted to sheltered, shaded conditions. And while one group of plants will be happy in the moister soil at the foot of a slope, the drier conditions at the top are suited to drought-tolerant species.

If your garden was once a deciduous woodland, then its shade trees or even a mass of mature common lilacs can shelter shade-loving natives such as tall, white-spiked goatsbeard, pink-flowering fringed bleeding heart, and white-plumed false Solomon's-seal. A trio of Christmas ferns would amplify the woodsy atmosphere. For an exposed location in an arid, higher-elevation garden in the West, try *Penstemon eatonii* (firecracker penstemon), *Baileya multiradiata* (desert marigold), *Mirabilis multiflora* (desert four-o'clock), and *Melampodium leucanthum* (blackfoot daisy). These tough natives would endure the dry soil, desiccating winds, and severe temperature swings of hot days followed by near freezing nights—and reward the gardener with a vibrant display of red, yellow, magenta, and white blooms.

Soil Structure and Plant Habitats

The amount of humus or organic matter in your garden's soil in large part determines its structure and what wildflower habitat it resembles. And soil structure affects moisture retention as much as the topography of your property and its exposure to sunlight and wind *(pages 56-60)*.

The soils of eastern woodlands and of the tallgrass and mixed-grass prairies, for example, are porous because of their high organic content. The decayed remains of dead plants, worms, insects, and other animals retain moisture and return essential minerals to the soil. In desert habitats, by contrast, where the plant cover is sparser and supports a smaller animal population, such organic litter is relatively scarce.

Chrysanthemum leucanthemum (oxeye daisy)

Inspired by Nature's Plan

Gardening with wildflowers doesn't mean practicing benign neglect of a landscape. The controlling hand is always crucial, for nature seldom composes and preserves vistas that truly qualify as gardens. Nevertheless, wildflowers look good when they are arranged in a manner that is reminiscent of natural groupings. Enlisting the spirit of nature's design is one easy way to unite a diverse collection of native plants.

Unfenced garden areas, curved paths, and plants with soft, unpruned silhouettes contribute to an asymmetrical landscape evocative of nature, where layers of foliage advance randomly into open spaces. In the Southeast, place the coarse-textured native oakleaf hydrangea in a sinuous pattern in front of the taller, small-leaved evergreen *Myrica cerifera* (wax myrtle) to screen one wildflower environment from another. In the arid Southwest, mass the shrubby-looking cactus *Opuntia bigelovii* (teddy-bear cholla) at the perimeter of your wildflower garden and front it with a ground cover of the rugged *O. polyacantha* (plains prickly pear) for a seemingly artless transition to the desert beyond.

How a species tends to grow in the wild—in low drifts like *Callirhoe involucrata* (poppy mallow), in loose clumps like *Aster laevis* (smooth aster), or as isolated single specimens like *Dodecatheon meadia* (shooting star)—can suggest a garden arrangement. You could plant a swirl of poppy mallow feathering outward, fill in the curves with smooth aster, and use several shooting stars as accents.

For a more formal design, plant a geometric bed close to the house with elegant-looking wildflowers. Good choices are *Iris fulva* (copper iris), with red spring flowers and neat foliage; *Thermopsis villosa* (Carolina bushpea), with spires of yellow blooms in late spring to early summer; and *Veronicastrum virginicum* (Culver's root), whose clusters of small white flowers may reach a height of 6 feet. Cede the farther reaches of the property to less majestic natives such as the sprawling pink evening primrose; Drummond's phlox, a white to purple annual that blooms nearly all summer; and spiderwort, whose lavender flowers are set off by wide, grassy leaves. Your eye will run from the formal near at hand to less ordered garden fringes that hint of domestication dissolving into wilderness.

ONE GARDEN, TWO HABITATS
Powder blue Mertensia virginica (Virginia bluebells) and white Isopyrum biternatum (false rue anemone) flourish in the dappled light of a woodsy Wisconsin backyard (above). On another side of the same house (left), native herbs such as 2- to 3-foot whiteflowered Osmorhiza longistylis (smooth sweet cicely) and low, glossyleaved Asarum canadense (wild ginger) enjoy a few hours of direct sun each day.

CHAPTER TWO

Designing with Wildflowers

There are perhaps as many ways to use wildflowers as there are garden-
ers and garden styles. Some people plant them interchangeably, and in
concert, with nonnative plants. Others take a much more rigorous ap-
proach, devoting their gardens exclusively to natives of a particular re-
gion. However eclectic or purist the gardener's array of plants may be,
the American wildflowers it includes offer unlimited design possibilities.
They belong in traditional beds and borders and in cottage gardens and
cutting gardens. And, of course, they are essential for naturalistic plant-
ings like the Phoenix, Arizona, entrance garden at right, which blends
perfectly with the surrounding desert.

As you study the design ideas presented here, remember that no mat-
ter how they are used, regional natives generally fare better than imports,
since they have had eons to adapt to local rainfall patterns, extremes of
heat and cold, and indigenous pests and diseases. Art can't overcome na-
ture; a garden composition stands or falls on the vigor of its plant palette.

A. *Fouquieria splendens*
(ocotillo) (2) **B.** *Carnegiea*
gigantea (saguaro) (2)
C. *Olneya tesota (desert iron-*
wood) (1) **D.** *Penstemon par-*
ryi (Parry's penstemon) (1)
E. *Verbena gooddingii (ver-*
vain) (1) **F.** *Encelia farinosa*
(brittlebush) (3) **G.** *Justicia*
californica (chuparosa) (1)
H. *Opuntia basilaris (beaver-*
tail, prickly pear) (1) and
Opuntia santa-rita (Santa Rita
prickly pear) (1) **I.** *Larrea tri-*
dentata (creosote bush) (2)

The key lists each plant type and the total quan-
tity needed to replicate the garden shown. The
diagram's letters and numbers refer to the type
of plant and the number sited in an area.

Wildflowers for Every Garden

It is very likely that you are already growing wildflowers in your garden. Many of the old standbys of the traditional herbaceous borders that have long been the hallmark of English gardens trace their ancestry to North America. Such plantings would be far poorer without New World asters, wild indigos, columbines, lupines, coneflowers, coral bells, phloxes, and their progeny.

In many instances, the plants have been changed through selection and breeding. When horticulturists find a truly outstanding individual and want to reproduce it, they do so vegetatively, from cuttings or tissue culture. That way, the results will be clones, identical to the mother plant (as with children, when plants are grown from seed, the results are unpredictable). They call these clones *cultivars* (short for "cultivated variety"). Cultivars usually possess some distinctive quality—a long flowering period, an unusual color, small stature, or handsome foliage. They are not necessarily better than seed-grown plants, but they *are* predictable, identical, and, therefore, uniform in appearance. This is a great advantage in formal gardens.

A Formal Setting for Wildflowers

Nature is manipulated in all gardens, but in a formal garden the manipulation is part of the design. Shorn hedges, plants in rows,

DECEPTIVE DELICACY
The brilliant pink flowers and willowlike leaves of Epilobium angustifolium—called fireweed because it is one of the first plants to germinate after a fire—make a delicate tracery against a house in Crested Butte, Colorado. Fireweed can be invasive, but a less vigorous white variety is well behaved in a perennial bed.

symmetrical beds, subdued colors, and uniformity all testify to the controlling hand of the gardener.

A formal garden suits a formal house. When the owner of a Georgian-style house chooses straight-edged, geometric beds and opts for uniformity of foliage, it is because these features enhance the lines and express the spirit of the house. Next to a brick path, a discreetly hued, homogeneous block of a cultivar such as the pale yellow *Coreopsis verticillata* 'Moonbeam' (threadleaf coreopsis) enclosed by a trim hedge of dwarf edging boxwood yields a neat, tailored look that harmonizes with more formal architectural styles.

Wildflowers for Beds and Borders

The predictability of cultivars also makes them good choices for traditional perennial beds and borders because a particular color, height, or width is a given. Gardeners design such ornamental plantings around specific color schemes, so being able to count on a particular shade is all-important. For example, in a pink to purple border that is meant to be soothing, the vivid scarlet of *Lobelia cardinalis* (cardinal flower) might be jarring. Not so the quieter wine color of its cultivar 'Ruby Slippers'.

Of course, cultivars are not the only natives suitable for perennial borders. Dozens of others, often not as well known, serve beautifully. *Baptisia alba* (white wild indigo), a midborder star, has clusters of pea-like flowers for nearly a month in spring and remains a neat 30-inch shrub until frost. Also for the midborder is golden threadleaf coreopsis, which adds tiny flowers and airy volume. Like its better-known, shorter cultivars 'Zagreb' and 'Moonbeam', it blooms for weeks on end, carrying the border through the summer.

Designing for a Natural Look

When gardens take inspiration from nature rather than from architectural or traditional styles, they can look so natural that they almost seem to have evolved on their own. Rather than being geometric in form, the beds in such gardens flow and curve, following the contours of the land. Slopes and

stands of trees are good places to site freeform beds, where they will also save on maintenance by eliminating the need to mow.

The gardener augments this less constrained look by placing plants in irregular groups of mixed textures and varying sizes and heights. If shrubs are combined with the herbaceous plants, they should reflect the diversity found in nature; fewer than half should be evergreen. And save the task of regular shaping for some other part of the garden. Instead, allow deciduous shrubs like the native *Callicarpa americana* (beautyberry), with its long, arching stems and purple berries, to grow into their natural shapes.

The Versatility of Ornamental Grasses

Most herbaceous plants change with the seasons, tying the garden to the natural world, but the ornamental grasses do it with exceptional flair. In summer they serve as cool green and blue fillers, providing a subtly textured background for the shifting colors of perennials and annuals. In fall and winter, the grasses remain standing, turning shades of almond, russet, tan, and gold. Grasses also

USING FORM TO ENHANCE COLOR
Lively in form but restrained in color, the boltonia in the foreground above enhances the monochromatic color scheme of a formal garden in Potomac, Maryland. Blooming from late summer into fall, its airy flowers repeat the white of the umbrella and contrast with the thick, plushy texture of the lamb's ears that edge the border.

FRONT AND CENTER ON A TERRACE
A purple verbena and a yellow hymenoxys nestled between its trailing stems bask in the center of a wide walkway leading through a southern California garden (left). Planted in pockets between the paving stones, these perennials enjoy a cool root run (cool soil) and, simultaneously, the good air circulation and full sunlight they need for optimum growth.

color best in full sun and dry soil. Its dense, mounded form makes this grass a striking accent among trailing plants in a rock or trough garden *(pages 36-37)*. For textural contrast, mass blue fescue in front of the flattened, leathery pads of a prickly pear cactus. If form is paramount in a planting scheme, consider dividing this grass every 2 years, since it may lose its neat outline with age.

Two other evergreen or semi-evergreen grasses are *Muhlenbergia capillaris* (pink muhly) and *Deschampsia caespitosa* (tufted hair grass). Found growing in moist, rich soil in the Southeast, pink muhly makes a 1½-foot clump of extremely fine-textured arching leaves surmounted in fall by airy panicles of delicate pink flowers that are especially lovely when backlit by the afternoon sun. *Muhlenbergia rigens* (deer grass) is another delicate-looking species suitable for dry-climate gardens in the West.

In silhouette, tufted hair grass is similar to muhly grass, but its foliage is a darker green. Its delicate flowers open green, then change to buff, gold, or a purplish bronze, depending on the cultivar. One of the few ornamental grasses that tolerate shade, it is lovely juxtaposed against ferns and hostas or massed as a ground cover in a woodland garden.

Tall Grasses

Prairie grasses attaining heights of 4 feet and more are ideal for the back of a sunny border, but they needn't be relegated solely to supporting roles. If you have a pool in your garden, the slim, graceful leaves of *Panicum virgatum* (switch grass), *Sorghastrum nutans* (Indian grass), or *Andropogon gerardii* (big bluestem) would make elegant reflections on its surface. Placed in front of a dense, dark broadleaf evergreen such as the native *Ilex glabra* (inkberry), any of these grasses presents a striking contrast of color and texture. If you juxtapose them with anything red—the berries of *Aronia arbutifolia* (chokeberry)

AN IMITATION OF NATURE
Prairie wildflowers cover a sunny slope in the Wisconsin garden at left. In midsummer the white spires of Culver's root are surrounded by black-eyed Susans and pink bee balm. Later in the season, the feathery plumes of goldenrod will dominate. After frost the slope is peppered with the dark round seed heads of the black-eyed Susans.

bring movement and sound to the garden when their thin, elongated leaves stir and rustle in the wind.

The Low-Growing Grasses

The arching leaves of grasses spilling onto a paved terrace, driveway, or walk make a pretty edging. Among the low-growing grasses suitable for this purpose are *Sporobolus heterolepis* (prairie dropseed), whose ¹⁄₁₆-inch-wide emerald green leaves form a fountain-like hummock. Prairie dropseed grows well in dry soil, as does the dwarf evergreen *Festuca ovina glauca* (blue fescue). Sometimes no more than 6 inches in height, blue fescue has dome-shaped tufts of needlelike leaves that

or the scarlet autumn leaves of *Itea virginica* (Virginia sweetspire), for instance—the composition fairly sparkles.

The height and mass of these grasses equip them to serve as architectural elements within the garden. To turn an area of lawn open to public view into a private seating area, partially surround it with clumps of grass planted in a sinuous curve or, for a more formal look, in an L shape. Because a tall grass reaches its mature size about 3 years after planting, the new garden room it defines will assume its character sooner than it would if shrubs were used.

Along a property line, a tall grass makes a low-key three-season herbaceous hedge that is cut to the ground by late winter to make way for new growth. A less restrained, more colorful alternative is to embellish the leafy screen with stately wildflowers. Choose a mix of annuals, biennials, and perennials ranging in height from 3 to 6 feet or more: *Helianthus maximiliani* (Maximilian sunflower) and *H. annuus* (common sunflower); *Ipomopsis rubra* (standing cypress), with brilliant red flowers that are magnets for hummingbirds; goldenrods; a dusky purple *Vernonia* (ironweed); yellow-flowered *Agastache nepetoides* (giant hyssop); or splashes of blue from *Baptisia australis* (blue wild indigo). Your choices will depend not only on growing conditions but also on the space available. A useful guideline is to limit the height of the tallest plant to no more than half of the width of the planting.

Meadows and Prairies

Whether growing in hedges, beds, or borders, ornamental grasses interplanted with colorful wildflowers evoke prairies or meadows. *Prairie,* the French word for meadow, denotes the complex, grass-dominated, treeless ecosystem that once covered much of the central United States and Canada. The special, untamed beauty of an expanse of flowering plants and grasses in a treeless clearing has caught the eye and won the heart of many a gardener.

Even though most people notice the flowers first, grasses are the major component of a prairie, making up more than 50 percent of its biomass. Such proportions account for the subtle, color-flecked green of the prairie, compared with the intense color of a conventional bed or border. If the grasses tone down the brilliance of the flowers, they also help to hide their demise. And in winter when other herbaceous plants have withered to dry sticks, grasses add volume and a tawny presence.

A pleasing possibility for the gardener who yearns for a bit of the prairie but has a small yard is a "pocket meadow," which is simply a prairielike mixture of flowering plants and grasses scaled down in height and mass to suit the space. By choosing plants that stay under 3 feet tall, a gardener can create a meadow in as few as 60 to 100 square feet.

A pocket meadow looks best when it is framed with a fence or shrub border as a background. In front, a path or a row of a grass with a mounding habit, such as prairie dropseed, gives it a logical, finished edge. Another alluring option is to mow a curving path through the meadow. Even in a small space where the plants are only hip high, a path gives the illusion of greater depth. It also allows whoever walks on it the wonderful sensation of being surrounded by a miniature ecosystem alive with the sound and sight of insects drawn to the flowers.

Establishing a pocket meadow is not substantially different from planting a border. Within the allotted space, intersperse grasses and flowering plants at intervals of a foot or so. Position flowering plants in irregular drifts. Even though the end product will appear to have evolved naturally, the young plants require care. Mulch the meadow well, and keep it watered and weed free while the plants establish themselves *(page 66).*

***SUPPORTING ROLES
FOR NATIVES***
A cooling sight on a hot July day in Milwaukee, a man-made garden pond (right) features the cupped blossoms of a nonnative water lily. Natives include the dark green fringe of sedge in the foreground and two clumps of dark green arrowhead that offer a vertical accent to the water lily's flat round leaves.

Tough Plants for Tough Places

Wildflowers that have adapted to conditions the opposite of those held up as the cultural ideal—moist, loamy soil, moderate temperatures, shelter from rough weather—are godsends when the gardener has an area vexing to manage because the drainage is poor or the light too low or too intense. The solution is to find a plant that grows to perfection in these conditions—even demands them.

Almost every garden has a hot spot—frequently next to a sidewalk or driveway—with little or no relief from the sun all day. The soil dries out so quickly that turf grasses and other drought-sensitive plants are doomed to struggle. Conversely, trying to maintain grass in the shade of closely spaced trees is just as unrewarding. In the first case, gaillardias and other dry-prairie natives will appreciate the qualities of the site; in the second, drifts of woodland natives are the solution.

For wildflowers from rocky, sandy soil or from the mountains, excellent drainage is imperative if they are not to succumb to diseases like root rot. A fast-draining steep or rocky slope provides the opportunity to try plants such as the creamy-flowered *Eriogonum compositum* (wild buckwheat) from California's Coastal Range.

A low place that holds water after a rain makes a good home for perennials from meadows that are wet for a portion of the year, such as Joe-Pye weed. If space allows, add a moisture-tolerant native tree or shrub such as *Magnolia virginiana* (sweet bay magnolia), which has fragrant white flowers, or the red-fruited *Ilex verticillata* (winterberry).

Plants for Dry, Sunny Places

Agave spp.
(agave)
Balsamorhiza sagittata
(balsamroot)
Baptisia spp.
(wild indigo)
Bouteloua curtipendula
(sideoats grama)
Erigeron spp.
(fleabane)
Gaillardia spp.
(Indian blanket)
Melampodium leucanthum
(blackfoot daisy)
Oenothera spp.
(evening primrose)
Verbena spp.
(verbena)
Yucca filamentosa
(Adam's-needle)
Zauschneria californica
(California fuchsia)
Note: The abbreviation "spp." stands for the plural of "species"; where used in lists it means that many, but not all, of the species in a genus meet the criterion of the list.

GRACE NOTE FOR A HOT SPOT
Kept comfortably hot and dry by the adjacent concrete sidewalk, Oenothera speciosa (showy evening primrose), from the shortgrass prairies of southern Kansas and Texas, grows luxuriously even in the moist climate of Bethesda, Maryland (below). Two evening primroses with showy lemon yellow flowers, O. missourensis and O. brachycarpa, can also be counted on to flourish in full sun and dry soil. Deadheading prolongs their season of bloom.

Plants for a Fast-Draining Slope

Aquilegia caerulea
(Rocky Mountain
columbine)
Campanula rotundifolia
(bellflower)
Eriogonum spp.
(wild buckwheat)
Eschscholzia californica
(California poppy)
Iris douglasiana
(Douglas iris)
Lewisia rediviva
(bitterroot)

Penstemon spp.
(beardtongue)
Sedum ternatum
(stonecrop)
Silene laciniata
(Mexican campion)
*Note: The abbreviation
"spp." stands for the plural
of "species"; where used in
lists it means that many,
but not all, of the species
in a genus meet the criterion of the list.*

EXPLOITING A ROCKY SLOPE

*Glowing orange California pop-
pies, whose petals close on overcast days and at night, flourish
on a rocky incline in the Berke-
ley, California, garden at left.
Also native to the area are the
creeping blue California lilac
in the foreground and the man-
zanita trees, whose arching
branches echo the contour of
the slope. Beyond the manzani-
tas is a drift of pale blue Douglas irises, a species ideal for
West Coast gardens.*

A WOODLAND VIGNETTE

*A derelict few square
yards of sparse lawn
under old shade trees
in a Connecticut gar-
den was transformed
into the inviting minia-
ture woodland shown
at left. The path of
rough stones allows for
closeup enjoyment of
a wild bleeding heart's
pink spring flowers
and, nodding above it,
the bicolored flowers
of wild columbine.*

Plants for Eastern Shade Gardens

Arisaema dracontium
(green dragon)
Asarum spp.
(wild ginger)
Aster divaricatus
(wood aster)
Dicentra eximia
(wild bleeding heart)
Eupatorium coelestinum
(hardy ageratum)
Geranium maculatum
(wild geranium)
Mitchella repens
(partridgeberry)
Podophyllum peltatum
(May apple)
Polygonatum biflorum
(Solomon's-seal)
Smilacina spp.
(false Solomon's-seal)
Tiarella cordifolia
(foamflower)
Viola spp.
(violet)
*Note: The abbreviation "spp."
stands for the plural of
"species"; where used in lists it
means that many, but not all,
of the species in a genus meet
the criterion of the list.*

BEAUTIFYING A DAMP SPOT

*The graceful foliage and nodding pale
green seed heads of river oats give
a lush look to the part of a garden
where water stands after a rain, then
evaporates in dry weather (above).
Found growing in the wild in the rich,
moist soils of lightly shaded stream
banks, this adaptable grass tolerates
occasional flooding and also does
well in average garden soil.*

Plants for Damp Spots

**Andropogon
glomeratus**
(bushy bluestem)
Anemone canadensis
(Canada anemone)
Asclepias incarnata
(swamp milkweed)
Camassia quamash
(camass)
**Chasmanthium
latifolium**
(river oats)
Iris brevicaulis

(Lamance iris)
Monarda didyma
(bee balm)
Physostegia virginiana
(obedient plant)
**Thalictrum
dasycarpum**
(meadow rue)
**Veronicastrum
virginicum**
(Culver's root)
Zephyranthes atamasco
(atamasco lily)

Wildflowers for All Seasons

To have something in flower throughout the growing season, experienced gardeners grow a selection of perennials that bloom at different times and in appealing compositions. This sequence of bloom does more than keep the garden showy: Plants that flower in succession make the garden seem neater because each new flush of bloom draws attention away from its fading predecessors.

Native annuals do the same thing. They also provide color over a very long season, so there is always something to fill any gaps between the bloom periods of perennials. Some short-lived wildflowers can also be used as handsome elements of the garden's foliage framework. In its first season, for example, the finely divided and lobed leaves of the biennial *Phacelia bipinnatifida* (spotted phacelia) are a fresh, pretty presence in moist shade; in its second year, the plant produces violet-blue flowers over a long period in spring.

A BORDER FOR SULTRY SUMMERS
Heat-loving natives in pink tints flank a non-native yellow verbascum (above). In the foreground are clumps of daisy-flowered purple coneflower and, at far left, bergamot. To the rear are two clusters of queen-of-the-prairie.

NATIVE WOODLANDERS
In spring a Maryland garden (left) blends the soft blue of wood phlox with the bright hues of yellow wood poppy and an orange azalea. At right, maidenhair fern masks the fading foliage of early-blooming ephemerals.

Early-Blooming Perennials

Many very early blooming woodland perennials help furnish the garden for only part of the growing season. These ephemerals, such as Virginia bluebells, spring beauty, and Dutchman's-breeches, flower under still-leafless trees. By early summer, when the canopy has filled out, they disappear completely.

Even though their disappearance leaves bare places for the gardener to fill, the rule that plants look best in large numbers of fewer kinds is especially true of ephemerals. When grown in great number, they make up for their fleeting delicacy in one grand, unforgettable stand. A hillside of bloodroot in fragile white bloom is as short-lived as a late snowfall, and just as lovely.

The best way to handle ephemerals is as you would bulbs such as tulips or daffodils—interplant them with companions that come up as they fade. Ferns, unfurling in late spring, are perfect for this purpose. So are summer- or fall-flowering woodland perennials—*Aster divaricatus* (white wood aster), *Solidago caesia* (wreath goldenrod), *Cimicifuga racemosa* (cohosh bugbane), and *Aralia racemosa* (spikenard). These send up their handsome foliage to take the places vacated by ephemerals and stay attractive until hard frost.

Flowers to Take the Heat

In most parts of North America, summers are hot. Plants such as hardy geraniums of European origin, which bloom all summer long in their cool native climates, flower promisingly in American gardens during spring and early summer, then go quickly to seed the minute the mercury rises. In order to have flowers

during the summer months, choose wildflowers that are adapted to bloom in the heat.

Not surprisingly, some of these are the same species that flower with bright abandon in fields and along roads—goldenrods and sunflowers (*Solidago* spp., *Helianthus* spp.), bee balms and sneezeweeds (*Monarda* spp., *Helenium* spp.). If you think that the wild species are too big, too ordinary, or too undisciplined for your garden, there are some attractive cultivars to choose from. *Solidago rugosa* 'Fireworks', for instance, is named for the graceful downward curves of its flower heads' many branches, which bloom long and showily through the steamy dog days. Where *Helenium autumnale* (sneezeweed) can grow to 5 feet or more and is a back-of-the-border plant, the rich, warm yellows, oranges, and brownish reds of the shorter cultivars move forward in the border. In the 2-foot range are 'Bruno', with reddish flowers, and 'The Bishop', with yellow flowers.

Sometimes, however, even a stalwart native

may succumb to extreme conditions. In a garden with high humidity and poor air circulation, mildew often plagues bee balm. Several cultivars, including the hot pink 'Marshall's Delight' and 'Gardenview Scarlet', are less susceptible to the disease than the species.

Plants for Fall and Winter

Late-blooming wildflowers make delightful company while you work in the fall garden. *Chelone lyonii* (pink turtlehead), *Physostegia virginiana* (obedient plant), and some species of *Helianthus* (sunflower) bridge the gap from late summer into fall, as does *Salvia azurea* (azure salvia), which has sky blue flower spikes and neat, slender gray-green foliage on 3- to 4-foot stems. There are also plants that bloom earlier in the season, then contribute to the garden anew in fall. The early-summer flowers of *Amsonia hubrechtii* are as pretty as its common name—Arkansas bluestar—suggests, but in autumn, its large, whorled leaves turn a knockout yellow.

Paramount among natives for the fall season are the asters. They come in all sizes, shades, and shapes from the recumbent, dark-stemmed *Aster divaricatus* (white wood aster) that makes its home in dappled shade to the tall, sun-loving *A. novae-angliae* (New England aster) and its fine cultivars such as 'Harrington's Pink' and the purple-flowered 'Hella Lacy'.

Ornamental grasses such as prairie dropseed are attractive after frost. Not only do they retain volume, but their colors may also actually be showier in winter than in summer. Prairie dropseed turns an almond tan, while *Schizachyrium scoparium* (little bluestem) glows rusty orange. Massed in a meadow setting, these native grasses make pleasing, subtle compositions with the tans, browns, and grays of the winter landscape. They are also handsome against a backdrop of evergreens.

Plant these winter combinations where they can be seen from inside, or site them beside the driveway or next to the front door so they can be admired in passing. Grasses usually stay presentable until late winter. When they no longer please, simply cut them to the ground before new spring growth appears.

Besides those that fade gracefully, there are wildflowers that are fully or partially evergreen. Low-growing species of *Heuchera* (alumroot) work well as edgings, framing dormant perennials and keeping the garden neat and attractive through winter. Their visible green keeps alive the promise of spring.

A GREEN CARPET FOR WINTER
Neatly bisected by a pale midvein, the rounded, leathery leaves of partridgeberry in a Vermont garden provide an evergreen foil for scarlet maple leaves and for its own red berries, which last into winter. At home in acid woodland, partridgeberry will tolerate dry shade once it is established. In spring, it produces pairs of tiny white flowers tinged with pink.

Late-Blooming Perennials

***Aster* spp.**
(aster)
Boltonia asteriodes
(boltonia)
***Chelone* spp.**
(turtlehead)
***Eupatorium* spp.**
(boneset)
Helenium autumnale
(sneezeweed)
Helianthus maximiliani
(Maximilian's sunflower)
Lobelia siphilitica
(great blue lobelia)
Physostegia virginiana
(obedient plant)
Rudbeckia hirta
(black-eyed Susan)
***Solidago* spp.**
(goldenrod)
Vernonia noveboracensis
(ironweed)
***Zauschneria* spp.**
(California fuchsia)

Plants with Winter Presence

Antennaria plantaginifolia
(pussy-toes)
Asarum arifolium
(evergreen wild ginger)
Chasmanthium latifolium
(river oats)
Deschampsia caespitosa
(tufted hair grass)
***Heuchera* spp.**
(alumroot)
Mitchella repens
(partridgeberry)
Panicum virgatum
(switch grass)
***Rudbeckia* spp.**
(black-eyed Susan)
Schizachyrium scoparium
(little bluestem)
Sporobolus heterolepis
(prairie dropseed)
***Yucca* spp.**
(Adam's-needle)
Note: The abbreviation "spp." stands for the plural of "species"; where used in lists it means that many, but not all, of the species in a genus meet the criterion of the list.

Broadening Your Options

Some wildflowers are so appealing that they tempt us to try to grow them in places where they would not make it on their own. This usually requires changing existing conditions—soil, moisture, drainage—to suit the needs of the desired plant. If you are going to tamper with conditions, think small. It's less expensive and less work, and your landscape will gain a pretty, jewel-like feature.

A Flowery Lawn

Sometimes even if conditions *are* right, your dream garden isn't. You may long for a tall, wild-looking meadow but live in a community where covenants won't allow it. In that case, consider a lawn studded with low-growing wildflowers.

An easy, conservative starting point is a small, confined area of existing lawn—a strip between a driveway and a hedge would be ideal. To this area, add multiples of a single diminutive species, spacing the plants at in-

tervals of a foot or so in an irregular drift. An excellent choice for this situation is a little violet such as the 3-inch *Viola labradorica*, with handsome purplish foliage. If you like the effect, add more low-growing natives. Crocuses, chionodoxas, and other nonnative bulbs are also good candidates.

When using spring-blooming bulbs, postpone the year's first mowing until the foliage withers. Thereafter, time mowings to spare flowers and those in the bud stage. Also, set the blade of the mower high—3 inches for bluegrass, Bermuda grass, and St. Augustine grass, and 4 inches for tall fescue.

A flowery lawn of blue grama or buffalo grass, two western natives that also succeed in the East, may need only one mowing a year. This gives the gardener the option of using wildflowers that reach 10 or 12 inches in height. *Chrysopsis villosa* (golden aster), California poppies, or trailing *Callirhoe involucrata* (winecups) are three that are perfect for this purpose.

It is important to keep at least half of a

A TAPESTRY OF BLADE AND BLOSSOM
In a dry-climate version of the flowery lawn, photographed outside Phoenix, Arizona, drifts of blue annual lupine and yellow California poppy flow around clumps of purple three-awn, a foot-tall bunch grass named for the vibrant color of its summer seed heads.

Plants for a Flowery Lawn

Allium cernuum
(wild onion)
Antennaria **spp.**
(pussy-toes)
Chrysopsis villosa
(golden aster)
Claytonia virginica
(spring beauty)
Eschscholzia caespitosa
(California poppy)
Iris tenax
(grass iris)
Sisyrinchium **spp.**
(blue-eyed grass)
Verbena canadensis
(rose vervain)
Viola **spp.**
(violet)

Note: The abbreviation "spp." stands for the plural of "species"; where used in lists it means that many, but not all, of the species in a genus meet the criterion of the list.

Building a Bog Garden

To create a bog like the one pictured at right, first dig a sloping basin 18 inches deep. Line it with an inch of sand; cover the sand with heavy-gauge plastic sheeting. Put a 1-foot layer of equal parts of peat humus and sharp sand into the basin and top with 6 inches of sphagnum moss. Water until the moss is saturated. After 6 weeks test the pH. If it is above 6, add ground sulfur to accommodate species needing more acid conditions, such as the yellow pitcher plants shown here.

The drawing below shows the degree of wetness various wildflowers prefer. Bog-garden species occupy the saturated middle ground. In the higher, drier soil *(below, left)*, bushy bluestem and river oats tolerate occasional flooding, while pickerelweed, cattails, and water lilies must be rooted in water *(below, right)*.

(1) Andropogon glomeratus
(bushy bluestem)
(2) Chasmanthium latifolium
(river oats)
(3) Filipendula rubra
(queen-of-the-prairie)
(4) Lobelia siphilitica
(great blue lobelia)
(5) Chelone lyonii
(pink turtlehead)

(6) Asclepias incarnata
(swamp milkweed)
(7) Lobelia cardinalis
(cardinal flower)
(8) Hibiscus coccineus
(rose mallow)
(9) Iris fulva
(copper iris)
(10) Iris versicolor
(blue flag)

(11) Iris prismatica
(slender blue flag)
(12) Rhexia virginica
(meadow beauty)
(13) Hymenocallis occidentalis
(spider lily)
(14) Lysichiton americanum
(yellow skunk cabbage)
(15) Sarracenia purpurea
(pitcher plant)

(16) Symplocarpus foetidus
(skunk cabbage)
(17) Pontederia cordata
(pickerelweed)
(18) Sagittaria latifolia
(arrowhead)
(19) Typha angustifolia
(cattail)
(20) Nymphaea odorata
(fragrant water lily)

MOIST .... **WET**

flowery lawn in grass. A ratio of up to 1 to 1 of turf to flowering plants yields color, but the area will still be perceived as lawn. With more flowers than grass, it will begin to look like an unkempt flower bed. Be vigilant about weeds, hand pulling them as they appear.

A Small-Scale Backyard Bog

A bog garden, another lovely bit of artifice, can be wrought from a low spot in the garden supplied with enough moisture, either naturally or by irrigation, to keep the soil saturated or muddy *(page 35)*. If the bog is small, plant it with diminutive species such as the charming

foot-tall *Rhexia mariana* (meadow beauty) in white and tints of lavender, pink, and rose. Two imposing 8-foot ornamentals, *Filipendula rubra* (queen-of-the-prairie), with deep pink blossoms, and pink-flowered *Hibiscus moscheutos* ssp. *palustris* (rose mallow), are splendid choices for a broader boggy expanse.

A World in a Container

Container plantings are another way to greatly expand the range of plants you can grow in a manageable way. Alpine plants are classic subjects for containers, both for aesthetic and for cultural reasons. Generally small and dainty, they are perfect in scale for this purpose.

MATERIALS FOR A TROUGH
20" long, 12" wide, and 8" high

For the forms:
One 2' x 4' sheet of 2" polystyrene foam
Duct tape
One large tuna can, top and bottom removed
Twelve 4" nails

For the hypertufa:
30 lbs. Portland cement
1 cu. ft. peat moss, sieved through ¼" hardware cloth
1½ cu. ft. perlite
Two concrete mixing tubs or large buckets

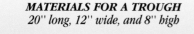

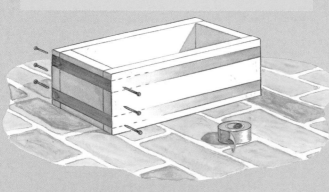

1. To make the outer form, cut two 8" x 24" side pieces and two 12" x 8" end pieces. Arrange the pieces to make a box and join them with three nails at each corner (above). Wrap two strips of duct tape around the form to strengthen it. For the inner form, cut two 6½" x 17" side pieces and two 6½" x 5" end pieces. Assemble as described above.

2. Wearing a dust mask and waterproof gloves, divide the hypertufa ingredients into two batches for easier mixing. Combine the ingredients for each batch in a concrete mixing tub. Stirring the mixture constantly, add enough water to moisten it evenly. Still stirring, add water a little at a time, until a handful of hypertufa holds together in a firm, slightly crumbly ball when squeezed.

Making a Trough

The process described here yields a handsome, one-of-a-kind trough durable enough to last a lifetime. It is made of hypertufa, whose principal ingredient is Portland cement. This material also includes perlite, which adds volume with minimal weight, and peat moss, which darkens the mixture and mimics the patina of age. Reinforcing fibers, available at masonry supply stores, strengthen the mixture. You may use premixed concrete in place of the Portland cement and reinforcing fibers. If you do, screen it to remove the gravel in it before proceeding. The two polystyrene forms used for casting the hypertufa can be taken apart and reused.

3. Place the outer form on a large sheet of plastic spread out on a level surface. To make the trough's drainage hole, place the tuna can in the center of the form. Fill the bottom of the form with a layer of hypertufa equal in depth to the tuna can (below). Pack the hypertufa down firmly with a blunt piece of wood to remove any air pockets.

They also demand a porous, fast-draining gritty soil, a condition very hard if not impossible to supply in many gardens, especially those with heavy clay soil.

Alpine fanciers have long favored stone troughs for their plantings. Originally used for feeding and watering animals, the genuine articles are expensive and not easy to find, but a very good-looking substitute can be made from cement, perlite, and peat moss as shown below. Because it is not as heavy as a stone trough of the same size, moving a cement trough is less daunting a task.

Your trough need not be restricted to lewisias, saxifrages, or other alpines. With the right soil mixture and exposure to light, it can house almost any type of wildflower you wish to grow, becoming an enchanting miniature garden world unto itself. You can create a meadow; the floor of a miniature woodland; or a bit of desert.

As to a growing medium, a basic mixture suitable to a wide range of plants consists of one part loam or commercial topsoil, one part poultry grit (available at feed and seed stores), and one part leaf mold. For alpines, substitute stone chips for half of the loam or topsoil. To raise the pH for alkaline-loving plants, add up to a half part of crushed limestone. For a more acid mixture, replace the leaf mold with two parts of peat moss. To avoid transporting a heavy load, put the soil mixture into the trough after you've moved it to the place it will occupy.

6. To give the trough the look of stone, *round its corners and top edge with a paint scraper and texture the sides with a wire brush. Then wet the trough and, with a helper, slip a 39-gallon plastic bag around it and seal the bag tightly. After 1 month, remove the trough from the bag. Leave it exposed to the weather for 3 months so that rain—or weekly hosings if the weather is dry—will leach out excess lime.*

4. Nest the inner form inside the outer form, *centering it carefully; the sides of the forms should be 1½ inches apart at every point. Put the hypertufa into the mold by handfuls, packing it down firmly as described in Step 3. When the mold is filled to the top, cover it with a plastic sheet to retard drying.*

5. After 24 hours, scratch the top edge of the trough with your fingernail. *If it has hardened enough that your nail doesn't leave a mark, scratch it with a screwdriver; the trough is ready to unmold when a fingernail won't mark the hypertufa but a screwdriver will. Gently ease out the inner mold. With a helper, carefully turn the trough upside down. Ease off the outer mold and remove the tuna can.*

7. To ready the trough for planting, *cover the drainage hole with a 6" square of fiberglass screening, spread an inch of pebbles on the bottom, and fill with an appropriate soil mix to within an inch of the rim. For plants from dry habitats such as the daisy-flowered hymenoxys below, arrange rocks around them to radiate heat and help keep the foliage dry.*

Domesticating Nature's Bounty

All gardening brings contentment, but gardening with wildflowers confers extra rewards. On a practical level, it reduces maintenance because well-sited native plants, once established, all but look out for themselves—even when combined in plantings with nonnatives. There is no need for prodigious watering or fertilizing, or for cumbersome winter protection.

A deeper satisfaction may come in knowing that by planting nursery-propagated wildflowers or starting your own by division or from seeds, you are helping to preserve our native plant heritage. Additionally, when you plant wildflowers native to your region, your garden gains a wonderful sense of place. A garden that includes native plants captures the unique character of the land around it, blending artfully into the natural world. Examples of such gardens appear on the following pages; for a list of plants and a planting guide for each garden, see pages 50-53.

HOT COLORS FOR A COOL CLIMATE
The flower power of natives Asclepias tuberosa (butterfly weed), with bright orange blooms (bottom left), and Coreopsis lanceolata (lance coreopsis), with deep yellow flowers (center), balances the vibrant hues of daylily hybrids 'Stella de Oro' (lower right) and 'Nuthatch' (upper right) in a Milwaukee garden. Beyond the fence, red Monarda didyma 'Cambridge Scarlet' mingles with yellow Lysimachia punctata (yellow loosestrife).

STRIKING GOLD

Bright orangey gold Eschscholzia californica (California poppy) contrasts vividly with a pair of nonnatives—Nepeta mussinii (catmint), with its cool blue flowers, and Achillea ptarmica 'The Pearl', with pristine white daisylike blooms—as they snuggle up to a low wall of glacial rock in this Washington State garden. Fields of the brilliantly hued native poppy proliferate in sunny, semiarid grasslands (above) from Washington south through California, where the wide, cup-shaped blooms close up at sunset.

FRONTING FRESH WATER

*Arching green lances of Iris versicolor (blue flag) and a shrubby back-
ground of Cephalanthus occidentalis (buttonbush) tame the dazzling red
flashes of Lobelia cardinalis (cardinal flower) abloom in July in this northern Illinois garden. Cooling pond breezes, direct sunlight, and wet soil
create an ideal environment for these three moisture-loving natives. Cardinal flower, at home in a perpetually moist, sunny tallgrass prairie in
Wisconsin (above), reaches 5 feet high with flame red stalks of nectar-laden
blooms that hummingbirds find irresistible.*

A NORTH-FACING SITE
In this Missouri garden of humid summers and cold winters, a stand of native Rudbeckia subtomentosa (sweet coneflower) (top, left) forms a backdrop punctuated by yellow ironweed and Boltonia asteroides 'Pink Beauty'. Lavender mist flower (center foreground), rose pink false dragonhead, and rose verbena front the planting. Another well-known Rudbeckia native, R. hirta (black-eyed Susan), flourishing in the Illinois meadow above, is shorter than its perennial cousin but just as flamboyantly colored. It tolerates light shade and temperature extremes, isn't fussy about soil, and reseeds prolifically in the wild.

ENRICHING POOR SOIL
*Ubiquitous in the Texas rangeland, Lupinus texensis (Texas bluebonnet),
with its white buds and blue flowers (above), thrives in alkaline, infertile
soil because of its ability—and that of other members of the legume family—to convert atmospheric nitrogen into nutrients. In the light clay soil
of this arid Phoenix garden, purple-blooming Lupinus sparsiflorus (Coul-
ter's lupine) benefits its native plant partners—pink-spired penstemon,
Mexican gold poppy, and brittlebush (rear center)—by making valuable
nitrates available to them.*

A BORDER OF LATE BLOOMERS

Selected for their similar mature heights, striking colors, and overlapping bloom periods—late summer through fall—sedum cultivars 'Autumn Joy' and 'Variegatum', with russet and white mopheaded flowers, bloom along a Missouri fence next to natives Solidago nemoralis (gray goldenrod), with fluffy deep yellow flowers, and spiky rose pink false dragonhead. Another native goldenrod, Solidago canadensis, shown above in a Wisconsin meadow, also enjoys a sunny setting and the same bloom time as gray goldenrod but grows to twice its height, making it an ideal choice for a larger garden.

**HOT COLORS FOR
A COOL CLIMATE**
pages 38-39

A. *Asclepias tuberosa* (4)
B. *Hemerocallis 'Hyperion'* (1)
C. *Lilium 'Enchantment'* (3)
D. *Monarda didyma
'Cambridge Scarlet'* (6)

E. *Chrysanthemum x superbum
'Alaska'* (3)
F. *Hemerocallis 'Nuthatch'* (1)
G. *Lysimachia punctata* (3)
H. *Coreopsis lanceolata* (1)
I. *Hemerocallis 'Stella de Oro'* (1)

*NOTE: The key lists each plant type and the total quantity needed to replicate the garden shown.
The diagram's letters and numbers refer to the type of plant and the number sited in an area.*

STRIKING GOLD
pages 40-41

A. *Eschscholzia californica* (many)
B. *Nepeta mussinii* (2)
C. *Achillea ptarmica 'The Pearl'* (3)
D. *Hemerocallis spp.* (1)

FRONTING FRESH WATER
pages 42-43

A. *Lobelia cardinalis* (4)
B. *Iris versicolor* (large clump)
C. *Symplocarpus foetidus* (2)
D. *Cephalanthus occidentalis* (1)

A NORTH-FACING SITE
pages 44-45

A. *Rudbeckia subtomentosa* (3)
B. *Verbesina alternifolia* (2)
C. *Juniperus virginiana* (1)
D. *Boltonia asteroides 'Pink Beauty'* (2)

E. *Quercus imbricaria* (1)
F. *Helianthus salicifolius* (8)
G. *Solidago nemoralis* (3)
H. *Liatris scariosa* (4)
I. *Eupatorium coelestinum* (14)

J. *Physostegia virginiana* (4)
K. *Verbena canadensis* (1)

ENRICHING POOR SOIL
pages 46-47

A. *Eschscholzia mexicana* (from seed)
B. *Lupinus sparsiflorus* (from seed)

C. *Encelia farinosa* (5)
D. *Penstemon spp.* (10)
E. *Sphearalcea ambigua* (4)

NOTE: The key lists each plant type and the total quantity needed to replicate the garden shown. The diagram's letters and numbers refer to the type of plant and the number sited in an area.

A BORDER OF LATE BLOOMERS
pages 48-49

A. *Ceratostigma plumbaginoides* (3)
B. *Sedum x 'Autumn Joy'* (2)
C. *Sedum spectabile 'Variegatum'* (2)
D. *Solidago nemoralis* (2)
E. *Physostegia virginiana* (3)
F. *Juglans nigra* (1)

Installation and Maintenance

Any garden—a foliage border, a perennial bed, a wildflower meadow—requires some maintenance if you are to keep the site from reverting to a wild state. However, because wildflower gardens are designed to work in harmony with nature's intention, chores such as fertilizing and deadheading can be kept to a minimum. In the North Carolina garden pictured at right, for example, natives white boltonia, pink seashore mallow, and dark purplish Joe-Pye weed have grown as they please—providing a haven for butterflies and birds.

In fact, the lion's share of the labor of a wildflower garden is in preparation rather than in upkeep. This chapter will take you through the steps of getting a garden started in a variety of habitats as well as provide tips for the garden's care. If you want to welcome native plants in more limited ways, the following pages will also show you how to introduce them into an existing bed of nonnatives or create an easy-care medley in a container to spruce up a corner of your patio or garden.

A. *Boltonia asteroides 'Snowbank' (boltonia) (3)*
B. *Kosteletzkya virginica (seashore mallow) (1)*
C. *Eupatorium fistulosum 'Selection' (compact Joe-Pye weed) (3)*

The key lists each plant type and the total quantity needed to replicate the garden shown. The diagram's letters and numbers refer to the type of plant and the number sited in an area.

Preparing Your Wildflower Beds

Designing any successful garden requires matching your plants to your particular garden conditions. But wildflower gardening means working hand in gardening glove with your habitat—be it woodland, grassland, desert, or a region in between. With the object of knowing the microclimates on your property so that you can make the best possible plant choices and create the optimum home for them, you must study the site and chart all the features that affect its growing conditions.

Sun and Shade

The first step is to take note of the kind of light that falls on your property during the growing season. This can range from full, direct sun for 6 or more hours during the middle of the day to varying degrees of shade. Partial shade is usually defined as 4 to 6 hours of sun each day, and full shade as 4 hours or less. Buildings, fences, trees, slopes, and time of year all affect the amount of light your garden receives. Under tall deciduous trees, shade will deepen as the growing season progresses and the trees leaf out; if you have your heart set on a regional wildflower that needs a bit more sun than a particular spot offers, consider pruning away low limbs or removing some trees altogether to admit more light.

Lightening Clay Soil

Before it can sustain most wildflowers, a sticky, heavy, clayey soil needs a combination of amendments to improve its structure, nutrient content, and drainage. To prepare a garden site with such soil, first break up the earth with a spading fork. Then cover the area with about 2 inches of coarse sand and, using a spade or shovel, dig it into the top 6 inches of your soil. Don't use beach or play sand, which may contain salt.

Next, spread 4 inches of organic matter over the bed—any combination of compost, leaf mold, or well-rotted manure mixed with straw will serve well. Dig the amendments into the soil, taking care not to stand on the soil and compact it. Also, avoid overcultivating, since tilling soil too finely actually breaks down its structure and makes the organic matter decompose too fast. In the end, you'll have a total depth of 12 inches of good garden soil.

Precipitation

To a great extent, the amount of moisture that reaches your soil, combined with how well the soil retains that moisture, will determine what plants you can grow in your landscape. Dig a few holes to a depth of several inches in different locations around your property to check the moisture level. In forest or grassland areas, dig down at least 12 inches—the depth to which roots of native plants in those regions penetrate. If you've had a heavy rainfall, wait 2 days or more before conducting the test.

Ideally, the soil at the bottom of the hole should be moist and cool to the touch. If water seeps into the hole, the soil there can be classified as wet, and you'll need to plant the area with flowers that tolerate wet feet. A high moisture level may not be obvious at a glance, however, so pick up a handful of soil from the bottom of the hole and squeeze; any oozing or dripping signifies wet conditions.

In desert areas, where annual rainfall is minimal, your soil is likely to contain very little moisture, limiting your choice of plants. However, topography affects how much precipitation stays in the soil. Check for soil moisture at the bottoms of any slopes shaded from afternoon sun. If the soil is moist and cool at a depth of 6 to 8 inches, you'll be able to plant a wider array of wildflowers on your site.

Soil Structure, Drainage, and pH

The structure of your soil is yet another factor determining how much water your plants can absorb. Soils with high levels of clay hold lots of water and can actually drown your plants; at the other extreme, sandy soils drain very quickly and can leave plants thirsting for moisture and vital nutrients. Loamy soils—balanced combinations of clay, sand, and silt particles—are best for most plants, although the beauty of many natives is that they can tolerate all sorts of adverse conditions.

Your geographical area will generally have a particular type of soil, but the builder of your

NATIVE COLOR IN A NATURAL BORDER
Regional grasses and wildflowers such as yellow core-opsis (center, left), red hibiscus, and brownish mauve Joe-Pye weed thrive in this North Carolina garden, where the soil has been prepared to bring out the best in plants already at home in their native conditions.

house may have removed the topsoil and replaced it with infertile fill dirt. To find out what kind of soil you're dealing with, dig up a handful and form it into a ball. If it crumbles readily, you have a sandy soil. If it holds the shape, roll the ball between your hands and try to form a cylinder. If you can, next pinch the soil out into the shape of a ribbon. The longer and thinner you can make it, the more clay you have in your soil. If the pinched soil crumbles rather than forms a ribbon, you have loamy soil. Repeat this test in several spots; you may get varying results.

If your idea is simply to add plants to an area where natives already grow, you can leave the soil pretty much as it is—as long as you select plants that are perfectly matched to it. However, if you want to plant gardens that thrive rather than subsist and that support a slightly broader array of plants, take steps to improve the soil. Even if you add wildflowers to an existing bed or border *(pages 58-59),* you should make use of the opportunity to get the soil in top shape.

Whether your soil is sandy or clayey, incorporating organic amendments such as compost and leaf mold will improve drainage. (For clayey soils, you can add sand as well; see the recipe for lightening heavy soils opposite.) These amendments also add nutrients and help keep your soil pH in the slightly acid range preferred by most plants. This pH—between 6 and 7 on the 14-point pH scale, where the upper range indicates greater alkalinity—keeps nutrients at their most soluble. However, desert plants don't mind neutral or somewhat alkaline soils, and certain woodland plants do well in soils more acidic than 6. Test your soil with a kit or meter available from a nursery or garden center, or send samples of your soil to the local Cooperative Extension Service office.

Ordinarily, amending and regularly top-dressing the soil with organic matter should eventually correct any minor pH problems. However, if your soil turns out to be significantly more alkaline than is normal for your region, you can lower the pH by incorporating powdered gypsum (chemically, calcium

Renovating a Border with Native Plants

One way to incorporate wildflowers into your landscape is to take an existing bed or border and renovate it. This allows you to clear out old plants that you may no longer wish to keep, divide others that have become too crowded *(page 80)*, and amend the soil with organic matter to improve drainage and add nutrients.

The best time to tackle this project is in midspring, when you can see where your plants are coming up. A springtime renovation gives your new and newly divided plants almost a full season in which to establish or reestablish themselves. Another reason to make these changes in the spring is that if you redo the bed later, you'll have to live with a sparse appearance all season, whereas a spring makeover allows you to fill in the bare spots with colorful annuals.

1. Lay a tarp adjacent to the bed. *With a spading fork or spade, dig out all the existing plantings. As much as possible, keep the plants' root systems intact by digging at least 2 to 3 inches outside of their drip lines. Then, lift the plants out of the bed and place them on the tarp. If you won't be completing the project within a few hours, cover the roots with wet newspaper to protect them from wind and sun, and keep them watered.*

If the project is going to take longer, opt to heel in your plants. First dig a shallow trench approximately 10 inches deep, then lay each plant on its side with the rootball in the trench, and cover the roots with soil and mulch (inset). Plants can often remain heeled in for up to several weeks as long as they receive sufficient water and light. The sooner your plants can be set in place, however, the better they'll keep their health and vigor.

2. Break up the bed's soil with a spading fork. *If the soil has become very compacted you may want to use a mattock. Apply 4 to 5 inches of any combination of leaf mold and compost and work them into the soil to the depth of one spade length (left). This is also a good opportunity to adjust your soil's pH level by adding either limestone to overacid soil or gypsum to very alkaline soil. Follow package directions. Work in small sections, moving from one end of the bed to the other. When working inside the bed, stand on a flat board to distribute your weight more evenly and thus minimize any soil compaction.*

3. Situate your plants on the bed's surface to visualize the design. When digging holes for your old plants and for new ones purchased in containers, make the holes slightly larger than the plant's rootball. Gently remove any plant from its container and loosen compacted soil around the rootball; place the plant in the hole, spreading the roots out evenly. The planting depth of both the container plants and your old plants should be the same as it was previously in the container or in the garden (above).

If you are setting in new bare-root plants, soak their roots in lukewarm water for an hour before planting—longer if they were fairly dry when they arrived in the mail. To plant, dig a hole as deep and as wide as the plant's longest roots. Then mound up some soil in the center of the hole. Set the plant on top of the mound and spread the roots out evenly all around (inset). Make sure that the plant's crown—where the stems and roots meet—is flush with the soil's surface. Holding the plant in place, fill the hole with soil and firm it in.

After planting the bed, water it thoroughly, then cover it with a 2-inch layer of organic mulch such as shredded hardwood. Be sure to keep the bed well watered during the first few weeks to make sure all the transplants become established.

sulfate), following package directions. To raise a very low pH, or decrease acidity, "sweeten" the soil with ground limestone.

Soil Needs of a Forest Garden

If you're planting a wildflower garden in a northeastern deciduous forest area, plan on supplying your soil with plenty of organic matter. Many plants native to this region adapted to the fertile, moist, acidic soil that existed before development took out stands of trees that carpeted the ground with leaves. Your plants will thrive if you restore as much as possible the original humusy condition of the soil.

To prepare a new garden site, use a spading fork to turn the soil and incorporate compost, leaf mold, ground bark, well-rotted manure, or any combination of these. Work to a depth of at least 8 inches—and 12 is better. To improve the drainage of clayey soils, add sand as described on page 56. If your soil is nutrient-poor replacement fill dirt, plan to add as much as 50 percent of the soil's original volume in amendments and new topsoil. Aim for a loamy soil that drains to a depth of 6 or 7 inches in a 24-hour period and has a pH between 6 and 6.5.

If your soil is so rocky that you are unable to dig deeply without using special equipment, consider building raised beds. The job needn't be complicated by constructing enclosures. Simply mound at least 8 to 12 inches of amended loamy soil in the spots where you want to put your plants.

In the southeastern United States, the pine-dominated forest habitats tend to have sandy, acidic soil. To bring it up to planting form, you'll need to add only organic matter for good drainage. Western mountain forests typically have a thin layer of stony topsoil at the feet of the towering conifers. You'll need to add compost and other organic matter to help improve the soil's water-holding capacity and increase its depth. But since the plants native to conifer forests are adapted to the poorer

soil of these areas and the soil generally contains a moderate supply of sand, gravel, and small rocks to assist drainage, you don't need to add as much organic matter to support native plants as you might in the Northeast.

Gardens in the Grasslands

In grassland habitats—characterized by full sun, adequate precipitation, and drying winds—the natural soil is fairly rich and runs deep, enabling plant roots to reach far down for water. The farther west the habitat, the rockier and less fertile the soil becomes.

Generally, because plants native to these areas are well adapted to heat, cold, drought, and wind, little soil improvement is needed. Add more topsoil if the existing layer is thin, but take care not to overenrich your grassland garden since high fertility will cause leggy growth; use compost or leaf mold at a rate of less than one part organic matter to three parts soil. Using a spade or spading fork, dig in amendments—the deeper the better, to imitate the natural habitat. The deep roots of native grasses, interplanted with your wildflowers, will help keep the garden soil well drained and aerated. In the semidesert grasslands of the Southwest, add composted sawdust to improve drainage if your soil is heavy.

A Desert Garden

Natural desert soil is sandy, gritty, very low in humus, and often alkaline, with a pH as high as 8.4. In the hot summer sun, organic matter decomposes so quickly that you would need to amend the soil weekly to make it more fertile. Instead, plan on making use of those wildflowers that survive the baking, infertile conditions of the region, and apply chelated synthetic fertilizers to the soil. These slow-release products are formulated so that nutrients are not washed away in fast-draining soil.

Desert plants have very shallow but wide root systems to capture and store the precious little rain that falls. As a result, you need only cultivate the soil to a depth of 6 to 8 inches to support them. Using a spade or spading fork, amend the garden site with topsoil to improve the soil texture, and add a chelated fertilizer, following package directions. Your plants will do best if the soil's pH is 7 to 7.5; if it is above 7.5, lower the pH with gypsum.

A LIKELY PAIR OF GARDEN MATES
Spikes of pink Palmer's penstemon and low mounds of fragrant valerian reach their full potential in this walled Arizona garden, where conditions of sun and light shade and well-drained, average soil are just as these wildflowers most prefer.

Buying and Planting Wildflowers

Once you have prepared your site for its new occupants and determined which plants will do best there, the fun of picking them out and bringing them home begins. Garden centers typically group all plants of a particular genus together. For example, you might find the native *Clematis texensis* you're looking for nestled among other clematis species, cultivars, and hybrids. Since you probably won't find a section dedicated to true local natives, you're more likely to select the right plants if you know in advance their complete botanical names *(Cross-Reference Guide to Plant Names, page 101, and encyclopedia, pages 102-149).* However, a good nursery should be able to provide you with information.

Perennials are usually offered in 4-inch pots; annuals can come in pots or as smaller plants in cell packs. As with any plants, look for those with vigorous, healthy-colored foliage, and check for insect or disease damage. The soil should be moist, and the roots should not be growing more than a couple of inches out of the bottom of the pot. Don't always buy the tallest or largest; it's wiser to choose a thrifty plant that has bushy, uniform growth. Last, make sure the plant has not been acquired by unethical means *(right).*

Native plants are enjoying greater popularity in recent years, but you're still likely to find a wider selection in mail-order catalogs than in local nurseries. Look for catalogs that specifically cater to your region to find the best matches for your conditions. Small plants will be shipped either bare-root or in small pots and should be planted right away in prepared soil. Catalogs also sell seed, which you can sow directly in the garden or start in containers *(pages 76-79)* for later transplant to the garden.

General Planting Rules

The two best times to transplant wildflowers are in spring, when the plants are just coming out of dormancy and beginning a cycle of vigorous growth, or in fall, when they are going dormant. At these times the plants are most able to concentrate on growing roots and getting established. Also, in both spring and fall,

---

TIPS FROM THE PROS

Acquiring Wildflowers Responsibly

According to F. M. Oxley, senior botanist at the National Wildflower Research Center in Austin, Texas, 600 North American native plant species are in danger of extinction in coming years, and some 3,000 others are threatened. Two powerful enemies of native wildflowers are loss of habitat and overwhelming competition from invasive exotics. But a third enemy is—ironically—recent renewed interest in the plants themselves. Ignoring laws that protect threatened species, individual and commercial collectors strip seeds, take cuttings, or dig out entire plants from the wild by the thousands.

Irresponsible collection disrupts the reproductive cycles of wild plants and devastates whole stands. When you buy wildflowers, counsels Oxley, make sure you are not buying plants taken illegally. Probably hundreds of species are wrongfully brought to market from the wild—among them many members of the orchid, lily, and iris families, whose blooms are popular and whose propagation is slow.

Learn what plants are threatened or endangered in your area; local nature centers and state agriculture departments are good sources of information. Never dig plants in the wild unless you see them in the path of destruction through development, and even then get written permission from the landowner to salvage them. It is acceptable to take seeds from wild plants, but only a few from each plant.

When you shop for wildflowers, ask how a nursery gets its plants, particularly if it offers endangered or threatened species. Look for the term "nursery propagated"; a label of "nursery grown" may mean the plant was taken from the wild and grown larger in the nursery. Reputable nurseries will tell you how they propagate their stock; if a nursery representative is evasive or ambiguous, don't buy there.

Be on the lookout for signs of transplant shock: weak stems, wilted leaves, leggy growth, sparse foliage, or poor color. These are clues that a plant has been recently lifted from the wild. You may also conclude that a plant did not grow in the pot in which it is being offered if it is potted off-center; if it is potted in compacted clay, in a mix of different soils, or with rocks; if several salable species are in the same pot; or if it has scars left by nibbling wildlife.

If you spot wild-gathered plants for sale, tell the nursery manager why you aren't buying them. Patronize nurseries that do their own propagation; a growing market will help them expand their operations. And inquire through garden clubs or plant societies in your area about ways to meet other wildflower fanciers with plants to trade, sell, or give away.

the soil is moist and warm—the condition most conducive to the plant's settling in.

Choose a cool or cloudy day, if possible, to move your plants into the prepared soil of your bed or border. This way you'll have an easier time keeping roots moist during the process. Use the guidelines described in Step 3 on page 59 for planting both container and bare-root plants; the guidelines are the same regardless of your habitat.

In deciding how to space your transplants, take into consideration the width of the mature plant and how fast it will grow. If you want a garden that looks full within a season or two—and if you are willing to put extra time into thinning and dividing your plants—put them closer together. Or you can space them farther apart, with their ultimate size in mind, and let them fill in over a period of years.

A Naturalistic Woodland Garden

Spacing may not be an issue at all if you want your wildflowers to present a very natural look in a woodland garden where trees and shrubs form an established framework. On a forest slope, for example, a small rock garden can present an enchanting, natural display with a few well-placed plants *(right)*.

In larger garden sites, lay out paths that curve among the trees by clearing swaths about 3 feet wide and putting down a carpet of shredded bark, woodchips, or pine needles. Then plant individual plants or small groups of plants in strategic spots: shade lovers in raised mounds of prepared soil under the trees, and other varieties in sunnier patches. Mulch around all of your woodland wildflowers with a 1- to 2-inch layer of shredded leaves to keep the soil cool and moist.

Sowing a Meadow Garden

If you have the space for it—and if you are a patient gardener—consider planting a wildflower meadow. Meadows do well in both forest and grassland regions, as long as they get plenty of sun and are filled with the native plants best suited to them. Expect it to take about 5 years for your plantings to reach maturity and for the meadow to achieve the right balance of desired plants—over time they will crowd out unwanted vegetation.

Creating a Rock Garden

Many wildflowers that naturally thrive in soil pockets on stony hillsides will also perform in a rock garden you construct yourself. Rock gardens look most at home on a slope. In cool alpine regions, choose a site that gets full sun; in areas with hot, dry summers, northern or eastern exposures will help keep plants cool and moist. You can also locate a rock garden on a shaded forest hillside, using shade-loving wildflowers and other plants. Whatever the habitat, seek out stones that are native to the area, similar in color and texture, and about equally weathered. Use the largest ones you can handle to keep the finished design from appearing cluttered, and arrange them in a way that looks natural, not studied.

1. At the bottom of your slope, dig a hole about half as deep as one of your largest stones. Slant the hole downward into the slope to promote surface drainage and to direct moisture to the roots of the plants. Settle the stone in place and pack the soil tightly around it. Seat other large rocks beside it to form a bottom row. If strata are visible in the stones, position them so the strata are parallel. Bury each stone at least halfway for stability and for the look of an outcrop exposed by weathering.

2. Make a second row by digging holes and inserting stones as described in Step 1; stagger the stones so that they do not sit directly above those in the bottom row. Add a third row if you have room. Aim for an arrangement that is by itself attractive, even without plants, and seems part of the landscape. You may want to seat another rock grouping nearby. For the most natural look, vary the number and configuration of rocks in each grouping.

An easy, inexpensive way to plant a meadow is by broadcasting seed by hand. Start with a site that has been cleared of existing vegetation and prepared for planting. Using a triangular hoe or the corner of a square chopping hoe, cut furrows into the soil that are 2 inches deep and 12 to 18 inches apart. Seed at a rate of 1 pound of seed per 1,000 square feet, using a mix that contains at least 50 percent native grasses and the remainder a combination of annual and perennial wildflowers. The annuals will provide immediate, bright color while the perennials are getting established. You can purchase mixes formulated for your area—particularly from regional catalogs—or create your own.

Mix your seed with an equal volume of sand in a pail and walk between the furrows, dropping pinches of the seed and sand in the furrows. Using the flat side of a rake, pull a quarter inch of soil across the furrows to cover the seeds. Then tamp in the seeds, either with a lawn roller or by walking down the planted furrows.

Sow in either spring or fall. If you're planting in spring, water the seeded meadow every day with a light spray for at least a week until the seeds start to germinate. As the seedlings grow, check the moisture of the soil frequently and water if necessary. For fall plantings, tamp the soil in place and allow nature to take its course. Don't water the seeds; they will rest in a dormant state over the winter and sprout in the spring.

3. When you have settled all the stones, fill the gaps between them with an appropriate soil mix. For alpine plants, use a gritty mixture of 3 parts topsoil, 2 parts peat moss, and 1.5 parts sand. For small woodland plants in a shady rock garden, add 1 part compost or leaf mold to this mixture for a more fertile but quick-draining medium. Put in your largest plants first, then the smaller ones, using a narrow trowel to settle them into the crevices. Firm the soil gently around them and water each plant thoroughly as you go.

Planting a Desert Garden

If you are planting a wildflower garden in the hot, dry conditions of a desert habitat, your best bet is to start with young plants rather than seeds, which need a lot of moisture to germinate. Generally, the larger, stockier, and stronger the plant you're transplanting, the better it will adapt to the environment—and the higher its chances of survival.

Depending on the size of the transplant, use a trowel, spade, or shovel to dig a hole at least twice the size of the rootball. If the soil is extremely poor, make the hole even larger. Line the hole with a mixture of 70 percent original soil and 30 percent peat, well-rotted manure, or sawdust that has been treated with nitrogen. Also add a slow-release chelated fertilizer to the mix, following package directions. Plant as you would any new plant,

Wildflowers for a Rock Garden

Aquilegia
(columbine)
Asarum
(wild ginger)
Erythronium
(trout lily)
Gentiana
(gentian)
Iris
(iris)
Lupinus
(lupine)
Phlox
(phlox)
Silene virginica
(fire pink)

4. Next, spread a mulch of gravel that blends with your stones between the plants to hold in moisture, deter weeds, and help keep plants cool in the summer. In the weeks after planting, water frequently and weed carefully by hand. Consult the list at left for a few of the many wildflowers suitable for rock gardens; check the encyclopedia that begins on page 102 to select ones that will thrive in your region.

A Container Garden of Annual Wildflowers

To dress up a patio or add a subtle accent to your garden, try planting an array of different wildflowers in an attractive container. First choose a pot at least 8 inches deep and cover the drainage hole in its bottom with pottery shards or stones. Fill the container to within 2 inches of the rim with a commercial potting soil.

Before planting, decide on the arrangement: Tall flowers should be placed in the center or back of the container, while shorter plants and those that cascade should go near the front or sides, as illustrated at left. Remove healthy young annuals from their cell packs or other containers, and gently spread apart the bottom of each rootball. With a trowel, make a hole slightly larger than the rootball and place it in the hole, spreading the roots out evenly. Fill the hole with soil and press firmly; water well. Cover the soil with a little bark mulch or sphagnum moss to help retain moisture and give the container a finished look. Water often, especially in hot weather, to keep the plants healthy.

and water well. Mulch with stones to help the soil retain moisture, and shield the new plants with shade or with wind blocks until they are established.

Special Planting Needs of Boggy Gardens

In wet soils as well as in dry, desert conditions seedlings take hold better than seed, which is often washed away. For each seedling, use a trowel or a spade to dig a hole twice the size of the rootball, and line the cavity with a mixture of original soil, sand, and gravel to assist drainage. Plant the seedling so that the crown is just slightly above the soil surface to discourage root rot, then firm the soil around the plant very gently to avoid compacting the soil and eliminating vital air pockets. Later watering and root growth will further stabilize the seedling in the ground.

Gaillardia pulchella (Indian blanket)

Easy-to-Grow Annual Wildflowers

Campanula americana
(bellflower)
Centaurea americana
(basket flower)
Chamaecrista fasciculata
(partridge pea)
Chamaecrista nictitans
(sensitive plant)
Cleome serrulata

(Rocky Mountain bee
plant)
Coreopsis tinctoria
(tickseed)
Eschscholzia mexicana
(Mexican gold poppy)
Euphorbia marginata
(snow-on-the-mountain)
Gaillardia pulchella

(Indian blanket)
Geranium carolinianum
(wild geranium)
Gilia tricolor
(bird's-eyes)
Helianthus annuus
(sunflower)
Lupinus aureus
(golden lupine)
Lupinus nanus
(sky blue lupine)
Lupinus texensis
(Texas bluebonnet)
Machaeranthera tanacetifolia
(Tahoka daisy)
Mirabilis
(four-o'clock)
Monarda citriodora
(horsemint)
Oenothera deltoides
(fragrant primrose)
Phacelia minor
(wild Canterbury bell)
Phlox drummondii
(Drummond's phlox)
Salvia farinacea
(mealy-cup sage)

Maintaining Your Wildflower Garden

By carefully matching your wildflower plants to the conditions of your geographical region and the microhabitat of your garden site, you'll drastically reduce your maintenance chores. However, the plants still need some help from you if they are to give their very best performance. Mulching, weeding, watering, soil maintenance, and a few grooming habits all have their place in the wildflower garden, and for most backyard habitats, the ground rules are the same.

Mulching

Of all gardening tasks, mulching is the biggest bargain. Mulches limit the growth of weeds by discouraging them from taking root or, for those that do, by depriving them of the sunlight they need to survive. By shielding the soil from the sun, wind, and other elements, mulches reduce evaporation of water and limit temperature extremes, conserving water and keeping your plant roots moist and healthy. Serving as a buffer, they even protect against heavy rains that could compact or erode soil. And an attractive covering of mulch unifies and neatens your beds and shows off your plants.

Use mulches that are appropriate to your plants and habitat. An enormous benefit of organic mulches is that they help keep the soil fertile by adding nutrients as they break down. Choose acidic pine needles in forest habitats, cooling straw in warm areas, attractive shredded bark and shredded leaves wherever organic mulches are suitable, or nutrient-laden compost, depending on the conditions of your region. Also check in your area for local commercial by-products, such as cotton burs in Texas or crushed crab shells in Maryland. The essential feature of mulch is a coarse, loose texture that will let water drain through it.

Use organic mulches liberally, spreading them in layers 2 to 4 inches deep around your plants in midspring and again in late fall. Keep mulch an inch or two away from any plant crowns or stems to avoid rot.

Among inorganic mulches, which have the advantage of being long-lasting, gravel is the most suitable for wildflower gardens. It is especially appropriate in rocky areas, where the stones blend in with the landscape and where the natural soil doesn't need the nutrients supplied by organic mulches. Black plastic sheeting or porous landscape fabric, while appropriate for other types of gardens, will prevent your flowers from propagating by seed and aren't in keeping with the spirit of wildflower gardening.

Mulching is not recommended at all for wildflower gardens on the southern West Coast, where the majority of native flowering plants are spring-blooming annuals that manufacture seed for next year's crop and then disappear by May. Mulch would only bury the seed or smother next year's seedlings.

Cutting Back

In fall, after the growing season, the dried stems of perennial wildflowers should be clipped to 1-inch stubs (above). To promote self-seeding, be sure to wait until seed pods have died back. The next spring, locate the stubs and cut them to the ground. Your new growth should be uniform and tidy.

Maintaining a Meadow with Mowing

Among the best reasons for planting a meadow rather than a lawn or more conventional garden is its minimal upkeep. A wildflower meadow—like the sea of color in Washington State pictured below—requires far less in the way of most chores. Watering, for example, is usually left to nature, and no fertilizing is ever necessary. However, the meadow does need some help keeping out the shrubs, saplings, and weeds that spring up from seeds that invariably find their way in. This is especially true in its first years, before your wildflowers and grasses have thoroughly filled in the soil and crowded out other vegetation. After the meadow is established, however, all you have to do to keep it beautiful is mow it—and only once a year at that.

During your meadow's first spring, mow at a height above your seedlings to cut the tops off any weeds that are taller than they are; this will keep the weeds from going to seed. Shorter weeds should be hand pulled. After that, control both weeds and woody invaders by mowing in the fall, after all of your desired plants have set seed.

Use a rotary power mower if you can set the blades at least 4 inches off the ground—this is necessary to keep from cutting the crowns of your perennial wildflowers. Make sure the blades are sharp, since dull blades tear the plants and leave them vulnerable to disease. If your mower can't be set high enough, use a power weed cutter or a scythe instead. Run the mower's engine at its highest speed to minimize stalling in the thick vegetation. Walk slowly as you cut, overlapping your previous swath so that you don't leave unattractive ridges of unclipped grass and stems. Because leaving a heavy blanket of long clippings on the ground may hinder the next year's growth, collect and remove most of them. Your mower may be equipped with a bag; otherwise, use a wide leaf rake. If you keep a compost pile, make sure it is hot enough to kill any pathogens before you add the clippings to it. Otherwise, throw them in the garbage.

Mowing will also scatter desirable wildflower seeds, many of which will sprout the next spring. If your meadow is mature and you don't mind losing some seed, you may delay mowing until late winter and let the birds feed on the seed heads. In this case, the vegetation may be so matted that you'll have to cut it with a scythe or a weed eater.

Neither do bog gardens need mulching, because a living layer of sphagnum moss serves the same purposes *(page 35, top).*

Weeding

In any habitat, pull perennial weeds early before they develop stubborn roots or spread, and you'll weed far less often. One hour spent weeding in spring saves many hours later in the season. Weed when the soil is moist—such as after a good rain—because damp soil releases the roots more easily.

Watering Techniques

If you choose wildflowers that are indigenous to the area and site them well, they should not need watering. When rainfall falls below normal, however, watering infrequently but slowly and deeply will satisfy the needs of most wildflowers—and defeat many weeds in the process. Sprinkling devices left on for several hours accomplish this, and, like rain, help to wash dust and pollutants from plant leaves. But they also keep foliage wet, inviting fungal diseases *(pages 91-93).* Instead, use a drip-irrigation or soaker-hose system that seeps water into the soil over a period of hours. If the area is small, you can water by placing a regular garden hose on the soil beside the plants and letting the water run gently until the soil is saturated; move the hose from time to time to be sure you water evenly. Your aim is to get an inch or so of water into the soil once a week. Water permeating the top 6 to 8 inches—12 inches in grasslands and forests—helps plants establish and maintain strong, deep root systems that will anchor them in the ground and help see them through drier times.

The best time to water is in the morning of a sunny day, when leaves can dry quickly. A regular source of water is especially critical in spring, when seedlings are sprouting and perennials are coming of dormancy; keep the soil moist, but not soggy, until the plants are under way. Afterward, consider watering after any week without rain. If plants look wilted or dull and the top 2 inches of soil are dry, it's time to give them a drink.

Fertilizing

In most areas of the country, top-dressing your established wildflower garden with organic matter such as composted yard waste or well-rotted manure is all the fertilizing you will have to do. Spread a couple of inches of the organic matter and, using a spading fork, work it into the top few inches of soil around each plant once a year—and more often in the South, where hot weather speeds organic decomposition. If you mulch with compost in the spring, dig it into the soil in the fall before laying down another layer as mulch. You can also add a commercial balanced slow-release fertilizer if you want to make absolutely sure that your plants are receiving the full complement of nutrients. In desert areas, apply chelated fertilizers, following package instructions.

Propagating Wildflowers

Although a number of favorite wildflowers are available from garden centers and nurseries, many beautiful species can be difficult to come by. Often the only way to introduce native plants you admire into your garden is by taking cuttings from other, carefully chosen plants or by propagating them yourself from seed you've gathered or purchased. Raising wildflowers from seed will not only expand your collection but will also offer an exciting lesson in nature as you observe and assist the life cycle of a plant from seed to maturity.

Most plants, including the white evening primrose, spiky bluebonnet, and red autumn sage shown at left blooming in a Texas garden, can be propagated by more than one method. The following pages will show you how to nurture new plants in a variety of ways—from seeds, cuttings, and division—to increase both the number and the variety of interesting and beautiful plants growing in your wildflower garden.

A. *Oenothera speciosa (white evening primrose) (6)* **B.** *Salvia farinacea (mealy-cup sage) (2)* **C.** *Calylophus berlandieri (formerly C. drummondiamus) (square-bud primrose) (1)* **D.** *Engelmannia pinnatifida (Engelmann daisy) (1)* **E.** *Salvia greggii (autumn sage) (2)* **F.** *Verbena bipinnatifida (Dakota vervain) (1)*

The key lists each plant type and the total quantity needed to replicate the garden shown. The diagram's letters and numbers refer to the type of plant and the number sited in an area.

Collecting and Preparing Wildflower Seeds

One of the greatest pleasures—and challenges—of growing wildflowers is raising new plants from seeds that you've collected yourself. Wildflower seeds can be gathered from your own garden if you want to increase your stock, or, if new plants are your goal, can be obtained from the garden of an obliging friend or neighbor. If you've spotted an appealing native plant on land belonging to someone you don't know, be sure to obtain permission before taking seeds. But if you are drawn to a plant growing on public lands, it's best to admire from afar; the seeds—like the plants themselves—should be left alone unless they are going to be destroyed by construction.

Watching Seed Development

The ideal time to begin your search for wildflower seeds is while the plants are in bloom. Tie a piece of brightly colored yarn or surveyor's tape—also called flagging and available

HOW SEEDS ARE SPREAD IN THE WILD
Nature disperses wildflower seeds in a number of ways. When the seeds of jack-in-the-pulpit (near left) ripen in the fall, the berries encasing them darken, luring birds that will then eat them, pass the seeds through their digestive systems, and leave them in a new location. The fruits of milkweed (far left) split open when mature, so that the wind can scatter the seeds. The pink blossoms of Joe-Pye weed turn brown (top), signaling that its fruits are beginning to mature. When fully ripe, the fruits will appear as fuzzy brown pods and the seeds will simply fall out and onto the ground, usually to sprout near the mother plant.

from hardware stores—near the base of the plants you wish to propagate; this will help you find them after the flowers have faded. You may also want to record the location and a description of the species in a gardening log.

The next step is to watch the plants as their blooms fade and form seed-bearing fruits. These fruits will be either dry or fleshy. Generally, meadow wildflowers, such as milkweed and those plants with daisylike blooms, develop dry seed heads where the flowers used to be. By contrast, the seeds of some spring-blooming woodland wildflowers, such as jack-in-the-pulpit, are embedded in fleshy berries, which can grow in dense clusters, in small groups, or individually on the stem.

Fruits disperse their seeds in a variety of ways. If you know what sort of fruit is produced by your tagged wildflowers, you'll be well prepared to collect them properly and at the right time. The dry fruits of some plants, such as Joe-Pye weed, simply drop whole to the ground when ripe, whereas others—milkweed, for example—split or crack open while still attached to the plants' stalks, letting the wind blow the seeds to new locations. Still others forcibly eject their seeds. The fruit of sky lupine, for example, explodes with a popping sound, shooting seed up to 10 feet away.

Capturing Seeds

1. To trap the seeds of a wild-flower *that disperses them quickly—such as the columbine shown here—enclose the fruits while they are still green in bags made from 6-inch lengths of nylon stockings. Slip the bags over the pods and gently secure both ends with twist ties.*

2. Inspect the plant every few days *to see whether the fruits have fully ripened and begun to drop their seeds into the bags. If they have, gently shake the flower stalks to dislodge any seeds remaining in the pods. Then remove the bags from the stalks one by one and carefully shake the loose seeds into a paper sack. Label the sack with the plant name and the date of collection.*

Preparing Seeds of Nonfleshy Fruits

Proper cleaning and storage is essential to keeping your wildflower seeds viable. As soon as you return home from harvesting nonfleshy fruits, set them out to dry; a few days later you can extract the seeds, then clean and store them, following the easy steps below. If you find that insects are present—as is often the case with summer-blooming wildflower seed—fumigate the seeds as well to keep the bugs from destroying your bounty.

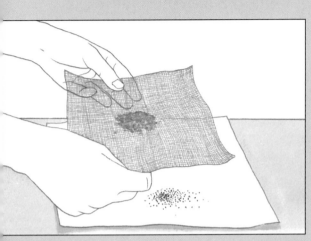

CLEANING *To remove chaff and litter mixed with the seeds, place them in a sieve or on a screen fine enough to trap most of the debris. Rubbing lightly with your fingers, let the seeds fall through to a clean sheet of paper. Then blow very gently on the seeds to remove the fine pieces of chaff that have come through the sieve.*

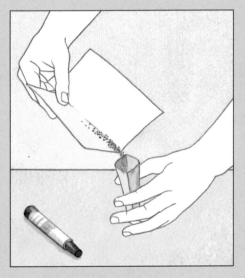

STORING *Let the cleaned seeds air-dry for several days on the paper. Then crease the paper down the middle and carefully pour the seeds into a small paper bag or envelope. Fold down the top of the bag and label it. Place the bags in a jar with a drying agent, such as a quarter cup of uncooked white rice; cap the jar and store in the refrigerator.*

FUMIGATING *If insects are present in your seeds, fumigate them after packaging them in paper envelopes but before storing. Put on gloves and cut a 1-inch square from an insecticide strip. Place it in a widemouthed jar, cover it with a layer of crumpled tissues, and then put your envelope or bag of seeds in the jar. Seal the jar, let it stand for 4 to 6 days, and then remove the seeds and store them, as above.*

Fleshy-fruited seeds are spread by birds and small mammals, which eat but cannot digest them. Birds especially like the bright colors of ripe berries, and may quickly strip them from the plants. Even the lowly ant plays a part in dispersing the seeds of some wildflowers—in particular, bloodroot and trout lily. Enticed by an oily substance on the surface of the seeds, the insects carry them away from the parent plant back to their nest.

Harvesting the Seeds

The goal of the seed collector, then, is to gather fruits as soon as they are ripe. A rough rule of thumb is that plants produce mature seed about 1 month after they flower; however, both flowering and fruiting dates for a plant can vary greatly from year to year, depending on local weather. Your best bet is to check the plant every few days once the flowers have begun to fade. When you've determined that the seed is ripe *(page 71)*, gather it as soon as possible, before the wind or a hungry bird or animal gets there first.

To harvest wildflower seeds you'll need gloves, small paper bags or envelopes to put the fruits in, and a pencil or pen to label the bag with the name of the plant, the date, and the location. Plastic bags can be useful for collecting and transporting fleshy-fruited seeds, which may be messy in paper packaging.

Pick the fruits directly from the plants, being careful not to damage the plant or spill the seed. For dry-fruited plants that release their seed as soon as it is ripe, you'll need to plan ahead so that you can capture the seed as the pod frees it *(page 71)*. Do not pick up seeds from the ground, where they are more likely to have become infected by fungus or infested with insects. In fact, you should examine all seeds for pest or mold damage before you collect them, to avoid contaminating the rest of your harvest. Also, be sure to limit your take to one-third of the seeds from a given plant so that enough are left to increase the stand.

Processing Seeds from Dry Fruits

As soon as you've reached home with dry-fruited wildflower seed, take the liberated seeds or the pods out of their collection bags

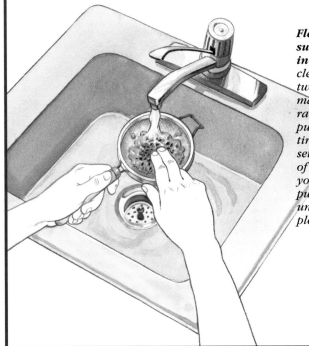

Podophyllum peltatum (May apple)

Wildflowers with Fleshy-Fruited Seeds

Arisaema dracontium
(green-dragon)
Arisaema triphyllum
(jack-in-the-pulpit)
Asarum arifolium
(wild ginger)
Asarum canadense
(snakeroot)
Asarum caudatum
(British Columbia
wild ginger)
Clintonia
(bead lily)
Mitchella repens
(partridgeberry)

Podophyllum peltatum
(May apple)
Polygonatum biflorum
(small Solomon's-seal)
*Polygonatum
commutatum*
(great Solomon's-seal)
Smilacina racemosa
(false Solomon's-seal)
Smilacina stellata
(starry false Solomon's-seal)
Trillium grandiflorum
(large-flowered trillium)
Trillium sessile
(red trillium)

and spread them in a single layer on sheets of newspaper. Leave them to air-dry for 2 or 3 days in a cool, well-ventilated room where the humidity is low. This step is extremely important, because any moisture in the seeds will cause them to rot later on.

After they have dried for a few days, the intact pods may split open unassisted and shed their seeds. To make sure you get all the seeds, crush the pods with your fingers. Fruits of foamflower and native mints, which crack as they dry, can be placed in a paper bag for drying and then shaken vigorously to free their seeds a few days later. Seed pods that remain closed after 3 days of drying can be crushed with a rolling pin or a mallet to free the seeds.

However you extract the seed, it is likely to have some chaff and litter mixed with it. The most convenient way to separate out the debris is by using a mesh screen or sieve. The illustrated instructions opposite show you how to clean, dry, and store your dry-fruited wildflower seeds—and how to fumigate them as well, since you may find that despite your best efforts some of the seed is infested with in-

Cleaning Fleshy-Fruited Seeds

Fleshy-fruited seeds, such as those of jack-in-the-pulpit, should be cleaned within a day or two after collection. After mashing the fruit, separate the seeds from the pulp by placing your entire batch in a strainer set under a gentle stream of running water. Use your fingers to press the pulp through the strainer until the seeds are completely clean.

sects. Properly handled, your dry-fruited wild-flower seeds should be viable for at least 2 or 3 years should you want to wait more than a season to plant them.

Processing Seeds of Fleshy Fruits

The moist seeds from fleshy fruits need to be separated from the pulp within 2 days of getting them home; this will prevent mold from setting in and killing them. If the pulp is fairly hard, you can soften it by leaving the fruits in plastic bags in a warm spot, such as on top of the refrigerator, for a day or two. Don't leave them any longer or they may begin to ferment, and you'll lose your hard-won seed.

If you have only a few berries, pull the seeds out with your fingers; if more, gently mash the fruits by hand or with a wooden block before picking out the seeds. Fruits that have softened in plastic bags may be kneaded in the bags to break up the pulp.

Clean the seeds by rinsing them in a sieve as shown on page 73. If you don't have a sieve, place the crushed fruits in a container of water for not more than 1 hour. Healthy seeds will sink to the bottom, allowing you to skim floating debris off the top. A bonus of using this method is that nonviable seeds will also rise to the surface, so you won't waste any effort with seeds that won't germinate.

Like the seeds of dry fruit, fleshy-fruited seeds do best when they are air-dried before storage. Package them in paper envelopes labeled with the name of the plant and the date and place of collection, and put the packets into a jar to which you've added a handful of uncooked rice to absorb any moisture that would rot the seeds. A few tablespoons of powdered milk wrapped in a paper towel and closed with a twist tie will serve the same purpose equally well. Cap the jar and store it in the refrigerator until you are ready to prepare the seed for sowing.

Sowing Seeds Immediately

Some seeds, if stored before sowing, may not grow in your garden for several years, because drying sends them into a very long dormancy. Instead of processing these seeds *(list, opposite),* sow them immediately after you've collected and cleaned them.

Seed Dormancy

Whether you collect the seeds yourself or purchase them, all seeds are dormant until the right combination of environmental factors—usually warmth and moisture—induces them to wake up and start growing. In nature, seed dormancy is linked to survival. Many species that live in climates with warm summers and cold winters produce seeds that will germinate only after they have endured a period of moist cold. This is nature's way of preventing them from producing tender seedlings in autumn that would soon be killed by winter frost. Other plants may produce seeds that are covered by hard outer coatings—an armor that can keep them dormant for any number of years by sealing out moisture. This tactic of nature reduces the risk that an entire crop will die out in a single season as the result of harsh conditions, because seeds produced by the same plant one season may germinate over a range of years.

Helping Seeds Germinate

To break the dormancy of seeds that usually sleep through the winter, you need to fool them with a good chilling—a process known as stratification. Stratification must be started 8 to 12 weeks before you intend to sow your seeds. The list opposite identifies many of the wildflower species whose seeds need to be chilled before they will germinate.

To start the process, mix equal parts of peat moss and coarse sand, and moisten the mixture to create a damp but not wet medium. Thoroughly mix the seeds with the medium in a small plastic bag, seal it tightly, label with the date, and refrigerate. Check from time to time to see whether any seeds have sprouted; if so, they should be planted immediately. Otherwise, let the seeds chill for 2 to 3 months—a little longer won't hurt. At this point they are ready for sowing *(pages 76-79).*

For germination to occur in species with hard-coated seed, such as lupine and purple prairie clover, the coat must be penetrated somehow. Outdoors, the natural action of soil or microorganisms eventually breaks down the barrier, thus allowing water to reach the embryo—the viable part of the seed that will grow into a plant. You can imitate the process using a technique known as scarification. If

A RIPENING WILDFLOWER
The vibrant flower spikes of wild lupine (Lupinus perennis) ripen by turning to green seed pods (above, right). If they are collected rather than left to follow nature's course, the tough pods will need to be broken through— or scarified—before the seeds can germinate.

Seeds That Need Special Treatment

SOW IMMEDIATELY AFTER COLLECTING

Asarum
(wild ginger)

Clintonia
(clintonia)

Dentaria
(toothwort)

Dicentra
(Dutchman's-breeches)

Erythronium
(trout lily)

Sanguinaria
(bloodroot)

Trillium
(trillium)

STRATIFY

Aquilegia
(columbine)

Asclepias
(milkweed)

Echinacea angustifolia
(purple coneflower)

Geranium maculatum
(wild geranium)

Iris
(iris)

Lobelia cardinalis
(cardinal flower)

Mertensia
(bluebells)

Phlox
(phlox)

Podophyllum peltatum
(May apple)

Polygonatum
(Solomon's-seal)

Silene virginica
(campion)

Smilacina racemosa
(false Solomon's-seal)

Tephrosia virginiana
(goat's-rue)

Thalictrum
(meadow rue)

SCARIFY

Amsonia
(bluestar)

Baptisia
(wild indigo)

Centaurea americana
(basket flower)

Lupinus
(lupine)

Sidalcea malviflora
(checkerbloom)

Tephrosia virginiana
(goat's-rue)

Thermopsis macrophylla
(false lupine)

your seeds are large, first sacrifice one or two by cutting them open to see how thick the outer coat is. Then carefully give the coats of the remaining seeds a light nick with a sharp knife, taking care not to penetrate to the seed inside. To scarify smaller seeds, shake them in a bag with some sand or rub them between sheets of sandpaper to scratch their hulls.

After nicking or abrading the seeds, heat a large pot of water to between 170° and 200°F; remove the pot from the heat, add the seeds, and let them soak overnight. (In the case of some plants, such as bluestar, the soaking not only gets moisture to the seed but also deactivates chemicals that inhibit germination.) Plan to sow the next day, while the seeds are still wet or damp. A number of wildflowers whose seeds need to be scarified are listed at right. If you are processing seeds that need both scarification and stratification, such as those of goat's-rue, stratify them first.

Geranium maculatum (wild geranium)

75

In nature only a small fraction of the seeds produced by wildflowers ever sprout; fewer still mature into viable plants. You can better the odds for the seeds you've collected or purchased by providing them with an environment that encourages germination and growth. In most cases, this can be done either outdoors or in, depending on how much space you have, the number of seedlings you want to grow, and how much time and energy you're prepared to invest in the project.

Starting seeds indoors *(box, opposite)* gives you the greatest amount of control over the growing environment—and as a result, as high a germination rate as possible. On the other hand, seedlings that sprout outdoors are often healthier, and outdoor sowing methods generally require less of your time to nurse the seedlings along.

Seeds can be started outside in either fall or spring. Fall planting of seeds you've collected that year means that the germination requirements of most of the seeds will be met naturally. Most will then sprout the following spring, although some stragglers may sprout in subsequent years. The easiest method of sowing outdoors is by casting seed on top of the soil. Some gardeners lightly scratch the seeds into the soil, but many just leave them to survive without assistance, much as Mother Nature does. It's best to scatter the seeds in early fall so that cold fall rains can soak them into the soil; if you do it earlier, you may lose a high proportion to birds and insects.

This method is most appropriate for creating a wildflower meadow *(pages 62-63)*. It's also a good strategy to follow if you don't know what the seed needs to break dormancy, because sooner or later the germination requirements of seed that survives and stays put will be met outdoors. The number that actually do survive and germinate is likely to be low, however, so if you don't have a lot of seed, you may want to use a more effective method.

Starting Seeds in Flats

Starting seeds outdoors in flats and nurturing them into garden-ready plants requires considerably more effort than casting them onto prepared soil, but in return you'll end up with more wildflowers for the seeds you plant. You can do this in the fall, or in the spring if you've stratified and scarified seeds that need it.

The flats you use need not be large—3 or 4 inches deep is fine. Just make sure they have holes in the bottom to allow good drainage; although the seeds need constant moisture to keep from drying out, they'll rot if they stay too wet. Fill your flats with a light, porous growing medium. An equal mix of coarse sand and milled sphagnum moss is ideal, or you may purchase a commercial medium that is specially prepared for starting seeds; although such products contain no actual soil, they are typically called soil mixes.

Sow the seeds in your flats as described in Steps 1 and 2 on pages 78-79. It's best to sow them sparingly to avoid crowding later. Small seeds can be sown at a rate of three or four per square inch, but large seeds should be spaced as much as an inch apart. Larger seeds should be just barely covered with planting mix; leave small seeds uncovered.

Set the planted flats outdoors in a place protected from direct sunlight and wind. If you're sowing in the fall, protect the seeds from winter's fluctuating temperatures by placing the flats next to a wall and covering them with evergreen branches, as shown in Step 3 on page 79. You can also place them in a cold frame if you have one, but leave it uncovered; if the top is left on, temperatures may get too warm for seeds that need a cold period to germinate.

Flats set out in the fall must maintain a steady chill throughout the winter to prevent premature germination. Evergreen boughs placed on the flats or cold frame will serve this purpose by keeping the warming sun off the seeds. Except for making sure that the soil stays moist, the flats should need little attention until the seedlings start to emerge. Begin checking a few weeks before the last frost, and remove the boughs when the new plants begin to appear.

If you are sowing the flats in spring, set them outdoors in a shaded area where the emerging seedlings won't be damaged or killed by the hot sun. Check daily to make sure the growing mix stays moist.

Transplanting Seedlings

Soon after your seedlings emerge, they will be ready to move to individual pots or a cell pack, where they'll have the necessary room to grow. Transplant the seedlings *(Steps 4-7, pages 78-79)* after they've developed their second set of leaves but before the next set comes in. The first set of leaves to appear on a plant—the cotyledons—are not true leaves. They contain a reserve supply of food to nourish the seedling as it grows and produces its first few sets of true leaves. Although moving the plants before the second set of leaves appears could damage soft leaf, stem, and root tissues, there is a far greater risk to the plant if you try to do it later: Once the seedlings' roots have tangled with one another, you could rip the roots when pulling them apart.

Seedlings that produce new growth at the tip of the stem, such as wild indigo, should be positioned in their new pots so that the surface of the soil mix is just below the cotyledons. Wildflower seedlings that grow by forming rosettes, such as black-eyed Susan and cardinal flower, must go into the mix at the same depth they enjoyed in the flat. For rosette seedlings with dense, hairy leaves—such as purple coneflower—mound the pot-

Starting Seeds Indoors

Starting wildflower seeds indoors offers two advantages over any outdoor method: You get a higher proportion of seedlings, and you can force your seeds to germinate early, thus giving the plants a head start on the growing season. By the last average frost date for your area, you could already have good-sized seedlings to be moved outdoors. In fact, the foamflower shown below is small and vulnerable for so long after germinating from its tiny seed that it should always be started indoors to give it adequate time to prepare for the outdoor elements.

Time your indoor planting so that the seedlings can be moved outside as soon as all danger of frost is past. In general, seedlings need 3 to 4 weeks in a seed flat and then another 5 or 6 weeks in individual pots. Sow seeds—which should already have been treated to break dormancy, if necessary—in flats according to Steps 1 and 2 on pages 78-79. Plant them in rows with one species per container for easy transplanting later on. Next, push sticks or pencils into the growing medium at the edges of the flat, and drape a plastic bag over the props to form a tent that will keep the seeds warm and moist. Prick the plastic for ventilation. Place the flats in a shallow tray, set them in a warm place, and water them from the bottom by pouring water into the tray. Check the soil daily; add water to the tray as needed.

Once the seedlings emerge, acclimate them to the room's environment by folding back the plastic a little more each day so that in 7 to 10 days they are completely uncovered. Monitor on a daily basis to make sure the medium stays moist. Also, situate the seedlings so they get 6 to 8 hours of light per day. Grow lights set a few inches above the flat are ideal, although you can also place the seedlings in a window. Be careful to avoid direct sunlight, however, which can damage the tender plants. Rotate the flat daily so the seedlings don't bend toward the light.

When the plants show their second pair of leaves, transplant them into individual containers, as described in Steps 4 through 7 on pages 78-79. Continue to inspect daily for moisture.

Before the seedlings can be moved to your garden, they'll need to be hardened off. A week or so before planting outdoors, move the pots into a sheltered, shady location—a porch, under a tree or shrub, or a cold frame. Bring them back inside at night for the first few days, and after that only if the temperature drops below 45° F or if the weather is windy. Alternatively, you can leave the plants in place and, before the sun sets, cover them with a plastic sheet. This will hold enough heat to keep the seedlings happy overnight unless the temperature goes below about 28° F—a hard frost. If your plants are sun lovers, gradually increase their exposure over the next several days until they can tolerate a full day's worth of the sun's direct rays. At this time they should be ready for the ground.

ting medium at the base of the plant to encourage drainage. Otherwise the fine hairs on the leaves could trap water and cause leaf rot.

Seedling Maintenance

Set the potted seedlings in a well-ventilated location outdoors where they will receive adequate light but be shaded from the hot afternoon sun. Check them frequently during the first few days after transplanting. If the leaves start to wilt, shrivel, or turn brown at the edges, move them to a shadier spot. If the stems show signs of growing spindly, they need more light.

The most critical task in caring for seedlings is watering them properly. Keep the soil moist but not soggy, and water gently with a fine spray; a heavy spray or stream could damage the fragile shoots or wash the seedlings out of their pots. On sunny days, the seedlings may need more than one soaking to prevent them from drying out. Make sure not to overwater, however, or the plants may fall victim to damping-off, a fungal disease that causes plants to rot at the soil line. If you see any sign of rot at the soil line, spray with an appropriate fungicide, following package directions, to avoid losing your entire planting. In general, it's best to water before midafternoon, so that the leaves have time to dry before nighttime.

To promote faster growth, feed the seedlings weekly once they are established in their new containers with a weak solution of 20-20-20 fertilizer. Consult the product label for instructions. Take care not to give them too much: Overfertilizing can weaken and even kill seedlings by making them grow spindly or by burning the tender tissue.

Inspect the root growth each week. Once the roots reach the bottom of the container and show through the drainage holes or begin to curl up around the sides of the container, it's time to move the young plants to their final home in the garden—or into a larger pot if the garden site isn't ready or if you want the plants to grow more before planting.

Most seeds that have been started outside in the fall will sprout between midspring and early summer and be ready for transplanting to the garden in the fall. If sown in the spring, most species will sprout within a few weeks to 2 months, if dormancy needs have been satisfied, and be ready for the garden by fall.

Sowing Seeds for the Outdoors

1. To prepare the growth medium for your seeds, combine equal parts of coarse sand and milled sphagnum moss. Transfer to a seed flat about 3 inches deep with drainage holes. Fill the flat to within ¼ inch of the top, tamp the medium down and level it; add more soil if needed. Moisten the mixture from the bottom by placing the flat in a tray of water. Let the flat drain for 2 hours or so before you begin sowing seeds; the medium should be damp but not wet.

4. When the seedlings have emerged and grown their second set of leaves, they should be transplanted into a cell pack (right) or pots. To prepare a cell pack, combine equal parts of peat moss and perlite. Pile the mixture in the middle of the cell pack, smooth it into the individual cells, and tamp it down well.

5. Using a plant label or other flat, flexible tool, remove a small clump of seedlings—potting mix and all—from the flat. To avoid harming the stems, handle the seedlings by their stronger leaves. Carefully tease the roots apart, separating each plant one at a time; lay the seedling atop its own cell in the cell pack. Transplant only one small clump of seedlings at a time, and work quickly to prevent the roots from drying out.

2. For medium-sized and large seeds, *make furrows about 1 inch apart by dragging a pencil over the growing mix; the rows should be about the thickness of the seeds. Using one species of seed per flat, gently tap the seeds out of their packet and let them fall sparingly and evenly into the rows; place large seeds by hand. Cover with a thin layer of fresh planting mix, then mist. For very small seeds, sprinkle them evenly over the medium and spray well with a fine mist, which will create good contact between the seed and the medium. Label the flat with the species and date.*

3. Group planted flats outdoors in a location sheltered from sun and wind; *a spot close to the foundation of the eastern side of your house works well. Cover the flats with hardware cloth—a metal mesh—to keep birds and animals out. To keep flats that have been set out in the fall cool and sheltered all winter, shade them with evergreen boughs, which should go on after the weather has turned consistently cold and when the soil is likely to remain frozen. Remove when the soil has thawed in early spring.*

6. Using a dull-pointed pencil, *lightly press down on each seedling just below where its roots and stem meet, and nudge the roots into the potting mix. This should stand the seedling upright, but if it leans a bit let it alone; it will straighten up as it grows. After you have transplanted a clump of seedlings, mist them before moving on to the next batch.*

7. If you are growing more than one species in a cell pack, *you'll need to plant and label the seedlings so that you can identify them later. Starting at the near left corner and working front to back up each row, plant the seedlings in successive rows. Insert a label in the first cell for each species.*

Propagating by Division and Cuttings

In addition to increasing the numbers of wildflowers you grow by gathering and planting seeds, you can use the asexual, or vegetative, methods of propagating by division or cuttings. The encyclopedia at the back of this volume will tell you the various ways particular plants that interest you can be propagated.

Increasing by Division

Division involves separating a larger, mature clump of a species into smaller clumps or individual plants, called divisions. Perennial wildflowers should be divided when they are dormant. This generally means tackling early-spring-blooming plants in the fall and fall bloomers in the spring. Plants that bloom in late spring and in early to midsummer may be divided either when dormant in early spring, or in late summer.

Using a trowel or a spade, dig up a mature plant. Shake the roots to remove excess soil, and examine the crowns—the point where stems and roots meet. If a plant has several crowns, it can be divided into individual plants, each with its own root system. Separate the clump by hand, using your fingers to gently work apart the crowns. If the roots are too tangled, use a knife to slice through them. Working quickly to keep the roots from drying out, replant the divisions at the same depth as the parent plant and water them immediately.

New Plants from Cuttings

Taking cuttings from the stems or roots of established plants is another good way to multiply your stock of wildflowers. Stem cuttings can be taken anytime a plant is growing vigorously. Using a sharp, clean knife, cut off a 3- to 6-inch section of stem that bears at least two leaf nodes but no blossoms. Take cuttings from growth that is starting to firm up instead of from soft new growth, which may rot.

Working quickly to keep the cuttings from drying out, trim the bottom set of leaves from the stem and pinch off the tip to promote side shoots; keep the upper set of leaves, however. Dip the cut end of the stem in commercial rooting hormone powder and insert half of the cutting's length into a container filled with a moistened 50-50 blend of peat moss and perlite. This medium provides excellent drainage, needed to prevent rot.

Next, to seal in humidity, fashion a mini-greenhouse to place over the container. Insert pencils or other supports around the perimeter, and enclose the container in a large, clear plastic bag held up by the supports. Place it outside, away from direct sunlight, for 3 to 5 weeks, opening the bag daily for air circulation and occasional misting to prevent the cuttings from drying out. When the cuttings resist gentle tugging—a sign that roots have formed—remove the plastic and allow the new plants to harden off for several days. They can then be transplanted into individual pots or directly into the garden.

Taking Root Cuttings

Wildflowers that grow from clumps of thick fibrous roots, such as purple coneflower and bergamot, propagate easily from root cuttings. These cuttings are best taken from the parent plant when it is dormant. To take root cuttings, dig up a plant and shake or rinse the soil from its roots. With a sharp knife, cut several roots at least a quarter inch thick and 5 inches long from the crown of the plant. Wrap them immediately in damp sphagnum moss, since keeping them moist is essential to their viability. Replant the parent plant.

Next cut the roots into sections 2 to 3 inches long and lay the cuttings in rows in a flat filled with a moistened mixture of equal parts of commercial seedling mix and perlite. Lightly cover the cuttings with the growth medium, mist with water, and place the flat in a plastic-bag greenhouse. Check daily and mist to make sure the medium stays moist. In 4 to 6 weeks the cuttings should send up shoots and leaves. When the new plants are several inches high, they can be potted in individual containers or planted in your garden bed.

A Shortcut to Propagating Trilliums

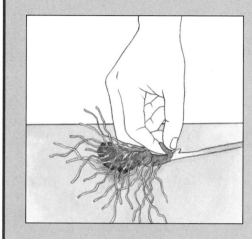

1. **To propagate trilliums that will bloom** in just a year or two—rather than the 5 years it may take if you grow them from seed—you must stimulate the plant's thick underground stem, or rhizome, to produce new plants. First, dig up a mature trillium after it has flowered, rinse the soil from the rhizome, and peel back the papery covering (left).

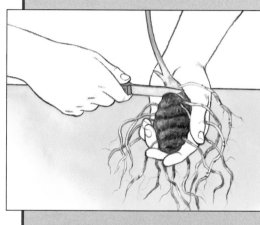

2. **Dip a sharp knife into a sterilizing solution of 10 parts water to 1 part chlorine;** rinse it thoroughly. Then carefully make a narrow, wedge-shaped cut around the rhizome at the growth ring near the top (inset). To keep the wound from rotting, dust it with a commercial fungicide according to the manufacturer's instructions. Work quickly to keep the roots from drying out.

Trillium ovatum (trillium)

3. **Replant the rhizome in a pot filled with a mixture of equal parts of loam,** sand, and organic matter. Bury the pot outdoors in a shady area and keep its soil moist. By the following spring, smaller trilliums should be nosing up around the base of the parent plant.

4. **In the fall, dig up the rhizome.** Slice off any offspring that have grown ⅛ to ¼ inch long and have developed their own roots. Plant the young trilliums in the garden or in containers. Repot the parent trillium, which should continue to produce offspring from the wound.

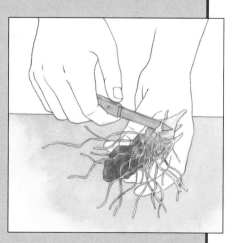

Answers to Common Questions

GARDEN DESIGN

I have a traditional landscape that includes an evergreen foundation planting, a number of specimen shrubs, and a large lawn. Is there some way I can incorporate wildflowers into existing plantings, or will I need to tear them out and start over?

You don't need to do anything drastic to incorporate wildflowers into your garden. Many of them are perfectly appropriate in a traditional garden that has a large proportion of nonnative plants. Your major concern will be to choose plants whose moisture, light, and soil requirements match the conditions of your site.

One of my gardening goals is to have color throughout the year. Is that possible with wildflowers?

With careful planning, year-round color is certainly possible. The encyclopedia in this book will help you pick species with bloom periods that overlap each other; as one species completes its life cycle, another species is beginning to bloom and will take its place. Be sure to plant a mix of perennials and annuals. The annuals will bloom for many weeks or even all season, providing continuous color and interest to fill any intervals between waves of perennial flowers. In fall and winter, foliage, fruits, and seed pods will offer a beauty unique to those seasons.

We are thinking of replacing some or all of our large lawn with a meadow of native plants. We want lots of showy flowers, but we also want a natural look. How do we go about striking the balance between different kinds of plants?

To create a meadow that looks like a wild landscape and is easy to maintain, healthy, and self-sustaining, at least half of the plants should be grasses. Besides adding texture and color, they provide support and protection for tall wildflowers; fill in spaces around wildflowers that would otherwise be occupied by weeds; prevent soil erosion; and provide food and cover for wildlife. As to the meadow's visual impact, there are many perennial and annual wildflowers adapted to meadow habitats with large, brightly colored blossoms for you to choose from.

Foliage is just as important to me as flowers when I choose plants for my garden, since the color, texture, or shape of their leaves can be assets all season long or even all year. I know that many wildflowers have spectacular blossoms, but how do they rate as foliage plants?

Gardeners can use many natives as attractive elements in a garden's foliage framework. Irises, for instance, are prized for their slender, rich green leaves, while goatsbeard and bugbane grow into big, bold, shrub-sized masses of ferny foliage in the woodland garden. For sunnier areas, choose fine-textured native clumping grasses such as little bluestem and prairie dropseed; snow-on-the-mountain for its white and green variegation; Culver's root for its strikingly regular horizontal whorls of lance-shaped leaves that remain fresh-looking all season; or the shrubby blue wild indigo, whose blue-gray leaves make a handsome backdrop for other flowering plants after its own spring blossoms fade. For evergreen foliage, some outstanding choices are the stiff gray-green fans of Adam's-needle; the rounded, mottled foliage of alumroots; silvery white sage; or wild ginger, with shiny dark green leaves.

Four years ago I planted a small meadow of wildflowers and native grasses from a commercial seed mix. It's beautiful, but some of the plants that bloomed heavily the first season aren't as dominant anymore. Is it normal for a meadow to change like this from year to year?

Yes. A wildflower meadow is a complex, interactive plant community that evolves over time. Annuals are its main source of color until the slower-developing perennials mature. Also, the species that are best adapted to a particular site will eventually come to dominate. In time the balance of species will tend to stabilize, but there will always be differences from year to year because of weather conditions such as a mild winter or a wet summer.

My yard is rather small, and it's already so full of plants that I'm not sure I can fit in any wildflowers. Is it worth trying to grow some in pots or in window boxes?

Growing wildflowers in containers is a wonderful way to enjoy the benefits of native plants where space is at a premium, and they are just as appropriate as other annuals and perennials. They provide concentrated splashes of color and can be moved as light conditions change or retired to an unobtrusive spot when their blooming season ends. They are also a great way to introduce children to the pleasures of growing plants. Among the many attractive natives for container plantings are baby-blue-eyes, bitterroot, clarkia, common stonecrop and wild stonecrop, California poppy, Drummond's phlox, mealy blue sage, purple saxifrage, and Tahoka daisy. Water plants suited to container gardening include fragrant water lily and pickerelweed.

SELECTING WILDFLOWERS FOR PARTICULAR PURPOSES

How can I make my garden more attractive to butterflies?

Nectar-rich wildflowers such as goldenrods and flowering onions are good food sources for butterflies. You'll also want to take flower color into consideration when you choose plants for your garden. Butterflies tend to prefer yellow, purple, blue, pink, and, sometimes, red flowers. Among their favorites are asters, Barbara's buttons, bee balm, butterfly weed, California fuchsia, cardinal flower, wild columbine, coyote mint, fire pink, gay-feather, goldenrod, Joe-Pye weed, mountain mint, partridge pea, passionflower, phlox, and pine lily.

My family enjoys watching the birds that visit our garden, and we also value them as a natural means of pest control. We already have a number of trees and shrubs with fruits that attract birds and would like to plant some wildflowers that would increase the food supply. What are some especially good choices for this purpose?

You can attract a variety of birds with an array of different seed- or fruit-producing annuals, perennials, and grasses such as asters, compass plant, fire pink, goat's-rue, goldenrod, jack-in-the-pulpit, mountain mint, partridge-berry, pickerelweed, purple coneflower, rudbeckia, Rocky Mountain bee plant, sideoats grama, spikenard, sunflowers, switch grass, tickseed, and wild geranium. Hummingbirds are attracted to nectar-producing flowers such as bee balm, cardinal flower, copper iris, columbine, lupine, monkshood, penstemon, fire pink, sage, spider lily, spigelia, verbena, wild four-o'clocks, wild hyssop, and yucca.

Are there any wildflowers that I could use as a ground cover to control soil erosion on a slope in my side yard?

New England aster, lanceleaf coreopsis, Indian blanket, and Rocky Mountain penstemon are all excellent choices for solving this problem.

Which wildflowers are suited to an exposed spot in a desert garden that is in full sun almost all day in summer?

Southwestern verbena, desert marigold, and desert mallow are just three of the many attractive wildflowers that will thrive in this hot, dry microhabitat.

Water drains from several neighboring properties into my backyard, so the soil is often damp and the lawn is growing poorly. Are wildflowers a sensible alternative to turf grass?

Though the majority of wildflowers would do no better than your lawn, some tolerate or even demand the soggy conditions you describe, including such fine ornamentals as sweet flag, swamp milkweed, rose mallow, blue flag, and cardinal flower. See page 35 for additional candidates.

One of the things I enjoy most about my garden is its wonderful range of sweet, spicy, and pungent scents. What are some natives noted for their fragrant flowers or aromatic foliage?

Wildflowers with fragrant flowers include Barbara's buttons, curly clematis, meadowsweet, Carolina phlox, Drummond's phlox, moss phlox, prairie phlox, summer phlox, spider lily, fragrant water lily, and sweet flag. For aromatic foliage, possibilities include bee balm and Oswego tea, which also have pleasantly scented flowers, coyote mint, flowering onions, giant wild hyssop, goldenrod, mountain mint, lyre-leaf sage, and the wild gingers.

I have a large cutting garden so that I can keep my house full of bouquets for as much of the year as possible. Should I consider adding some wildflowers for more variety?

The following plants are lovely additions to bouquets: asters, basket flower, blanket-flower, blue wild indigo, coneflower, Culver's root, flowering onions, flowering spurge, gay-feather, goldenrod, lupine, Mexican hat, obedient plant, pink verbena, purple coneflower, rattlesnake master, rudbeckia, sneezeweed, summer phlox, and tickseed.

For years there've been occasional reports of deer in our neighborhood, but the population has jumped since a tract of land nearby was cleared for construction. I like wildlife, but I don't want to see my garden eaten up. What are some natives that are safe from deer?

As you've discovered, deer will boldly invade well-populated gardens when the natural food supply isn't adequate. Only a few plants are so toxic that deer avoid them completely, but there are others that they normally shun except in extreme conditions. Among the unpalatable wildflower species are annual sunflower, black-eyed Susan, blackfoot daisy, gay-feather, milkweeds, nightshades, and Indian blanket. Ferns are also relatively deer resistant.

WILDFLOWERS FROM SEED AND FROM CONTAINERS

I'm planning a perennial wildflower border, and I would like to keep the cost down by starting the plants from seed. How long will I have to wait for the perennials to begin blooming?

Perennials usually do not bloom the first year after they are sown. Rather, they spend their time and energy establishing good, healthy root systems and will generally bloom the second or third year.

I have several unopened packets of wildflower seeds collected 2 years ago. Are the seeds likely to germinate after all this time?

The "shelf life" or longevity of seed varies from species to species. If harvested, cleaned, and stored properly, some seeds may be viable after as many as 10 years of storage, while others may not germinate after 2 years. Ideally, seeds should be planted within 1 year of collection.

I'd like to plant some wildflowers in my yard and was considering using a wildflower mix. Is this a good idea?

Seed mixes seem like a good idea in theory but in practice often produce more problems than they are worth. The vast majority of mixes are not formulated for a particular region and often contain a high percentage of species that are not native to the North American continent, much less a specific state. People who buy these "wildflower mixes" think they are planting hardy, native species, when in reality, they are planting exotics. You'll be better off putting together your own mix of species native to your area or buying a mix formulated by a nursery that specializes in wildflowers.

When I broadcast grass seed for a new lawn by hand, the coverage was very uneven. How can I avoid thin spots and clumps when I sow the seed for my small wildflower meadow?

For even sowing, first mix the seeds with fine, damp sand (roughly one part seed to four parts sand). Sow half of the mixture in one direction, then sow the other half in a direction at right angles to the first. Rake or tamp the seeds into the soil to ensure good seed-to-soil contact.

I thought blue wild indigo was supposed to be easy to grow, but I've lost all my seedlings. What did I do wrong?

The problem may be that the soil in which the seeds were sown lacks an essential microorganism. Like lupines, leadplant, and other members of the legume or pea family, wild indigos require bacteria that convert atmospheric nitrogen into a form the plants can use. Different legumes require different bacteria. The kind that wild indigos need, named *Rhizobium,* is available from wildflower nurseries in a preparation called an inoculum. Before sowing, wet the seed and coat it with the inoculum. When buying container-grown leguminous wildflowers, ask whether the soil has been inoculated with the appropriate bacterium.

How often should I water a newly seeded wildflower area?

Keep the top 1 or 2 inches of soil moist with a daily light sprinkling unless rain or overcast weather makes it unnecessary. If the weather is dry or windy, you may need to sprinkle the area twice a day to keep the soil from drying out. Continue this regimen until the seeds germinate and three or four leaves appear, then gradually reduce watering to two or three applications each week; water in the early morning to decrease the chance of root-rot disease and to minimize evaporation. As plants reach the flowering stage, provide deep-penetrating irrigation once a week.

When is the best season to plant container-grown wildflowers?

Fall is the best time for planting in Zones 7 to 11. Even though the air is cooler, the soil is still warm, which encourages root growth. In zones with colder winters, spring is the best time to plant. Wait until the average date of the last spring frost has passed before setting plants out.

Can you tell me what an "established" wildflower is?

An established wildflower is one that has reached a certain stage of development. Annual wildflowers are said to be established when the seedlings have grown enough to support six to eight sets of leaves and have started to branch out. Perennial wildflowers aren't established until the end of their first growing season.

SOIL AND FERTILIZER

I think my garden's soil is average. Do I really need to measure the pH?

Wildflowers need certain elements and nutrients to grow and reproduce. These must be absorbed from the soil, and the level of the soil's acidity or alkalinity influences the availability of these elements and nutrients. Every species is adapted to a particular pH range and, though plants may survive in soil that is more acid or alkaline than the ideal, they won't grow or flower well because their nutritional needs aren't being met properly.

Are there some rules of thumb for fertilizing wildflowers?

Grown in the soil, light, and climate conditions to which they are adapted, wildflowers don't need fertilizer to stay healthy. In fact, they usually grow better without fertilizer, which can produce rapid, excessive, soft, sprawling growth that is more susceptible to disease and insect attack.

How can I get my wildflowers to bloom for a longer period?

Deadheading—that is, removing blossoms that are past their prime—encourages wildflowers to bloom longer and more profusely, and it also keeps the plants looking fresh and tidy. This practice isn't appropriate if you want to collect seed from your wildflower garden for propagating, because it prevents seed production.

How important is it to mulch my wildflower beds?

Mulching with shredded bark, pine needles, or another organic material has many benefits. It controls weeds, reduces the need to cultivate the soil, slows evaporation of soil moisture, moderates soil temperatures, adds organic material to the soil as it decays, and gives the garden a finished look.

What is the best strategy for controlling weeds in my wildflower garden?

Weed regularly. It is much easier to eliminate an unwanted plant when it first appears than it is to dig out a mature root system later. Since most weeds are annuals and are killed by frost, pulling or cutting them before they set seed is a very effective way to sharply reduce or even eliminate next year's crop of weeds. Spot applications of a nonresidual herbicide such as glyphosate can be used for perennial weeds.

How often does an established wildflower garden need to be watered?

A watering schedule varies, depending on how old the plants are, sun exposure, time of year, and the type of soil in your garden. Plants with shallow root systems require more frequent watering than plants with deep root systems. Whatever frequency is called for, always water slowly and deeply to encourage deep, drought-resistant root systems. Annual wildflowers do not need to be watered after they have reached their peak of flowering. Many perennials, on the other hand, require continued watering throughout the growing season to maintain their health and vigor.

PESTS AND DISEASES

Very large caterpillars with black, white, and yellow stripes are eating the foliage of my butterfly weed. What should I do?

Don't do anything! It's worth tolerating a little damage, since the caterpillars are the larvae of the magnificent monarch butterfly. After feeding for 2 weeks or so, each larva encloses itself in a leaf green chrysalis studded with gold dots for the next stage of development. When metamorphosis is complete, the adult butterfly emerges from the chrysalis.

My neighbor said that the whitish growth on the foliage of my purple coneflower is powdery mildew. How do I get rid of it?

Although this disease detracts from a plant's appearance, it usually doesn't do any serious harm. An environmentally friendly treatment is to spray the affected plant with a baking-soda solution, then rinse it thoroughly with a fine spray from the garden hose. For other ways to manage powdery mildew, see page 92 of the Troubleshooting Guide.

Troubleshooting Guide

Although wildflowers seldom suffer serious damage from pests and diseases, problems can arise even in the best-tended garden. It's always better to catch an infestation or infection at an early stage, so make it a habit to inspect your plants regularly for warning signs. Remember that lack of nutrients, improper pH levels, and other environmental conditions can cause symptoms like those typical of some diseases. If wilting or yellowing appears on neighboring plants, the source is probably environmental; pest and disease damage is usually more random.

This troubleshooting guide is intended to help you identify and solve the occasional pest and disease problems that you may encounter. In general, good drainage and air circulation will help prevent infection, and the many insects, such as ladybugs and lacewings, that prey on pests should be encouraged. Natural solutions to garden problems are best, but if you must use chemicals, treat only the affected plant. Try to use horticultural oils, insecticidal soaps, and botanical insecticides such as neem. These products are the least disruptive to beneficial insects, and they will not destroy the soil balance that is the foundation of a healthy wildflower garden.

P E S T S

PROBLEM: Leaves curl, are distorted in shape, and may be sticky and have a black, sooty appearance. Buds and flowers are deformed, new growth is stunted, and leaves and flowers may drop.

CAUSE: Aphids are pear-shaped, semitransparent, wingless sucking insects, about ⅛ inch long and ranging in color from green to red, pink, black, or gray. Two slender, wax-secreting tubes project backward from the abdomen. Aphids suck plant sap and may spread viral disease. Infestations are most severe in spring and early summer, when pests cluster on new shoots, the undersides of leaves, and flower buds. Aphids secrete a sticky substance known as honeydew onto leaves, which fosters the growth of a black fungus called sooty mold.

SOLUTION: Spray plants frequently with a steady stream of water from a garden hose to knock aphids off plants and discourage them from returning. In severe cases, prune off infested areas and use a diluted insecticidal soap solution or a recommended insecticide. Ladybugs, green lacewings, gall midges, and syrphid flies prey on aphids and may be introduced into the garden. *POSSIBLE HOSTS: ASTER, BUTTERFLY WEED, CAMPANULA, COLUMBINE, COREOPSIS, CRANESBILL, DELPHINIUM, EUPHORBIA, GAILLARDIA, GOLDENROD, LUPINE, PURPLE CONEFLOWER, SUNFLOWER, VIOLET.*

PROBLEM: Small, round holes are eaten into leaves, leaf edges, and flowers. Leaves may be reduced to skeletons with only veins remaining.

CAUSE: Japanese beetles, iridescent blue-green with bronze wing covers, are the most destructive of a large family of hard-shelled chewing insects ranging in size from ¼ to ¾ inch long. Other genera include Asiatic garden beetles (brown), northern masked chafers (brown with dark band on head), and Fuller rose beetles (gray), as well as blister beetles (metallic black, blue, purple, or brown), flea beetles (shiny dark blue, brown, black, or bronze), and sunflower beetles (cream and pale yellow, dark striped wing covers). Japanese and other adult beetles are voracious in the summer. Beetle larvae feed on roots of plants and are present from midsummer through the following spring, when they emerge as adults.

SOLUTION: Handpick, shake, or jar small colonies out of foliage *(Caution: Use gloves when picking blister beetles)*, placing them in a container filled with soapy water. Japanese beetles can be caught in baited traps. Place traps in an area away from susceptible plants so as not to attract more beetles into the garden. The larval stage can be controlled with parasitic nematodes and milky spore disease, which can be applied to the whole garden. For heavy infestations, contact your local Cooperative Extension Service for information on registered pesticides and the best times to apply them in your region. *POSSIBLE HOSTS: ASTER, COLUMBINE, DELPHINIUM, GAILLARDIA, PENSTEMON, PHLOX, PURPLE CONEFLOWER, ROSE MALLOW, SUNFLOWER, VIOLET.*

PROBLEM: Holes appear in leaves, buds, and flowers; stems may also be eaten.

CAUSE: Caterpillars, including the larvae of violet sawfly, verbena bud moth, sunflower moth, and painted lady butterfly, come in a variety of shapes and colors and can be smooth, hairy, or spiny. These voracious pests are found in gardens in spring and summer.

SOLUTION: Handpick to control small populations. The bacterial pesticide *Bacillus thuringiensis* (Bt) kills many types without harming plants. If caterpillars return to your garden every spring, spray Bt as a preventive measure. Identify the caterpillar species to determine the control options and timing of spray applications. Several species are susceptible to sprays of insecticidal soap. Introduce beneficial insects that prey on caterpillars, including spined soldier bugs, assassin bugs, minute pirate bugs, and lacewings. Keep the garden clear of debris and cultivate frequently. Destroy all visible cocoons and nests.
POSSIBLE HOSTS: COLUMBINE, FALSE FOX-GLOVE, GENTIAN, GOLDENROD, IRIS, LUPINE, SOLOMON'S-SEAL, SUNFLOWER, VERBENA, VIOLET.

PROBLEM: Leaves and stems wilt. Sawdustlike castings are visible near small holes in the stems.

CAUSE: Columbine borer, a 1½-inch-long salmon-colored caterpillar with a pale stripe down its back, feeds in the stems and leafstalks of columbine in spring, then bores into the crown and roots to mature. It emerges as a large, reddish brown moth that lays its eggs on the surface of the soil near the plants. Bacteria and fungi may enter the plant through the columbine borer's holes.

SOLUTION: Cut off infested stems or destroy badly infested plants. Remove any mulch or debris around columbines in spring and cultivate the soil to get rid of any overwintering eggs.
POSSIBLE HOSTS: ALL COLUMBINES.

PROBLEM: Stems of emerging young plants are cut off near the ground; seedlings may be completely eaten. Leaves of older plants show ragged edges and chewed holes.

CAUSE: Cutworms, the larvae of various moths, are fat, hairless, and gray or dull brown in color. These 1- to 2-inch-long night feeders do the most damage in the spring. In the daytime, they curl up into a C shape and are found under debris or below the soil surface next to the plant stem.

SOLUTION: Place barriers called cutworm collars around the base of a plant. Introduce beneficials that prey on cutworms, including parasitic braconid wasps and tachinid flies. Use crushed eggshells, wood ashes, and oak-leaf mulch around plants to discourage cutworms. To reduce hiding places and discourage egg laying, keep the area weeded and free of debris. Apply *Bacillus thuringiensis* (Bt).
POSSIBLE HOSTS: YOUNG SEEDLINGS AND TRANSPLANTS.

PROBLEM: White or light green serpentine tunnels or blotches appear in leaves; leaves may lose color, dry up, and die. Seedlings may be stunted or die.

CAUSE: Leaf miners—minute (1/16 to 1/8 inch long) translucent, pale green larvae of certain flies, moths, or beetles—are hatched from eggs laid on the leaves of plants. During spring and summer, the larvae eat the tender interior below the surface of the leaf, leaving behind trails of blistered tissue known as mines. In the fall, fully grown miners crawl into the soil to overwinter.

SOLUTION: Damage may be unsightly but is usually not lethal. Pick off and destroy infested leaves as they appear. In the fall, cut infested plants to the ground and destroy. Remove and destroy leaves with egg clusters. Cultivating the soil around the plants in the fall exposes miners to birds and the elements. Use a systemic insecticide, timing applications at proper intervals, before leaf mining becomes extensive.
POSSIBLE HOSTS: ASTER, COLUMBINE, DELPHINIUM, MONKSHOOD.

PROBLEM: Light-colored sunken brown spots appear on the upper surfaces of leaves. Foliage may wilt, discolor, and fall from the plant. Shoots may be distorted or blackened. Flower buds may be deformed.

CAUSE: Plant bugs include the four-lined plant bug, lygus bug, black stink bug, lace bug, yucca plant bug, and tarnished plant bug. Active from early spring to early summer, these 1/4-inch-long sucking insects are brown, black, green, yellow, or brightly colored or patterned and have antennae and wings.

SOLUTION: In most cases, plants recover from the feeding injury, and control is often unnecessary. If infestation is severe, eliminate debris that could be breeding grounds. Introduce beneficials into the garden, including tachinid flies, big-eyed bugs, and damsel bugs. Spray plants with water or a diluted soap solution, or use an insecticidal soap to control nymphs.
POSSIBLE HOSTS: ALUMROOT, ASTER, BEARD-TONGUE, COLUMBINE, MONKSHOOD, PHLOX, PURPLE CONEFLOWER, RUDBECKIA, YUCCA.

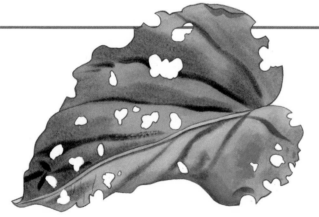

PROBLEM: Ragged holes are eaten in leaves, especially those near the ground. New shoots and seedlings may disappear. Telltale silver streaks appear on leaves and garden paths.

CAUSE: Slugs or snails hide during the day and feed on low-hanging leaves at night or on overcast or rainy days. They prefer damp soil in a shady location and are most damaging in summer, especially in wet regions or during rainy years.

SOLUTION: Keep garden clean to minimize hiding places. Handpick slugs or trap them by placing saucers of beer near plants. Slugs will also collect under a board laid on the ground or under inverted grapefruit halves or melon rinds. Salt kills slugs and snails but may damage plants. Barrier strips of coarse sand or cinders or copper garden edging also act as deterrents. Encourage rove beetles, which prey on slugs. Spading in the spring destroys dormant slugs and eggs.
POSSIBLE HOSTS: WILDFLOWERS WITH TENDER FOLIAGE INCLUDING BUGBANE, CAMPANULA, DELPHINIUM, GENTIAN, LILY, TRILLIUM, AND VIOLET. IRIS AND MANY OTHER KINDS OF WILDFLOWERS THAT ARE SELDOM BOTHERED BY SLUGS AND SNAILS WHEN MATURE ARE VULNERABLE WHILE THEIR FOLIAGE IS YOUNG AND TENDER.

PROBLEM: A slight yellowing along leaf veins occurs on young infected plants. As the disease progresses, the entire plant yellows. Flowers are small and have a yellow-green color. New root, flower, and leaf growth is distorted, and leaves are stunted. Plants wilt and die.

CAUSE: Aster yellows, a viral disease that despite its name attacks many different plants, can appear throughout the growing season.

SOLUTION: Remove and destroy infected plants. Six-spotted leafhoppers spread the virus, so remove perennial weeds in which leafhopper eggs may overwinter.
POSSIBLE HOSTS: ASTER, CAMPANULA, COLUMBINE, COREOPSIS, DELPHINIUM, GAILLARDIA, PURPLE CONEFLOWER, RUDBECKIA, SNEEZEWEED.

PROBLEM: Flowers are streaked with white, gray, or tan fuzzy growth. Stalks weaken, flowers droop, shoots wilt and fall over. Buds may not open or may wither and blacken. Discolored blotches appear on leaves, stems, flowers, and bulbs, and eventually form fuzzy mold. Stem bases blacken and rot. Affected plant parts eventually turn brown and dry.

CAUSE: Botrytis blight, a disease caused by several species of fungi, produces microscopic spores that are present in most soils and can be carried by the wind to spread infection. The disease is most likely to develop during damp, cool, cloudy weather.

SOLUTION: Avoid overwatering. Place plants in well-drained soil. Thin out plants so they get more light and air circulation, or transplant them to a dry, sunny location. Cut off and destroy diseased portions. Cut stalks to the ground in fall and destroy, since the fungus overwinters in decaying vegetation. As growth starts in the spring, spray with a labeled systemic fungicide.
POSSIBLE HOSTS: BLUE TOADFLAX BLOODROOT, CAMPANULA, COREOPSIS, EUPHORBIA, GENTIAN, JACK-IN-THE-PULPIT, JOE-PYE WEED, LUPINE, MAY APPLE, SUNFLOWER.

PROBLEM: Overnight, young seedlings suddenly topple over. Stems are rotted through at the soil line.

CAUSE: Damping-off is a disease caused by several fungi that form in the soil and attack seeds and the roots of young seedlings at ground level. The problem often occurs in wet, poorly drained soil with a high nitrogen content.

SOLUTION: Use fresh or treated seeds. Plant in sterile medium topped with a thin layer of sand or perlite to keep seedlings dry at the stem line. Plants in containers are more susceptible than those growing outdoors. Give them well-drained soil with plenty of light; avoid overcrowding. Do not overwater seed flats or seedbeds.
POSSIBLE HOSTS: SEEDLINGS OF MANY WILDFLOWERS.

PROBLEM: Leaves turn yellow. Angular pale green or yellow blotches appear on the upper surface of the leaf, with corresponding gray or tan fuzzy growths that resemble tufts of cotton forming on the underside. Leaves wilt, turn brown, and die.

CAUSE: Downy mildew, a disease caused by a fungus, thrives in cool, wet weather, most often in late summer and early fall.

SOLUTION: Grow resistant species and cultivars. Promote dry conditions by not watering plants overhead after morning. Space plants and thin stems to encourage air circulation. Remove and destroy blighted plant parts or the entire plant if the infection is severe.
POSSIBLE HOSTS: ASTER, CINQUEFOIL, CRANESBILL, GOLDENROD, JOE-PYE WEED, LUPINE, PURPLE CONEFLOWER, SNEEZEWEED.

PROBLEM: Yellow blotches that progress to brown may appear on leaves. Damaged areas are bound by large leaf veins. Eventually the leaf dies and becomes brittle. Young foliage curls and twists; growth is stunted. Symptoms appear first on older leaves, then move up the plant. Flowers and buds may also be affected.

CAUSE: Foliar nematodes, microscopic worms, feed on the outside of young foliage and the inside of mature foliage, spending most of their time inside a leaf. They thrive during warm, wet summers. Wet conditions help them migrate on films of water to infect plants and soil.

SOLUTION: Destroy infected plants. If plant is not severely infected, pull off affected leaves and their two closest healthy neighbors. In fall, cut plants to the ground and destroy stalks. Avoid wetting foliage. Add organic matter to the soil to stimulate the growth of predaceous fungi.
POSSIBLE HOSTS: ALUMROOT, IRIS, PHLOX, SOLOMON'S-SEAL, WILD INDIGO, WIND-FLOWER.

PROBLEM: Leaves develop small yellow spots that gradually turn brown. Spots are frequently surrounded by a ring of yellow or brownish black tissue. Spots often join to produce large, irregular blotches. The entire leaf may turn yellow, wilt, and drop. Extensive defoliation can occur, weakening plant. The problem usually starts on lower leaves and moves upward.

CAUSE: Leaf-spot diseases, caused by various fungi and bacteria, are spread by wind and splashing water. Most prevalent from summer into fall, these pathogens thrive when humidity and rainfall are high.

SOLUTION: Destroy infected leaves as they appear; do not leave infected material in the garden over winter. Water only in the morning. Thin plants to encourage air circulation. A fungicide can protect healthy foliage but will not destroy fungi on infected leaves.
POSSIBLE HOSTS: ALUMROOT, ASTER, BLOOD-ROOT, CARDINAL FLOWER, CLEMATIS, CORE-OPSIS, CRANESBILL, DELPHINIUM, FIREWEED, IRIS, JOE-PYE WEED, LOBELIA, MAY APPLE, MONKSHOOD, PHLOX, SPIDERWORT, STORK'S-BILL, WILD INDIGO.

PROBLEM: Leaves become mottled with light green or yellow spots or streaks. New growth is spindly, and plant growth is often stunted.

CAUSE: Mosaic viruses are a group of viruses that can occur at any time of the growing season.

SOLUTION: Viral infections cannot be controlled. They are spread when a diseased plant touches a healthy one and are also spread via hands, tools, and insects. Remove and destroy infected plants. Introduce lacewings and ladybugs to control virus-transmitting aphids.
POSSIBLE HOSTS: ASTER, COLUMBINE, CRANESBILL, DELPHINIUM, GAILLARDIA, PURPLE CONEFLOWER.

PROBLEM: White or pale gray powdery growth appears on upper leaves and is followed by leaf distortion, yellowing, withering, and leaf drop. The powdery growth may also be seen on stems and buds.

CAUSE: Powdery mildew, a fungal disease, is especially noticeable in late summer and early fall when cool, humid nights follow warm days. More unsightly than harmful, it rarely kills the plant.

SOLUTION: Grow mildew-resistant varieties. Place susceptible plants in areas with good air circulation, mist frequently, and spray with baking-soda solution or fungicide. Spraying infected plants with compost tea in the evening can limit the spread of the disease.
POSSIBLE HOSTS: ACHILLEA, ALUMROOT, ASTER, ASTILBE, BEE BALM, COREOPSIS, CRANESBILL, DELPHINIUM, FIREWEED, GOLD-ENROD, JOE-PYE WEED, LUPINE, MONKS-HOOD, PHLOX, PURPLE CONEFLOWER, RUD-BECKIA, SUNFLOWER.

PROBLEM: Leaves turn yellow or brown or are stunted and wilted; the entire plant may wilt and die. Roots are discolored dark brown or black and may rot off.

CAUSE: Root rot, a common soil-borne disease, is caused by a variety of fungi found in moist soils.

SOLUTION: Remove and destroy affected plants and surrounding soil. Plant in well-drained soil; do not overwater. Keep mulch away from base of plants. Avoid damaging roots when digging. A garden fungicide may be used in the soil. *POSSIBLE HOSTS: ASTER, BUTTERFLY WEED, CAMPANULA, DELPHINIUM, WILD INDIGO.*

PROBLEM: Upper leaf surfaces have pale yellow or white spots; undersides of leaves are covered with orange or yellow raised pustules. Leaves wilt and hang down along the stem. Pustules may become more numerous, destroying leaves and occasionally the entire plant. Plants may be stunted in severe cases.

CAUSE: Rust, a disease caused by a fungus, is a problem in the late summer and early fall and is most prevalent when nights are cool and humid. Rust spores are spread by wind and rainfall and may overwinter on plant debris.

SOLUTION: Grow resistant varieties. Water early in the day and avoid wetting leaves. Provide good air circulation. Remove and destroy infected leaves. Clean up garden debris to remove overwintering sites. Spray with sulfur or a fungicide. *POSSIBLE HOSTS: ASTER, BEE BALM, BUTTERFLY WEED, CAMPANULA, COLUMBINE, CONEFLOWER, COREOPSIS, CRANESBILL, DELPHINIUM, GAY-FEATHER, GAILLARDIA, GENTIAN, IRIS, LUPINE, PENSTEMON, PHLOX, RUDBECKIA, SHOOTING STAR, SUNFLOWER, WILD INDIGO.*

PROBLEM: Plant is wilted, yellowed, or stunted, and it may die. Sometimes roots have knots or galls.

CAUSE: Soil nematodes—microscopic worms that live in the soil and feed on roots—inhibit a plant's intake of nitrogen. Damage is at its worst in warm, moist sandy soils in sunny locations.

SOLUTION: Since nematodes are microscopic, only a laboratory test will confirm their presence. Dispose of infected plants and the surrounding soil, or solarize the soil by fixing a sheet of clear plastic over the ground and leaving it in place 1 to 2 months. Grow resistant species or cultivars; interplant with nonhost plants such as marigolds. Add nitrogen fertilizer. *POSSIBLE HOSTS: BLUE TOADFLAX, BUGBANE, CLEMATIS, COREOPSIS, CRANESBILL, GAY-FEATHER, PHLOX, VIOLET.*

PROBLEM: Entire plant becomes yellow, wilts, fails to grow, and eventually dies. Symptoms usually appear first on the lower and outer plant parts. A cut across the stem near the base reveals dark streaks or other discoloration on the tissue inside.

CAUSE: Vascular wilt caused by fusarium and verticillium fungi in the soil displays similar symptoms. Fusarium wilt is more prevalent in hot weather, and verticillium wilt is found in cool weather. In both diseases, the fungus responsible forms strands that penetrate the roots and stems and eventually clog the water-conducting vessels. Both fungi are long-lived, remaining in the soil for years after the host plant has died.

SOLUTION: Destroy infected plants; substitute resistant varieties. Wash hands and disinfect tools. Don't site susceptible plants in an area that has been infected previously. Solarize the soil by fixing a sheet of clear plastic over the ground and leaving it in place 1 to 2 months. *POSSIBLE HOSTS: ASTER, COREOPSIS, DELPHINIUM, GAILLARDIA, MONKSHOOD, SUNFLOWER.*

Plant Selection Guide

Organized by flower color, this chart provides information needed to select species and varieties that will thrive in the particular conditions of your garden. For additional information on each plant, refer to the encyclopedia that begins on page 102.

WHITE	ZONES										SOIL				LIGHT			BLOOMING SEASON				PLANT HEIGHT			NOTED FOR			
	Zone 3	Zone 4	Zone 5	Zone 6	Zone 7	Zone 8	Zone 9	Zone 10	Zone 11	Dry	Well-Drained	Moist	Boggy	Full Sun	Partial Shade	Shade	Spring	Summer	Fall	Winter	Under 2 ft.	2-3 ft.	Over 3 ft.	Long Bloom Season	Form	Distinctive Foliage	Fruit/Seed Heads
ALLIUM CERNUUM	✓	✓	✓	✓	✓	✓				✓	✓	✓		✓	✓			✓			✓						
ANEMONE CANADENSIS	✓	✓	✓								✓	✓		✓	✓		✓	✓			✓				✓	✓	
ASTER UMBELLATUS		✓	✓	✓	✓						✓	✓		✓	✓			✓				✓	✓	✓	✓		
CHELONE GLABRA	✓	✓	✓	✓	✓							✓			✓			✓				✓	✓				
CIMICIFUGA AMERICANA		✓	✓	✓								✓			✓			✓					✓		✓	✓	
CLINTONIA UNIFLORA		✓	✓	✓	✓							✓			✓	✓	✓				✓					✓	✓
DENTARIA LACINIATA		✓	✓	✓	✓	✓						✓			✓	✓	✓				✓					✓	
DICENTRA CUCULLARIA	✓	✓	✓								✓	✓			✓		✓				✓				✓	✓	
DODECATHEON DENTATUM		✓	✓	✓	✓							✓			✓	✓	✓				✓				✓	✓	
ERIOGONUM WRIGHTII			✓	✓	✓	✓	✓			✓				✓				✓	✓		✓			✓	✓	✓	
ERYNGIUM YUCCIFOLIUM		✓	✓	✓	✓	✓	✓			✓	✓	✓		✓				✓				✓	✓		✓	✓	
ERYTHRONIUM ALBIDUM VAR. ALBIDUM		✓	✓	✓	✓							✓			✓		✓				✓					✓	
EUPATORIUM RUGOSUM		✓	✓	✓	✓							✓	✓		✓	✓		✓	✓				✓	✓	✓	✓	
GAURA LINDHEIMERI			✓	✓	✓	✓				✓	✓			✓				✓	✓			✓	✓	✓	✓		
HEUCHERA MICRANTHA		✓	✓	✓	✓						✓	✓		✓	✓	✓	✓	✓			✓				✓	✓	✓
HYMENOCALLIS OCCIDENTALIS			✓	✓	✓	✓						✓	✓	✓	✓			✓	✓			✓			✓		
MELAMPODIUM LEUCANTHUM		✓	✓	✓	✓	✓				✓	✓			✓			✓	✓	✓		✓			✓	✓	✓	
MITCHELLA REPENS	✓	✓	✓	✓	✓	✓						✓			✓	✓	✓				✓				✓	✓	✓
NEMOPHILA MACULATA*											✓	✓		✓	✓		✓	✓			✓				✓	✓	
NYMPHAEA ODORATA	✓	✓	✓	✓	✓	✓	✓					✓	✓	✓				✓			✓				✓	✓	
OENOTHERA CAESPITOSA		✓	✓	✓	✓	✓				✓				✓			✓	✓			✓				✓	✓	
PENSTEMON CANESCENS			✓	✓	✓					✓					✓			✓			✓						
PODOPHYLLUM PELTATUM	✓	✓	✓	✓	✓							✓			✓	✓	✓				✓				✓	✓	✓
SAGITTARIA LATIFOLIA	✓	✓	✓	✓	✓	✓	✓						✓	✓				✓					✓			✓	
SANGUINARIA CANADENSIS	✓	✓	✓	✓	✓	✓					✓	✓			✓		✓				✓				✓	✓	
SAXIFRAGA CALIFORNICA			✓	✓	✓						✓	✓			✓		✓				✓				✓		
SCHIZACHYRIUM SCOPARIUM	✓	✓	✓	✓	✓	✓	✓			✓	✓			✓					✓	✓		✓	✓		✓	✓	✓
SEDUM TERNATUM		✓	✓	✓	✓						✓				✓	✓	✓	✓			✓				✓	✓	

* ANNUAL

Color	Plant	Zone 3	Zone 4	Zone 5	Zone 6	Zone 7	Zone 8	Zone 9	Zone 10	Zone 11	Dry	Well-Drained	Moist	Boggy	Full Sun	Partial Shade	Shade	Spring	Summer	Fall	Winter	Under 2 Ft.	2-3 Ft.	Over 3 Ft.	Long Bloom Season	Form	Distinctive Foliage	Fruit/Seed Heads
WHITE	SMILACINA RACEMOSA		✓	✓	✓	✓							✓			✓	✓	✓					✓			✓	✓	✓
	SMILACINA STELLATA	✓	✓	✓	✓	✓							✓	✓		✓	✓	✓				✓				✓	✓	✓
	TIARELLA CORDIFOLIA	✓	✓	✓	✓	✓							✓	✓	✓	✓	✓	✓				✓				✓	✓	
	VERONICASTRUM VIRGINICUM	✓	✓	✓	✓	✓							✓	✓	✓	✓			✓					✓		✓		
	VIOLA CANADENSIS	✓	✓	✓	✓	✓							✓		✓	✓	✓	✓				✓				✓	✓	
	YUCCA FILAMENTOSA			✓	✓	✓	✓	✓	✓		✓	✓			✓				✓					✓		✓	✓	✓
	ZINNIA ACEROSA					✓	✓	✓			✓	✓			✓	✓		✓	✓	✓		✓				✓	✓	✓
YELLOW	AGAVE PALMERI			✓	✓	✓	✓	✓			✓				✓				✓					✓		✓		
	ARALIA NUDICAULIS	✓	✓	✓	✓	✓					✓	✓			✓	✓	✓	✓				✓				✓	✓	
	ARTEMISIA LUDOVICIANA			✓	✓	✓	✓				✓				✓				✓					✓			✓	
	BALSAMORHIZA SAGITTATA			✓	✓	✓	✓	✓	✓		✓	✓			✓	✓		✓				✓				✓	✓	
	CHAMAECRISTA MARILANDICA	✓	✓	✓	✓	✓	✓	✓	✓		✓				✓				✓	✓			✓			✓	✓	✓
	CHRYSOPSIS GRAMINIFOLIA			✓	✓	✓	✓	✓	✓		✓				✓					✓		✓	✓			✓	✓	✓
	COREOPSIS VERTICILLATA	✓	✓	✓	✓	✓	✓				✓	✓	✓		✓	✓			✓			✓	✓		✓	✓		
	ERIOGONUM COMPOSITUM		✓	✓	✓						✓				✓			✓				✓				✓	✓	
	ERYTHRONIUM AMERICANUM	✓	✓	✓	✓	✓							✓			✓		✓				✓					✓	
	ESCHSCHOLZIA CAESPITOSA*											✓			✓			✓				✓					✓	
	GAILLARDIA ARISTATA	✓	✓	✓	✓	✓	✓						✓		✓				✓	✓		✓	✓		✓			
	HELENIUM AUTUMNALE	✓	✓	✓	✓	✓	✓						✓	✓	✓				✓	✓			✓					
	HELIANTHUS MAXIMILIANI	✓	✓	✓	✓	✓								✓	✓				✓	✓				✓				
	HELIANTHUS SIMULANS	✓	✓	✓	✓	✓	✓	✓					✓		✓	✓				✓				✓			✓	
	LUPINUS DENSIFLORUS VAR. AUREUS*										✓	✓			✓			✓				✓				✓	✓	
	LYSIMACHIA CILIATA	✓	✓	✓	✓	✓	✓	✓					✓		✓	✓			✓			✓	✓				✓	
	MIMULUS GUTTATUS			✓	✓	✓	✓	✓					✓		✓	✓		✓	✓				✓		✓			
	OENOTHERA MACROCARPA		✓	✓	✓	✓					✓				✓				✓			✓				✓	✓	
	PASSIFLORA LUTEA			✓	✓	✓	✓	✓				✓			✓	✓			✓					✓		✓	✓	✓
	RATIBIDA PINNATA	✓	✓	✓	✓	✓	✓				✓	✓			✓			✓	✓	✓			✓			✓		
	RUDBECKIA GRANDIFLORA			✓	✓	✓	✓	✓			✓				✓	✓			✓	✓			✓			✓		
	RUDBECKIA SUBTOMENTOSA			✓	✓	✓	✓	✓					✓		✓				✓	✓				✓		✓	✓	
	SARRACENIA FLAVA			✓	✓								✓	✓	✓	✓		✓	✓					✓		✓	✓	
	SENECIO AUREUS		✓	✓	✓	✓					✓	✓	✓		✓	✓		✓	✓			✓	✓			✓	✓	✓
	SENECIO DOUGLASII			✓	✓	✓	✓	✓			✓	✓	✓		✓	✓			✓	✓		✓				✓	✓	✓

* ANNUAL

Color	Plant	Zone 3	Zone 4	Zone 5	Zone 6	Zone 7	Zone 8	Zone 9	Zone 10	Zone 11	Dry	Well-Drained	Moist	Boggy	Full Sun	Partial Shade	Shade	Spring	Summer	Fall	Winter	Under 2 Ft.	2-3 Ft.	Over 3 Ft.	Long Bloom Season	Form	Distinctive Foliage	Fruit/Seed Heads
YELLOW	SOLIDAGO MISSOURIENSIS		✓	✓	✓	✓					✓				✓				✓			✓				✓		
YELLOW	SOLIDAGO ODORA	✓	✓	✓	✓	✓	✓	✓			✓				✓				✓	✓				✓	✓	✓	✓	
YELLOW	SOLIDAGO SEMPERVIRENS		✓	✓	✓	✓					✓				✓				✓	✓				✓		✓	✓	
YELLOW	THERMOPSIS MONTANA	✓	✓	✓	✓	✓					✓	✓			✓			✓	✓				✓				✓	✓
YELLOW	UVULARIA GRANDIFLORA	✓	✓	✓	✓	✓							✓			✓	✓	✓				✓				✓		
YELLOW	ZINNIA GRANDIFLORA		✓	✓	✓	✓	✓	✓	✓		✓	✓			✓			✓	✓	✓		✓				✓	✓	
ORANGE	ASCLEPIAS TUBEROSA	✓	✓	✓	✓	✓	✓	✓			✓	✓			✓				✓				✓			✓		
ORANGE	ESCHSCHOLZIA CALIFORNICA					✓	✓	✓			✓				✓			✓	✓	✓		✓			✓			
ORANGE	IRIS FULVA			✓	✓	✓							✓	✓	✓	✓			✓				✓			✓		
ORANGE	LILIUM CANADENSE		✓	✓	✓	✓						✓	✓		✓	✓			✓					✓		✓	✓	
ORANGE	LILIUM HUMBOLDTII			✓	✓	✓	✓	✓			✓	✓			✓				✓					✓		✓		
ORANGE	LILIUM PHILADELPHICUM		✓	✓	✓							✓	✓		✓				✓				✓	✓		✓		
ORANGE	SPHAERALCEA AMBIGUA			✓	✓	✓	✓	✓			✓				✓			✓	✓				✓			✓	✓	
RED	AQUILEGIA CANADENSIS	✓	✓	✓	✓	✓	✓				✓	✓	✓		✓	✓		✓				✓				✓	✓	
RED	ASARUM CANADENSE	✓	✓	✓	✓	✓							✓			✓	✓	✓				✓				✓	✓	✓
RED	CLEMATIS TEXENSIS			✓	✓	✓	✓				✓	✓			✓	✓			✓	✓				✓	✓	✓		✓
RED	DODECATHEON AMETHYSTINUM		✓	✓	✓						✓	✓	✓		✓	✓	✓	✓				✓				✓	✓	
RED	GAILLARDIA PULCHELLA*												✓		✓			✓	✓	✓		✓			✓			
RED	GAURA COCCINEA	✓	✓	✓	✓	✓	✓				✓	✓			✓				✓			✓				✓		
RED	LOBELIA CARDINALIS	✓	✓	✓	✓	✓	✓						✓		✓				✓	✓				✓	✓	✓		
RED	MONARDA DIDYMA		✓	✓	✓								✓		✓	✓			✓				✓		✓			
RED	MONARDELLA MACRANTHA					✓	✓	✓			✓	✓			✓				✓			✓					✓	
RED	RHEXIA VIRGINICA			✓	✓	✓	✓						✓	✓	✓				✓			✓				✓		
RED	SILENE LACINIATA				✓	✓	✓					✓			✓	✓			✓	✓			✓			✓		
RED	SILENE VIRGINICA		✓	✓	✓	✓	✓					✓			✓	✓		✓	✓			✓				✓		
RED	SPHAERALCEA PARVIFOLIA			✓	✓	✓	✓	✓			✓				✓				✓	✓			✓			✓	✓	✓
RED	TRILLIUM SESSILE		✓	✓	✓	✓							✓			✓	✓	✓				✓					✓	
RED	ZAUSCHNERIA CALIFORNICA					✓	✓	✓			✓	✓			✓				✓	✓		✓	✓			✓	✓	
RED	ZAUSCHNERIA LATIFOLIA					✓	✓	✓			✓	✓			✓				✓	✓		✓	✓			✓	✓	
PINK	ALLIUM STELLATUM		✓	✓	✓	✓					✓				✓				✓	✓		✓				✓	✓	
PINK	ANTENNARIA ROSEA	✓	✓	✓	✓	✓					✓				✓				✓			✓				✓	✓	✓
PINK	BRODIAEA ELEGANS				✓	✓	✓	✓	✓		✓		✓		✓	✓		✓	✓			✓			✓	✓		

* ANNUAL

Wildflower selection chart — Pink and Purple.

Name	Color	Zone 3	Zone 4	Zone 5	Zone 6	Zone 7	Zone 8	Zone 9	Zone 10	Zone 11	Dry	Well-Drained	Moist	Boggy	Full Sun	Partial Shade	Shade	Spring	Summer	Fall	Winter	Under 2 Ft.	2-3 Ft.	Over 3 Ft.	Long Bloom Season	Form	Distinctive Foliage	Fruit/Seed Heads
CALLIRHOE PAPAVER	PINK		✓	✓	✓	✓					✓	✓			✓	✓						✓	✓		✓			
CENTAUREA AMERICANA*	PINK											✓	✓		✓				✓					✓				✓
CLAYTONIA VIRGINICA	PINK		✓	✓	✓	✓	✓						✓			✓	✓	✓				✓				✓		
CLEOME SERRULATA*	PINK											✓			✓	✓			✓				✓	✓		✓		✓
DICENTRA CANADENSIS	PINK		✓	✓	✓	✓						✓	✓			✓	✓	✓				✓				✓	✓	
DODECATHEON MEADIA	PINK			✓	✓	✓					✓	✓	✓			✓	✓	✓				✓					✓	
ECHINACEA PURPUREA	PINK	✓	✓	✓	✓	✓					✓	✓			✓				✓					✓	✓			✓
EUPATORIUM FISTULOSUM	PINK		✓	✓	✓	✓						✓	✓		✓	✓			✓	✓				✓		✓		
FILIPENDULA RUBRA	PINK	✓	✓	✓	✓								✓		✓	✓			✓					✓		✓	✓	
GERANIUM VISCOSISSIMUM	PINK	✓	✓	✓	✓								✓		✓			✓	✓				✓			✓	✓	
HIBISCUS GRANDIFLORUS	PINK				✓	✓	✓						✓	✓	✓	✓			✓					✓		✓	✓	
LEWISIA COLUMBIANA	PINK		✓	✓	✓	✓						✓				✓			✓			✓					✓	
LIATRIS ASPERA	PINK	✓	✓	✓	✓	✓						✓			✓				✓				✓					✓
MARSHALLIA GRANDIFLORA	PINK			✓	✓	✓	✓				✓	✓	✓		✓	✓			✓			✓			✓	✓		
MUHLENBERGIA CAPILLARIS	PINK				✓	✓	✓	✓				✓			✓					✓	✓	✓	✓			✓	✓	✓
PENSTEMON GRANDIFLORUS	PINK	✓	✓	✓	✓	✓	✓					✓			✓	✓		✓					✓	✓		✓		
PHLOX PANICULATA	PINK		✓	✓	✓	✓							✓		✓	✓			✓				✓			✓		
PHLOX SUBULATA	PINK		✓	✓	✓						✓				✓	✓		✓				✓			✓	✓	✓	
RHEXIA MARIANA	PINK		✓	✓	✓	✓	✓						✓	✓	✓	✓			✓			✓				✓		
SALVIA SPATHACEA	PINK						✓	✓			✓	✓			✓	✓		✓				✓					✓	
SIDALCEA MALVIFLORA	PINK			✓	✓	✓	✓					✓	✓		✓	✓			✓				✓			✓		
SIDALCEA NEOMEXICANA	PINK		✓	✓	✓	✓	✓					✓	✓		✓	✓			✓				✓					
SILENE CAROLINIANA	PINK			✓	✓	✓						✓			✓	✓		✓				✓				✓	✓	
SPHAERALCEA COCCINEA	PINK	✓	✓	✓	✓	✓	✓	✓			✓				✓			✓	✓	✓			✓			✓		
TEPHROSIA VIRGINIANA	PINK		✓	✓	✓	✓	✓				✓				✓			✓	✓			✓				✓	✓	✓
VERBENA CANADENSIS*	PINK										✓				✓			✓	✓			✓			✓	✓		
ZEPHYRANTHES ATAMASCO	PINK				✓	✓	✓	✓					✓			✓		✓				✓				✓		
AGASTACHE SCROPHULARIIFOLIA	PURPLE	✓	✓	✓	✓	✓							✓		✓	✓			✓			✓			✓	✓	✓	
ANDROPOGON GERARDII	PURPLE		✓	✓	✓	✓							✓	✓	✓					✓	✓			✓			✓	✓
ASTER LAEVIS	PURPLE		✓	✓	✓	✓					✓	✓	✓		✓	✓				✓	✓		✓		✓	✓	✓	
CLARKIA CONCINNA*	PURPLE										✓				✓	✓		✓	✓			✓				✓		
COLLINSIA GRANDIFLORA*	PURPLE										✓	✓			✓	✓		✓				✓			✓			

* ANNUAL

97

Color	Species	ZONE 3	ZONE 4	ZONE 5	ZONE 6	ZONE 7	ZONE 8	ZONE 9	ZONE 10	ZONE 11	DRY	WELL-DRAINED	MOIST	BOGGY	FULL SUN	PARTIAL SHADE	SHADE	SPRING	SUMMER	FALL	WINTER	UNDER 2 FT.	2-3 FT.	OVER 3 FT.	LONG BLOOM SEASON	FORM	DISTINCTIVE FOLIAGE	FRUIT/SEED HEADS
PURPLE	ECHINACEA PURPUREA			✓	✓	✓					✓	✓			✓				✓				✓			✓		✓
	EPILOBIUM ANGUSTIFOLIUM	✓	✓	✓	✓	✓	✓	✓			✓	✓	✓		✓				✓					✓		✓	✓	
	ERIGERON PHILADELPHICUS	✓	✓	✓	✓	✓	✓	✓	✓			✓			✓	✓		✓	✓				✓			✓		
	EUPATORIUM COELESTINUM			✓	✓	✓	✓						✓	✓	✓	✓			✓	✓		✓	✓			✓		
	FRITILLARIA LANCEOLATA			✓	✓	✓	✓					✓				✓		✓					✓			✓		
	GERANIUM ERIANTHUM	✓	✓	✓	✓								✓		✓			✓	✓				✓			✓	✓	
	IRIS LONGIPETALA					✓	✓					✓	✓	✓	✓			✓					✓			✓	✓	
	LIATRIS CYLINDRACEA	✓	✓	✓	✓							✓			✓				✓			✓				✓	✓	
	MACHAERANTHERA TANACETIFOLIA	✓	✓	✓	✓	✓						✓			✓				✓	✓		✓				✓	✓	
	MIRABILIS MULTIFLORA			✓	✓	✓	✓	✓			✓	✓			✓				✓			✓				✓	✓	
	MONARDA FISTULOSA	✓	✓	✓	✓	✓						✓			✓	✓			✓			✓	✓		✓	✓		
	PANICUM VIRGATUM			✓	✓	✓	✓				✓		✓		✓				✓	✓				✓	✓	✓	✓	✓
	PASSIFLORA INCARNATA			✓	✓	✓	✓	✓				✓			✓	✓			✓					✓		✓		✓
	POLEMONIUM CARNEUM			✓	✓	✓					✓	✓			✓			✓	✓			✓				✓	✓	
	PONTEDERIA CORDATA		✓	✓	✓	✓	✓	✓					✓	✓	✓				✓	✓		✓				✓		
	PYCNANTHEMUM TENUIFOLIUM			✓	✓	✓	✓				✓	✓	✓		✓				✓				✓				✓	
	RUELLIA CAROLINIENSIS			✓	✓	✓					✓	✓			✓	✓			✓				✓			✓		
	RUELLIA HUMILIS		✓	✓	✓	✓	✓				✓	✓			✓	✓			✓	✓		✓				✓	✓	
	SARRACENIA PURPUREA	✓	✓	✓	✓	✓	✓							✓	✓	✓		✓	✓			✓				✓	✓	
	SAXIFRAGA OPPOSITIFOLIA	✓	✓	✓							✓	✓			✓			✓				✓				✓		
	SEDUM ROSEA SSP. INTEGRIFOLIUM	✓	✓	✓	✓	✓	✓					✓			✓			✓	✓			✓				✓	✓	
	SISYRINCHIUM DOUGLASII		✓	✓	✓	✓	✓				✓	✓	✓		✓	✓		✓	✓			✓				✓	✓	
	TRADESCANTIA VIRGINIANA		✓	✓	✓	✓	✓	✓			✓	✓			✓	✓		✓	✓			✓				✓		
	TRILLIUM ERECTUM	✓	✓	✓	✓							✓				✓	✓	✓				✓				✓		
	VERBENA HASTATA		✓	✓	✓	✓	✓	✓	✓				✓		✓				✓	✓				✓	✓	✓	✓	
	VERNONIA ALTISSIMA		✓	✓	✓	✓	✓					✓	✓		✓	✓			✓	✓				✓		✓		
	VERNONIA NOVEBORACENSIS			✓	✓	✓	✓					✓	✓		✓	✓			✓					✓		✓		
	VIOLA ROSTRATA			✓	✓	✓							✓			✓	✓	✓				✓				✓		
BLUE	ACONITUM COLUMBIANUM			✓	✓	✓	✓	✓					✓			✓			✓					✓	✓	✓	✓	
	AMSONIA TABERNAEMONTANA	✓	✓	✓	✓	✓	✓	✓				✓	✓		✓	✓		✓					✓	✓			✓	✓
	AQUILEGIA CAERULEA	✓	✓	✓	✓	✓						✓	✓	✓	✓	✓	✓	✓				✓				✓		✓
	BAPTISIA AUSTRALIS	✓	✓	✓	✓	✓	✓	✓			✓	✓			✓	✓		✓						✓		✓	✓	

* ANNUAL

COLOR	SPECIES	Zone 3	Zone 4	Zone 5	Zone 6	Zone 7	Zone 8	Zone 9	Zone 10	Zone 11	Dry	Well-Drained	Moist	Boggy	Full Sun	Partial Shade	Shade	Spring	Summer	Fall	Winter	Under 2 Ft	2-3 Ft	Over 3 Ft	Long Bloom Season	Form	Distinctive Foliage	Fruit/Seed Heads
BLUE	CAMASSIA SCILLOIDES			✓	✓	✓	✓					✓	✓		✓	✓		✓				✓						
BLUE	CAMPANULA ROTUNDIFOLIA	✓	✓	✓	✓						✓	✓			✓	✓			✓			✓			✓	✓		
BLUE	DELPHINIUM TRICORNE			✓	✓	✓	✓	✓				✓	✓			✓		✓	✓			✓	✓			✓	✓	
BLUE	ERIGERON SPECIOSUS		✓	✓	✓	✓	✓	✓	✓			✓			✓	✓		✓	✓			✓	✓			✓		
BLUE	GENTIANA ANDREWSII	✓	✓	✓	✓							✓	✓		✓	✓			✓	✓		✓				✓		
BLUE	GILIA ACHILLEIFOLIA*											✓			✓			✓				✓					✓	
BLUE	IRIS CRISTATA		✓	✓	✓	✓	✓	✓				✓	✓			✓		✓				✓					✓	
BLUE	LINUM PERENNE VAR. LEWISII			✓	✓	✓	✓					✓			✓	✓		✓				✓			✓			
BLUE	LOBELIA SIPHILITICA		✓	✓	✓								✓			✓			✓	✓			✓		✓			
BLUE	LUPINUS NANUS*										✓	✓			✓			✓				✓					✓	✓
BLUE	LUPINUS PERENNIS		✓	✓	✓	✓					✓	✓			✓			✓	✓			✓					✓	✓
BLUE	MERTENSIA CILIATA	✓	✓	✓	✓	✓							✓		✓	✓		✓	✓			✓	✓			✓		
BLUE	MERTENSIA VIRGINICA	✓	✓	✓	✓	✓							✓			✓		✓				✓				✓		
BLUE	PENSTEMON HETEROPHYLLUS					✓	✓	✓				✓			✓	✓		✓				✓					✓	
BLUE	PHACELIA CAMPANULARIA*											✓			✓	✓		✓				✓			✓	✓		
BLUE	PHACELIA SERICEA		✓	✓	✓	✓	✓					✓			✓				✓			✓					✓	✓
BLUE	POLEMONIUM OCCIDENTALE	✓	✓	✓	✓	✓	✓					✓	✓			✓		✓	✓				✓				✓	
BLUE	SALVIA DORRII			✓	✓	✓	✓				✓	✓			✓				✓				✓			✓	✓	
BLUE	SALVIA LYRATA			✓	✓	✓	✓				✓	✓			✓	✓		✓				✓				✓	✓	
BLUE	SISYRINCHIUM ANGUSTIFOLIUM	✓	✓	✓	✓	✓	✓	✓			✓	✓	✓		✓	✓		✓	✓			✓					✓	✓
GREEN	ANEMONE VIRGINIANA		✓	✓	✓	✓						✓	✓		✓	✓			✓				✓		✓			✓
GREEN	ARISAEMA TRIPHYLLUM	✓	✓	✓	✓	✓	✓					✓	✓			✓		✓				✓	✓			✓		✓
GREEN	CHASMANTHIUM LATIFOLIUM		✓	✓	✓	✓	✓	✓				✓	✓		✓	✓			✓	✓	✓		✓		✓	✓		✓
GREEN	EUPHORBIA MARGINATA*										✓	✓			✓				✓	✓		✓	✓				✓	
GREEN	HEUCHERA AMERICANA		✓	✓	✓	✓	✓					✓	✓		✓	✓	✓	✓				✓			✓	✓	✓	
GREEN	POLYGONATUM BIFLORUM	✓	✓	✓	✓	✓	✓	✓					✓			✓	✓	✓					✓			✓	✓	✓
GREEN	SPOROBOLUS HETEROLEPIS	✓	✓	✓	✓	✓	✓				✓				✓	✓			✓	✓		✓				✓	✓	✓
GREEN	THALICTRUM DASYCARPUM	✓	✓	✓									✓		✓	✓	✓		✓					✓	✓	✓		
GREEN	THALICTRUM POLYCARPUM			✓	✓	✓	✓						✓		✓	✓			✓					✓		✓		
BUFF	ANDROPOGON GLOMERATUS			✓	✓	✓							✓		✓					✓	✓			✓	✓	✓		✓
BUFF	BOUTELOUA CURTIPENDULA	✓	✓	✓	✓	✓	✓	✓			✓	✓			✓				✓	✓		✓			✓	✓	✓	✓
BUFF	MUHLENBERGIA LINDHEIMERI			✓	✓	✓	✓					✓			✓	✓				✓			✓	✓	✓	✓	✓	

* ANNUAL

A Zone Map of North America

A plant's winter hardiness is critical in deciding whether it is suitable for your garden. The map below divides North America into 11 climatic zones based on average minimum temperatures, as compiled by the United States Department of Agriculture. Find your zone and check the zone information in the Plant Selection Guide *(pages 94-99)* or the encyclopedia *(pages 102-149)* to help you choose the plants most likely to flourish in your climate.

Zone 1: Below -50° F

Zone 2: -50° to -40°

Zone 3: -40° to -30°

Zone 4: -30° to -20°

Zone 5: -20° to -10°

Zone 6: -10° to 0°

Zone 7: 0° to 10°

Zone 8: 10° to 20°

Zone 9: 20° to 30°

Zone 10: 30° to 40°

Zone 11: Above 40°

Cross-Reference Guide to Plant Names

Adam's-needle—*Yucca*
Alumroot—*Heuchera*
Arrowhead—*Sagittaria*
Atamasco lily—
    Zephyranthes atamasco
Baby-blue-eyes—*Nemophila*
Balsamroot—*Balsamorhiza*
Barbara's buttons—
    Marshallia
Basket flower—*Centaurea*
Bead lily—*Clintonia*
Beardtongue—*Penstemon*
Bee balm—*Monarda*
Bee plant—*Cleome*
Bellflower—*Campanula*
Bellwort—*Uvularia*
Bergamot—*Monarda*
Bird's-eyes—Gilia
Bitterroot—*Lewisia*
Black-eyed Susan—
    Rudbeckia hirta
Blackfoot daisy—
    Melampodium
Blanket-flower—*Gaillardia*
Blazing star—*Liatris*
Bleeding heart—*Dicentra*
Bloodroot—*Sanguinaria*
Bluebells—*Mertensia*
Bluebells—*Phacelia*
    campanularia
Blue-eyed grass—
    Sisyrinchium
Bluestar—*Amsonia*
Bluestem—*Andropogon*
Bluestem—*Schizachyrium*
Boneset—*Eupatorium*
Bowman's root—
    Veronicastrum
Buckwheat—*Eriogonum*
Bugbane—*Cimicifuga*
Butterfly weed—
    Asclepias tuberosa
California fuchsia—
    Zauschneria
California poppy—
    Eschscholzia
Campion—*Silene*
Cardinal flower—*Lobelia*
Checkerbloom—
    Sidalcea malviflora
Checker lily—*Fritillaria*

Columbine—*Aquilegia*
Coneflower—*Ratibida*
Coneflower—*Rudbeckia*
Cranesbill—*Geranium*
Culver's root—
    Veronicastrum
Dogtooth violet—
    Erythronium
Dropseed—*Sporobolus*
Dutchman's-breeches—
    Dicentra cucullaria
Evening primrose—
    Oenothera
False lupine—*Thermopsis*
False Solomon's-seal—
    Smilacina
Fireweed—*Epilobium*
Five-spot—*Nemophila*
    maculata
Flax—*Linum*
Fleabane—*Erigeron*
Flowering onion—*Allium*
Flowering spurge—
    Euphorbia
Foamflower—*Tiarella*
Four-o'clock—*Mirabilis*
Gay-feather—*Liatris*
Glacier lily—*Erythronium*
    grandiflorum
Goat's-rue—*Tephrosia*
Godetia—*Clarkia*
Golden aster—*Chrysopsis*
Goldenrod—*Solidago*
Grama—*Bouteloua*
Green-dragon—
    Arisaema dracontium
Hair grass—
    Muhlenbergia capillaris
Hardy ageratum—
    Eupatorium coelestinum
Harebell—*Campanula*
Horsemint—*Monarda*
    punctata
Hyssop—*Agastache*
Indian blanket—*Gaillardia*
    pulchella
Ironweed—*Vernonia*
Jack-in-the-pulpit—
    Arisaema triphyllum
Joe-Pye weed—*Eupatorium*
Larkspur—*Delphinium*

Leather flower—*Clematis*
Loosestrife—*Lysimachia*
Mallow—*Hibiscus*
Mallow—*Sphaeralcea*
Mandrake—*Podophyllum*
May apple—*Podophyllum*
Meadow beauty—*Rhexia*
Meadow rue—*Thalictrum*
Meadowsweet—*Filipendula*
Merry-bells—*Uvularia*
Mesquite grass—*Bouteloua*
    curtipendula
Mexican hat—*Ratibida*
    columnifera
Milkweed—*Asclepias*
Mint—*Monardella*
Mint—*Pycnanthemum*
Mist flower—*Eupatorium*
    coelestinum
Monkey flower—*Mimulus*
Monkshood—*Aconitum*
Muhly—*Muhlenbergia*
Oswego tea—*Monarda*
    didyma
Partridgeberry—*Mitchella*
Partridge pea—
    Chamaecrista fasciculata
Pasqueflower—*Anemone*
    patens
Passionflower—*Passiflora*
Pickerelweed—*Pontederia*
Pink—*Silene*
Pitcher plant—*Sarracenia*
Poppy—*Eschscholzia*
Poppy mallow—*Callirhoe*
Prairie beard grass—
    Schizachyrium
Purple coneflower—
    Echinacea
Pussy-toes—*Antennaria*
Queen-of-the-meadow—
    Eupatorium fistulosum
Queen-of-the-prairie—
    Filipendula
Ragwort—*Senecio*
Rain lily—*Zephyranthes*
Rattlesnake master—
    Eryngium
Sage—*Artemisia*
Sage—*Salvia*
Senna—*Chamaecrista*

Shooting star—
    Dodecatheon
Snakeroot—*Asarum*
    canadense
Snakeroot—*Cimicifuga*
    racemosa
Snakeroot—*Eryngium*
    yuccifolium
Snakeroot—*Eupatorium*
    rugosum
Sneezeweed—*Helenium*
Snow-on-the-mountain—
    Euphorbia marginata
Solomon's-seal—
    Polygonatum
Spider lily—*Hymenocallis*
Spiderwort—*Tradescantia*
Spikenard—*Aralia*
    racemosa
Spring beauty—*Claytonia*
Squirrel corn—*Dicentra*
    canadensis
Stonecrop—*Sedum*
Sundrops—*Oenothera*
Sunflower—*Helianthus*
Switch grass—*Panicum*
Tahoka daisy—
    Machaeranthera
Texas bluebonnet—*Lupinus*
    texensis
Thimbleweed—*Anemone*
Tickseed—*Coreopsis*
Toothwort—*Dentaria*
Trout lily—*Erythronium*
Turtlehead—*Chelone*
Vervain—*Verbena*
Wake-robin—*Trillium*
Water lily—*Nymphaea*
Wild Canterbury bell—
    Phacelia minor
Wild ginger—*Asarum*
Wild hyacinth—*Brodiaea*
Wild hyacinth—*Camassia*
    scilloides
Wild indigo—*Baptisia*
Wild oats—*Chasmanthium*
Wild oats—*Uvularia*
Wild sarsaparilla—*Aralia*
Windflower—*Anemone*
Winecups—*Callirhoe*
    involucrata

Encyclopedia of Wildflowers

Presented here is a selection of North American wildflowers that includes annuals, perennials, bulbs, vines, and grasses. The plants were chosen for their ornamental qualities, ease of cultivation, and commercial availability. If local nurseries do not carry a species you want, there are many excellent mail-order nurseries that offer wildflowers. Wherever you shop, make sure that the plants have not been collected from the wild, a practice that threatens the natural environment.

The encyclopedia lists plants alphabetically by their botanical names; common names appear beneath the Latin. If you know a plant only by its common name, check the name against the cross-reference chart on page 101 or in the index.

The information given on hardiness zones refers to the USDA Plant Hardiness Zone Map (page 100). Plants grown outside the recommended zones may do poorly or fail to survive.

Aconitum
(ak-o-NY-tum)
MONKSHOOD

Aconitum columbianum

Hardiness: *Zones 4-9*

Flowering season: *summer*

Height: *2 to 6 feet*

Flower color: *blue, white*

Soil: *moist, rich*

Light: *partial shade*

The showy, hooded flowers of monkshoods are borne in loose spikes and attract hummingbirds and hawk moths. These perennials are found along stream banks and in moist woodlands. All parts of the plant are poisonous to humans.

Selected species: *A. columbianum* (western monkshood)—2 to 6 feet tall with palmately lobed dark green leaves up to 6 inches wide. The long-lasting, deep purplish blue flowers begin opening at the base of the spike and progress upward. *A. delphinifolium* (northern monkshood)—up to 28 inches tall with dark blue flowers and glossy palmate leaves. There is also a white-flowered variety.

Growing conditions and maintenance: Monkshoods thrive in partial shade and require abundant moisture. *A. columbianum* may need staking. Propagate by division of tubers in spring or by sowing freshly collected seed or the bulbils produced in leaf axils in outdoor flats in fall.

Agastache
(a-GAH-sta-kee)
GIANT HYSSOP

Agastache foeniculum

Hardiness: *Zones 3-8*

Flowering season: *mid- to late summer*

Height: *2 to 5 feet*

Flower color: *purplish red, blue, white*

Soil: *rich, moist to sandy, well-drained*

Light: *full sun to shade*

The giant hyssops are aromatic perennials of the mint family. They provide a long season of bloom in a mixed herbaceous planting.

Selected species: *A. foeniculum* (fragrant giant hyssop, anise hyssop)—2 to 4 feet tall, with neat, oval toothed leaves and fat terminal spikes of blue flowers. Both leaves and flowers have a distinct anise scent when crushed. The variety 'Alba' has white flowers. *A. scrophulariifolia* (purple giant hyssop)—2 to 5 feet tall with erect purplish stems bearing oval toothed leaves. It produces terminal spikes of purple-red flowers with purple bracts.

Growing conditions and maintenance: *A. foeniculum* prefers a dry, open site in full sun or partial shade. It is well suited to sandy soils and tolerates summer heat. *A. scrophulariifolia* prefers a shady site with rich, moist soil. Propagate giant hyssops by seed or by cuttings taken from nonflowering lateral shoots in the summer.

Agave
(a-GAH-vay)
AGAVE

Agave parryi

Hardiness: *Zones 6-10*

Flowering season: *summer*

Height: *6 inches to 15 feet*

Flower color: *white, yellow*

Soil: *dry, rocky*

Light: *full sun*

These succulent perennials form neat basal rosettes of fleshy sword-shaped leaves. They require several years of growth before flowering, after which the plant dies. Most are natives of deserts, high plains, or arid mountains.

Selected species: *A. lecheguilla* (lecheguilla)—8 to 13 feet with leathery yellow-green leaves. A stiff stalk bearing pinkish white tubular flowers rises from the center of the rosette. *A. neomexicana* (century plant)—stiff bluish green 6- to 18-inch leaves and yellow flower clusters at the top of its stalk. *A. palmeri* (palmer agave)—pale green leaves up to 30 inches long and greenish yellow flowers on a 15-foot stalk. *A. parryi* (Parry agave, mescal)—gray-green 12-inch leaves. Sends up a 15-foot stalk topped with red flower buds that open to creamy yellow blossoms.

Growing conditions and maintenance: Agaves thrive in poor, dry, rocky soil and full sun. Propagate by seed, by separation of offsets, or by division of the rhizomes.

Allium
(AL-lee-um)
FLOWERING ONION

Allium cernuum

Hardiness: *Zones 3-9*

Flowering season: *spring, summer, fall*

Height: *3 inches to 3 feet or more*

Flower color: *white, pink, lavender*

Soil: *moist to dry, rich to rocky*

Light: *full sun to partial shade*

The clusters of small, soft-colored flowers that characterize these perennials lend an air of delicacy to woodland gardens, mixed borders, or rock gardens.

Selected species: *A. cernuum* (nodding onion)—white to pink flowers arranged in loose, nodding clusters on 1- to 2-foot stalks in summer; most effective planted in groups; native across the United States; Zones 3-8. *A. falcifolium* (sickle-leaf onion)—flowers ranging in color from deep rose pink to nearly white borne on 3- to 5-inch stalks from early spring to early summer; produces two thick, flat leaves slightly taller than the flower stalks; its small size suits it to rock gardens; West Coast native; Zones 8-9. *A. stellatum* (prairie onion) —tufts of slender leaves 1 to 2 feet tall appear in spring, then wither in late summer just before stalks bearing 3- to 4-inch round clusters of showy rose pink to lavender flowers emerge; Zones 4-8. *A. tricoccum* (ramp, wild leek)—two or three strongly scented glossy oval leaves 8 to 12 inches long emerge in early spring, then die back in summer before 6- to 10-inch stalks with dome-shaped

clusters of creamy white flowers appear; native to northeastern deciduous forests; Zones 4-7. *A. validum* (swamp onion)—tight clusters of purplish pink flowers carried on stalks 3 feet or more in height from early to late summer; a native of the mountains of the Northwest; Zones 4-8.

Growing conditions and maintenance: *A. cernuum* prefers a humus-rich neutral to alkaline soil. It grows in full sun to light shade and dry or moist conditions. Clumps benefit from division about every 3 years. *A. falcifolium* thrives in full sun in dry, rocky soil. *A. stellatum* also prefers a dry, rocky soil, with full sun or partial shade. *A. tricoccum* prefers a slightly acid to neutral soil with sun in early spring and summer shade.

Allium tricoccum

A. validum requires moist soil and full sun. All can be propagated by seed or division of offsets.

Amsonia
(am-SO-nee-a)
BLUESTAR

Amsonia tabernaemontana

Hardiness: *Zones 3-10*

Flowering season: *late spring to summer*

Height: *1 to 3 feet*

Flower color: *blue*

Soil: *well-drained*

Light: *full sun to partial shade*

Bluestars are easy-to-grow, long-lived perennials native to the southeastern and south central United States. They bear tubular blue flowers that flare to a star shape. Use bluestars in a herbaceous border or at the edge of a woodland garden.

Selected species: *A. ciliata* (blue funnel lily)—erect 3-foot stems clad with narrow, fine-textured leaves and topped by loose clusters of blue flowers; Zones 7-10. *A. tabernaemontana* (bluestar)—1 to 3 feet tall with narrow oval leaves that turn gold in the fall. Flowers are steel blue; Zones 3-9.

Growing conditions and maintenance: Both species thrive in full sun or partial shade in a rich, well-drained soil. They benefit from added organic matter and supplemental watering during dry periods. Cut them back after flowering to promote bushiness. Propagate by seed, division, or cuttings.

Andropogon
(an-dro-PO-gon)
BLUESTEM

Andropogon gerardii

Hardiness: *Zones 3-9*

Flowering season: *late summer, fall*

Height: *2 to 8 feet*

Flower color: *green, pinkish, purplish*

Soil: *dry, sandy to moist*

Light: *full sun*

Bluestems are perennial bunch grasses found in prairies, open woods, and lowlands over much of the United States. The narrow leaves are blue-green in spring and summer and copper or maroon in fall.

Selected species: *A. gerardii* (big bluestem, turkeyfoot)—clumps 4 to 8 feet tall with purplish late-summer flowers in branched clusters resembling a turkey's foot. Leaves blue-green in summer and maroon to tan in fall; Zones 4-9. *A. glomeratus* (bushy bluestem)—clumps 2 to 5 feet tall with silvery green to pinkish flowers in bold feathery racemes surrounded by salmon sheaths in fall followed by fluffy white seed heads. Leaves and stems turn coppery after frost and remain attractive in winter; Zones 6-9.

Growing conditions and maintenance: *A. gerardii* grows best in a sandy loam and withstands periodic flooding. *A. glomeratus* prefers a moist site. Both need full sun and should be cut or mowed to the ground in late winter or early spring. Propagate by seed or division.

Anemone
(a-NEM-o-nee)
WINDFLOWER

Anemone canadensis

Hardiness: *Zones 1-9*

Flowering season: *spring, summer*

Height: *4 inches to 3 feet*

Flower color: *white, yellow, blue, pink*

Soil: *moist to dry, sandy to rocky*

Light: *full sun to partial shade*

The following perennial anemones all have showy flowers made up of petal-like sepals surrounding prominent stamens and pistils held above deeply cut foliage. Native habitats of the various species include moist woodlands, meadows, and dry prairies.

Selected species: *A. canadensis* (meadow anemone)—1 to 2 feet tall with deeply lobed basal leaves and 1½-inch white flowers with golden centers on leafy flower stems in late spring; native of damp meadows; Zones 2-6. *A. caroliniana* (Carolina anemone)—6 to 12 inches tall with numerous 1½-inch white flowers with yellow centers in spring; native of dry prairies; Zones 6-8. *A. multifida* (early thimbleweed)—loose clump of silky-haired stems up to 20 inches tall with deeply divided leaves on long stalks; sepals of the ⅜-inch flowers that appear from late spring to summer are usually yellowish white but occasionally bright red; Zones 3-9. *A. patens* (pasque-flower)—6 to 12 inches tall with deeply cut basal leaves and solitary pale lavender flowers 2½ inches wide in spring; native of dry sandy prairies; Zones 3-6.

A. quinquefolia (wood anemone)—solitary 1-inch flowers on 4- to 8-inch stalks in spring, usually white but occasionally pink or pink tinged; disappears after flowering; Zones 4-7. *A. virginiana* (thimbleweed)—2 to 3 feet tall with 1-inch greenish white flowers with elongated, thimblelike centers in summer and cottony seed heads after frost; eastern United States; Zones 4-8.

Growing conditions and maintenance: Most species thrive in full sun or partial

Anemone quinquefolia

shade. *A. canadensis* prefers a moist, sandy soil and needs frequent division to prevent overcrowding. *A. caroliniana* and *A. patens* prefer a dry sandy soil. *A. quinquefolia* requires full to partial shade and moist to damp soil. *A. virginiana* tolerates dry, rocky to wet soil. Propagate by dividing in early spring or fall, by root cuttings in spring, or by seed.

Antennaria
(an-te-NAY-ri-a)
PUSSY-TOES

Antennaria rosea

Hardiness: *Zones 3-8*	
Flowering season: *spring, summer*	
Height: *2 to 16 inches*	
Flower color: *white, pink*	
Soil: *dry to moist, well-drained*	
Light: *full sun*	

Pussy-toes are easily grown perennials that form low-growing mats of attractive fuzzy leaves. Used as ground covers, they effectively control erosion on sunny banks. The fuzzy flower heads are silvery white or pink.

Selected species: *A. alpina* (alpine everlasting)—western mountain native with hairy leaves and white summer flowers on 4-inch stems; Zones 4-8. *A. plantaginifolia* (plantainleaf pussy-toes)—native to the eastern United States; woolly white leaves and silvery white flowers on 4- to 16-inch stems; Zones 3-7. *A. rosea* (rose pussy-toes)—western native with soft gray leaves that form a 2- to 3-inch mat; clusters of six to 10 small light pink flowers on 10-inch stalks in spring; Zones 3-7.

Growing conditions and maintenance: Grow alpine everlasting in moist, well-drained soil and the other two species in dry soil. Antennarias make good ground covers and in ideal conditions may become invasive. Propagate by seed or division in spring or fall.

Aquilegia
(ak-wil-EE-jee-a)
COLUMBINE

Aquilegia canadensis

Hardiness: *Zones 2-8*	
Flowering season: *spring, summer*	
Height: *1 to 3 feet*	
Flower color: *blue, white, red, yellow*	
Soil: *moist, well-drained*	
Light: *full sun to partial shade*	

Columbines provide a delicate beauty to rock gardens and borders. They bear bell-shaped flowers with curved spurs above mounds of finely cut leaves with rounded lobes.

Selected species: *A. caerulea* (Rocky Mountain columbine)—1 to 2 feet tall with large blue and white summer flowers; Zones 2-7. *A. canadensis* (wild columbine)—up to 2 feet with red and yellow spring flowers; native to much of the United States east of the Rockies; Zones 3-8. *A. chrysantha* (golden columbine)—up to 3 feet with long-spurred yellow flowers; native to the southern Rockies; Zones 3-8. *A. formosa* (scarlet columbine)—western species 2 to 3 feet tall with red and yellow flowers in summer; Zones 3-8.

Growing conditions and maintenance: Columbines are short-lived perennials that usually self-seed once established. They require a well-drained location and supplemental watering during dry periods. Propagate by seed or division.

Aralia
(a-RAY-lee-a)
WILD SARSAPARILLA

Aralia racemosa

Hardiness: *Zones 3-10*

Flowering season: *spring, summer*

Height: *1 to 6 feet*

Flower color: *greenish white, white*

Soil: *dry to moist, acid, fertile*

Light: *partial to full shade*

Aralias are perennials that grow in open woods over much of the United States. Their large compound leaves impart a lush appearance to a garden, and their berries attract birds to the garden.

Selected species: *A. nudicaulis* (wild sarsaparilla)—up to 1 foot in height with 6-inch doubly compound leaves, greenish white flowers from late spring to early summer, and purplish fall berries; use as a woodland ground cover; Zones 3-7. *A. racemosa* (spikenard)—6 feet tall with leaves up to 2½ feet long and large clusters of tiny white flowers tinged with yellow or green in early to midsummer followed by purple berries; Zones 4-10.

Growing conditions and maintenance: Aralias thrive in open woods and require little care once they have become established. Wild sarsaparilla prefers a dryish soil, while spikenard prefers a moist, fertile one. Mulch for winter protection. Propagate by seed or division in fall.

Arisaema
(a-ri-SEE-ma)
ARISAEMA

Arisaema triphyllum

Hardiness: *Zones 4-9*

Flowering season: *spring*

Height: *1 to 3 feet*

Flower color: *green*

Soil: *moist, humus-rich, acid*

Light: *partial shade*

Arisaemas can be found in moist woodlands throughout much of eastern and central North America. In addition to their unusual flowers, they have attractive bright red berries in summer.

Selected species: *A. dracontium* (green-dragon, dragonroot)—single stem 1 to 3 feet tall bearing one large compound leaf; small green flowers on a 5- to 6-inch fingerlike spadix, or stalk, that is partly surrounded by a modified leaf called a spathe. The spathe's very slender, elongated tip supposedly resembles a dragon's extended tongue. *A. triphyllum* (jack-in-the-pulpit, Indian turnip)—1 to 3 feet tall with one or two large compound leaves; 3-inch green spadix hooded by a canopy-like green spathe sometimes striped with red, purple, brown, or white; Zones 4-9.

Growing conditions and maintenance: Both species require little care if given a constantly moist shady place and mulched with several inches of leaves in winter. Propagate by seed or root division in fall.

Artemisia
(ar-tem-IS-ee-a)
WHITE SAGE

Artemisia ludoviciana

Hardiness: *Zones 5-8*

Flowering season: *summer*

Height: *1½ to 3 feet*

Flower color: *yellow*

Soil: *dry, rocky, shallow*

Light: *full sun*

White sage is grown for its attractive silver-gray foliage, providing a cool contrast to plants with brightly colored flowers in a mixed border.

Selected species: *A. ludoviciana* (white sage)—clumps of stiff, erect stems with leaves up to 4 inches long covered with a fine, dense coat of hairs; aromatic when crushed. Lower leaves are usually toothed, while upper leaves are notched; modest yellow flowers in summer. The varieties 'Silver King' and 'Silver Queen' have lighter, more silvery foliage.

Growing conditions and maintenance: White sage thrives in full sun in poor, dry soils, where it may spread quickly into large colonies unless divided regularly. In fertile soil white sage tends to become leggy, and the roots are subject to rot in wet soil. It is easily propagated by seed or by division in spring or fall.

Asarum
(a-SAR-um)
WILD GINGER

Asarum caudatum

Hardiness: *Zones 3-10*

Flowering season: *spring*

Height: *2 to 12 inches*

Flower color: *purple, brown*

Soil: *moist, acid, fertile*

Light: *shade*

The rich green, handsomely textured leaves of these ground-hugging perennials make beautiful carpets for the woodland garden. The dusky 1- to 2-inch spring flowers are often hidden by the leaves.

Selected species: *A. arifolium* (wild ginger)—2 to 4 inches high with triangular evergreen leaves up to 5 inches long, mottled with paler green; native to eastern North America; Zones 6-10. *A. canadense* (wild ginger, snakeroot)—hairy, deciduous heart-shaped leaves 3 to 6 inches wide on 12-inch arching petioles, or leafstalks; eastern North America; Zones 3-8. *A. caudatum* (British Columbia wild ginger)—glossy heart-shaped evergreen leaves 2 to 6 inches wide on petioles 7 or 8 inches long; Zones 4-8.

Growing conditions and maintenance: Wild gingers require shade and ample moisture. They benefit from the addition of organic matter to soil. Propagate by division, rhizome cuttings, or seed.

Asclepias
(as-KLEE-pee-as)
MILKWEED

Asclepias tuberosa

Hardiness: *Zones 3-9*

Flowering season: *spring to summer*

Height: *1 to 4 feet*

Flower color: *rose, purple, orange*

Soil: *boggy, rich to dry, infertile*

Light: *full sun to partial shade*

Milkweeds are showy perennials common to prairies, flood plains, and stream banks across much of North America. They attract monarch butterflies.

Selected species: *A. incarnata* (swamp milkweed)—2 to 4 feet high with narrow, lance-shaped leaves and an open, branched habit; terminal clusters of small, bright rose-purple flowers; Zones 3-8. *A. speciosa* (showy milkweed)—to 3 feet with blue-green leaves and round clusters of rose-colored flowers; Zones 3-9. *A. tuberosa* (butterfly weed)—to 3 feet with linear leaves and brilliant orange flower clusters; Zones 4-9.

Growing conditions and maintenance: Grow *A. incarnata* in full sun or partial shade in a rich, boggy to moist soil. *A. speciosa* prefers full sun and moist, well-drained soil. *A. tuberosa* is very drought tolerant, thriving in full sun and dry, sandy, infertile soil. Propagate by seed, division, or root cuttings.

Aster
(AS-ter)
ASTER

Aster novae-angliae

Hardiness: *Zones 3-8*

Flowering season: *late summer to fall*

Height: *1 to 6 feet*

Flower color: *white, purple, rose*

Soil: *moist, acid to dry, sandy*

Light: *full sun to partial shade*

Asters are easy-to-grow perennials whose daisylike flowers provide welcome color to the landscape in late summer and fall.

Selected species: *A. laevis* (smooth aster)—numerous clusters of pale lavender flowers with bright yellow centers on stout 2- to 4-foot stems in late summer and fall; smooth, dark green lance-shaped leaves; native of open woods and dry prairies; Zones 4-8. *A. macrophyllus* (large-leaf aster)—basal clump of attractive heart-shaped leaves 4 to 8 inches across and large, flat or rounded clusters of 1-inch white or violet flowers; native of open woods and clearings throughout much of the eastern United States; Zones 3-6. *A. novae-angliae* (New England aster)—3 to 6 or more feet in height with numerous loose clusters of showy flowers an inch across, usually deep violet-purple with yellow centers but occasionally blue, lavender, pink, or white, until frost; varieties include 'Harrington's Pink', with salmon pink flowers, and 'Purple Dome', an 18-inch dwarf with deep purple semidouble blooms; native from New England to the Southwest in woodlands, meadows, and prairies; Zones 3-7. *A. pilosus* (frost aster)—much-branched 3-foot stems with stiff, narrow leaves frequently covered with frosty-looking white hairs and showy white flowers with yellow centers; eastern North America; Zones 4-8. *A. umbellatus* (flat-topped aster)—rigid stems 2 to 5 feet or more in height with dense flattened clusters of 10- to 15¾-inch white flowers with yellow to pink centers; moist sites from eastern Canada to Gulf States; Zones 4-7.

Aster umbellatus

Growing conditions and maintenance: *A. macrophyllus* prefers partial shade. In full shade it makes an attractive ground cover but will not bloom. The other species grow in full sun or partial shade. *A. novae-angliae* and *A. umbellatus* thrive in moist, acid soils. *A. pilosus* prefers a dry to well-drained sandy soil. *A. laevis* and *A. macrophyllus* adapt to moist or dry soils. Asters can be propagated by seed planted outside in the fall, or damp-stratified and planted in the spring. Most species can also be propagated by division or by softwood cuttings taken in late spring.

Balsamorhiza
(bawl-sa-mo-RI-za)
BALSAMROOT

Balsamorhiza sagittata

Hardiness: *Zones 4-10*

Flowering season: *spring to summer*

Height: *24 to 32 inches*

Flower color: *yellow*

Soil: *sandy or gravelly, moderately dry*

Light: *full sun*

A perennial native to mountain grasslands and prairies of the West, balsamroot produces bright sunflower-like blossoms in late spring and early summer.

Selected species: *B. sagittata* (balsamroot, Oregon sunflower)—low clump of arrow- or heart-shaped leaves covered with silvery hairs and measuring up to 6 inches wide and 12 inches long; may be undivided or deeply divided into fernlike segments; flower stems up to 32 inches tall bear a single 2½- to 4-inch yellow flower.

Growing conditions and maintenance: Balsamroot thrives in full sun and deep, sandy soil, but it will tolerate poor, infertile soil. Because of its deep woody taproot, it does not transplant well. Propagate from seed sown in fall where you want the plants to grow. Balsamroot generally requires 2 years of growth to reach flowering size.

Baptisia
(bap-TIZ-ee-a)
WILD INDIGO

Baptisia australis

Hardiness: *Zones 3-9*

Flowering season: *spring, summer*

Height: *1 to 6 feet*

Flower color: *white, cream, blue*

Soil: *well-drained to dry, sandy, rocky*

Light: *full sun to partial shade*

The baptisias are shrubby perennials of the prairies and open woodlands of North America. Their pea-like flowers appear in late spring or early summer, and their blue-green foliage is an asset throughout the growing season.

Selected species: *B. alba* (white wild indigo)—2- to 3-foot stems topped with erect clusters of white flowers in early summer. *B. australis* (blue wild indigo)—clump of woody-based stems up to 6 feet tall with 4- to 16-inch spikes of blue-purple flowers in late spring. *B. leucophaea* (plains wild indigo)—1 to 3 feet tall with spreading branches and 12-inch terminal spikes of cream-colored flowers heavy enough to make the stems arch to the ground.

Growing conditions and maintenance: Wild (false) indigo thrives in full sun or partial shade and adapts to most well-drained to dry soils. Protect *B. leucophaea* from strong winds. Propagate by seed or by division.

Bouteloua
(boo-te-LOO-a)
GRAMA

Bouteloua curtipendula

Hardiness: *Zones 3-10*

Flowering season: *summer, fall*

Height: *1 to 2 feet*

Flower color: *purplish*

Soil: *well-drained to dry*

Light: *full sun*

These clump-forming drought-tolerant grasses are found in prairies, open woodlands, and on rocky slopes throughout much of the United States. They are useful for meadow plantings or as accents in a rock garden.

Selected species: *B. curtipendula* (sideoats grama, mesquite grass)—wiry clumps 1 to 2 feet tall; small flowers arranged in numerous spikelets with downward-pointing tips along one side of each flower stem in summer; in fall the seed heads bleach to a tan color and foliage often turns red or purple. *B. gracilis* (blue grama)—1 to 1½ feet tall with narrow, fine-textured foliage; forms a dense sod when mowed, making it a good turf grass for dry climates.

Growing conditions and maintenance: Grama grasses require full sun and a well-drained to dry soil. Both are excellent plants for low-maintenance gardens. To propagate, collect seed in fall and sow immediately, or stratify and sow in spring. Plants can also be divided while dormant.

Brodiaea
(bro-di-EE-a)
WILD HYACINTH

Brodiaea elegans

Hardiness: *Zones 5-10*

Flowering season: *spring, summer*

Height: *4 to 36 inches*

Flower color: *violet to purple*

Soil: *poor, dry to moist, heavy*

Light: *full sun to partial shade*

Brodiaeas are cormous plants from grasslands and plains in the West. They have grasslike foliage and terminal clusters of ½- to 1½-inch tubular flowers on wiry stems and go dormant after blooming, so place them where the foliage of other plants will fill in the space they leave. Use brodiaeas in groups of 12 or more in a perennial border, a rock garden, or naturalized in grass.

Selected species: *B. elegans* (harvest brodiaea)—mounds of foliage up to 16 inches tall and violet to purple flowers open in late spring to early summer on erect stems of about the same height as the foliage; Zones 7-10. *B. pulchella* [also called *Dichelostemma pulchella*] (wild hyacinth)—pinkish violet flowers in spring on stalks up to 2 to 3 feet tall; Zones 5-10.

Growing conditions and maintenance: *B. elegans* adapts to full sun or partial shade and to heavy soils ranging from dry to moist. *B. pulchella* prefers full sun and poor, dry soils; it tolerates drought. Propagate by seed or offsets. Seedlings take 3 to 4 years to flower.

Callirhoe
(ka-LEER-o-ee)
POPPY MALLOW

Callirhoe involucrata

Hardiness: *Zones 3-10*

Flowering season: *spring to summer*

Height: *6 inches to 4 feet*

Flower color: *red, purple*

Soil: *sandy, rocky, well-drained to dry*

Light: *full sun*

The genus *Callirhoe* includes annuals and long-blooming perennials native to open woods and dry plains over much of the United States. The showy, cup-shaped flowers are held above the foliage on slender stems. These drought-tolerant wildflowers have carrotlike taproots.

Selected species: *C. digitata* (fringed poppy mallow)—annual ranging from 1 to 4 feet in height with 2-inch rosy red to violet flowers beginning in spring. *C. involucrata* (purple poppy mallow, winecups)—trailing plant that grows 6 to 12 inches tall and 2 to 3 feet wide with attractive, deeply lobed hairy leaves; 2-inch magenta flowers with a white spot at the base of the petals in spring and summer, opening during the day and closing in the evening; Zones 4-8. *C. papaver* (poppy mallow)—prostrate stems as much as 10 feet in length and solitary 2- to 3-inch magenta flowers; Zones 5-8.

Growing conditions and maintenance: Poppy mallows thrive in full sun and dry soil. Extend flowering by deadheading. Propagate by seed that has been scarified.

Camassia
(ka-MAS-ee-a)
CAMASS, QUAMASH

Camassia quamash

Hardiness: *Zones 5-8*

Flowering season: *spring to early summer*

Height: *1 to 3 feet*

Flower color: *white, blue, lavender*

Soil: *moist, well-drained*

Light: *full sun to partial shade*

Camassias inhabit open woods, wet meadows, and prairies. They grow from bulbs and produce loose clusters of star-shaped flowers in spring and early summer. They are especially handsome planted in drifts in a woodland border or meadow.

Selected species: *C. quamash* (common camass, quamash)—western species with bright green grasslike leaves and 1- to 3-foot flower stalks bearing dozens of star-shaped flowers in white and shades from light blue to deep blue or lavender-blue; Zones 5-8. *C. scilloides* (wild hyacinth, eastern camass)—clump of leaves up to 16 inches long producing leafless 6- to 24-inch stems bearing loose clusters of fragrant white, blue, or lavender-blue flowers; native to central and southern United States; Zones 5-8.

Growing conditions and maintenance: Grow camassias in full sun to partial shade in a moist, well-drained site. After flowering they go dormant and do best with less water. Propagate from seed or offsets.

Campanula
(kam-PAN-yew-la)
BELLFLOWER

Campanula americana

Hardiness: *Zones 3-9*

Flowering season: *spring, summer*

Height: *4 inches to 6 feet*

Flower color: *white, blue, lavender*

Soil: *moist, well-drained to dry, sandy*

Light: *full sun to partial shade*

Bellflowers are native to many regions of the United States. The genus includes annuals, biennials, and perennials with showy, bell-shaped flowers.

Selected species: *C. americana* (American bellflower)—annual usually 3 to 4 feet tall but occasionally to 6 feet; lavender-blue, five-petaled flowers on the upper portions of the stems all summer. *C. rotundifolia* (harebell)—perennial 4 to 15 inches tall with loose clusters of nodding lavender flowers in summer; Zones 3-6. *C. scouleri* (harebell)—perennial 4 to 15 inches tall with white to pale blue flowers in loose clusters in late spring and summer; Zones 6-9.

Growing conditions and maintenance: *C. americana* thrives in moist, rich, well-drained soil in full sun to partial shade. *C. rotundifolia* prefers a sandy site and full sun to partial shade. *C. scouleri* grows in partial shade and adapts to a range of soils, from rich and moist to rocky and dry. Propagate by seed. *C. rotundifolia* can also be grown from cuttings.

Centaurea
(sen-TOR-ee-a)
KNAPWEED

Centaurea americana

Hardiness: *annual*

Flowering season: *summer*

Height: *1½ to 6 feet*

Flower color: *violet, lavender-pink*

Soil: *dry, well-drained*

Light: *full sun*

This genus includes both annuals and perennials, mostly of European origin. The following species is a lovely annual native to the dry prairies of the central United States that blooms throughout the summer.

Selected species: *C. americana* (basket flower)—up to 6 feet tall and 3 feet wide, bold and shrubby-looking with sturdy, well-branched stems clad in lance-shaped leaves up to 4 inches long; showy 4- to 5-inch lavender-pink flowers with cream-colored centers and a fringe of bracts that gives the flowers a thistlelike appearance. Basket flower is a good choice for the rear of a sunny border or a meadow garden, and it also makes a long-lasting cut flower. The variety *alba* produces white flowers.

Growing conditions and maintenance: *C. americana* is easy to grow in dry or well-drained soils and full sun, requiring no special care. Sow seed in place in late winter or early spring.

Chamaecrista
(kam-ee-KRIS-ta)
SENNA

Chamaecrista fasciculata

Chasmanthium
(kaz-MAN-thee-um)
WILD OATS

Chasmanthium latifolium

Chelone
(kee-LO-nee)
TURTLEHEAD

Chelone lyonii

Hardiness: *Zones 3-10*

Flowering season: *summer to fall*

Height: *1 to 4 feet*

Flower color: *yellow*

Soil: *sandy, wet to dry*

Light: *full sun to partial shade*

This genus, which is also listed as *Cassia,* includes both annuals and perennials that inhabit open woods and prairies in the eastern and central United States. Their bright yellow flowers are attractive in borders or as a transition between lawn and woodlands.

Selected species: *C. fasciculata* (partridge pea) and *C. nictitans* (sensitive plant)—annuals that grow to 2 feet and 12 inches respectively with yellow flowers arising from leaf axils and light green, pinnately compound leaves that fold together when touched. *C. marilandica* (wild senna)—semiwoody perennial that grows to 4 feet with bold yellow flower clusters and finely divided leaves; Zones 3-10.

Growing conditions and maintenance: Chamaecristas thrive in full sun. All three species grow well in well-drained to dry sandy soil, and *C. nictitans* also tolerates wet conditions. They benefit from soil inoculation with nitrogen-fixing bacteria, available from wildflower nurseries. Propagate by seed. *C. marilandica* can also be divided.

Hardiness: *Zones 5-10*

Flowering season: *summer*

Height: *2 to 4 feet*

Flower color: *green*

Soil: *moist, well-drained*

Light: *full sun to partial shade*

The genus *Chasmanthium* offers landscape interest during three seasons of the year. Its green flowers appear in drooping panicles in summer. In autumn the leaves turn bright yellow-gold. The panicles turn bronze and persist throughout winter, providing color and graceful movement.

Selected species: *C. latifolium* (wild oats)—clump-forming perennial grass from the east and central United States; 2 to 4 feet in height with blue-green, bamboolike leaves; fall foliage most intense in full sun; oatlike spikelets of flowers on slender, arching stems in summer. Wild oats is effectively used in borders and beside pools and streams.

Growing conditions and maintenance: Unlike most ornamental grasses, chasmanthium adapts well to partial shade, where it has darker green foliage and tends to grow taller than it does in full sun. Propagate by division or seed. It may self-sow.

Hardiness: *Zones 3-9*

Flowering season: *summer, early fall*

Height: *1 to 4 feet*

Flower color: *white, pink, purple*

Soil: *moist, rich*

Light: *partial shade to full sun*

Turtleheads are perennials native to marshes, stream banks, low meadows, and moist woodlands in much of eastern North America. Their distinctively shaped flowers, which somewhat resemble a turtle's head, appear in terminal racemes on erect stems. They are well suited to bog gardens or the edges of garden pools.

Selected species: *C. glabra* (white turtlehead)—1 to 4 feet tall with 6-inch, lance-shaped leaves; clusters of white or pale pink 1½-inch flowers at the tops of the stems in summer; Zones 3-8. *C. lyonii* (pink turtlehead)—2 to 3 feet tall with dark green foliage and clusters of pinkish purple flowers beginning in late summer; Zones 3-9.

Growing conditions and maintenance: Turtleheads thrive in moist soils in partial shade but will tolerate a sunny location if abundant water is supplied. Place them among stout plants to provide support for their slender stems. Propagate by seed, division, or cuttings.

Chrysopsis
(kri-SOP-sis)
GOLDEN ASTER

Chrysopsis mariana

Hardiness: *Zones 4-10*

Flowering season: *summer to fall*

Height: *6 inches to 5 feet*

Flower color: *yellow*

Soil: *wet to dry, sandy*

Light: *full sun*

The perennial golden asters are tough, vigorous plants that punctuate the landscape with long-lasting clusters of bright daisylike blossoms.

Selected species: *C. graminifolia* [also called *Pityopsis graminifolia*] (grass-leaved golden aster)—12-inch grasslike leaves and clusters of bright yellow flowers on 2½-foot stems; makes a good evergreen ground cover; Zones 5-10. *C. mariana* (Maryland golden aster)—18 to 30 inches tall with showy clusters of flowers on sturdy stems; Zones 4-9. *C. villosa* (golden aster)—as little as 6 inches to as much as 5 feet in height with flowers near the tips of stems that may be upright or trailing; Zones 4-9.

Growing conditions and maintenance: *C. graminifolia* and *C. villosa* are easy to grow on sunny, dry sites; they may do poorly in too rich a soil. *C. mariana* requires wet to moist soil. Propagate by seed.

Cimicifuga
(si-mi-SIFF-yew-ga)
BUGBANE

Cimicifuga racemosa

Hardiness: *Zones 3-8*

Flowering season: *summer*

Height: *3 to 8 feet*

Flower color: *white*

Soil: *moist, acid, rich*

Light: *full sun to partial shade*

Bugbanes are tall, stately perennials that are native to open moist woodlands of the eastern United States. Their spires of white flowers add a vertical accent to the rear of a mixed border.

Selected species: *C. americana* (American bugbane)—4 to 6 feet tall with slender stems bearing compound leaves; 1- to 2-foot erect wandlike clusters of creamy white flowers held above the foliage; Zones 4-8. *C. racemosa* (black snakeroot, black cohosh)—up to 8 feet with a bushy habit; tiny white, fuzzy flowers in narrow, upright clusters above doubly compound foliage.

Growing conditions and maintenance: Grow cimicifugas in rich soil with ample moisture. Incorporate organic matter into soil prior to planting. Provide a winter mulch. Propagate by seed or division in fall. Seeds take 3 or 4 years to flower.

Clarkia
(KLAR-kee-a)
FAREWELL-TO-SPRING

Clarkia amoena

Hardiness: *annual*

Flowering season: *spring to summer*

Height: *1 to 3 feet*

Flower color: *pink, red, purple, white*

Soil: *dry, sandy*

Light: *full sun to partial shade*

Clarkias are free-flowering annuals from the coastal ranges of the West. They are named after explorer William Clark, who collected their seed during the Lewis and Clark expedition. These species are also listed as *Godetia.*

Selected species: *C. amoena* (farewell-to-spring, satin flower) grows 1 to 3 feet tall. Throughout summer, 2- to 4-inch cup-shaped flowers appear in the axils of the upper leaves. The four petals are pink to lavender with a bright red splash at the base, and the four sepals are red. *C. concinna* (red ribbons) grows 1 to 2 feet tall and bears rose-purple flowers with deeply cut petals in late spring and early summer. *C. unguiculata* (mountain garland) produces erect reddish stems that reach 1½ to 3 feet. Purple, rose, or whitish flowers appear in small clusters in late spring.

Growing conditions and maintenance: Clarkias thrive in poor, dry soils, and should not be thinned, as crowding encourages flowering. Propagate by seed.

Claytonia
(klay-TOH-nee-a)
SPRING BEAUTY

Claytonia virginica

Hardiness: *Zones 4-9*

Flowering season: *spring*

Height: *4 to 12 inches*

Flower color: *pink, white*

Soil: *moist, rich*

Light: *shade to partial shade*

Spring beauties are low-growing perennials found in rich woodlands throughout much of the eastern and central United States. Their dainty flowers are pink or white with darker pink stripes on the petals and dark pink stamens. They are lovely planted in large drifts or scattered among other woodland flowers. The plants disappear shortly after flowering.

Selected species: *C. caroliniana* (broad-leaved spring beauty) grows from corms to produce two oval leaves, each 2 inches long. Throughout spring flowers are borne in loose clusters along the upper portion of the 4- to 12-inch stems. *C. virginica* (narrow-leaved spring beauty) is similar to the above species except that its leaves are slender and grasslike.

Growing conditions and maintenance: Claytonias will thrive and spread rapidly in a moist soil with high humus content. Incorporate generous amounts of organic matter into the soil prior to planting. Propagate by corms or seed.

Clematis
(KLEM-a-tis)
CLEMATIS

Clematis viorna

Hardiness: *Zones 5-9*

Flowering season: *spring, summer, fall*

Height: *9 to 12 feet*

Flower color: *lavender, red, purple*

Soil: *moist, rich to rocky, alkaline*

Light: *partial shade*

This genus includes several species of native perennial twining vines with small bell-shaped flowers.

Selected species: *C. crispa* (blue jasmine, marsh clematis)—southern species with stems to 10 feet in length; fragrant, ruffled flowers 1 to 2 inches long, usually lavender but occasionally blue, pink, or white appear in spring; Zones 6-9. *C. texensis* (scarlet clematis)—clusters of leathery ¾-inch scarlet flowers from late spring until frost on 6- to 12-foot stems; Zones 6-9. *C. viorna* (leather flower, vase vine)—10-foot stems with bright green lance-shaped leaves and solitary 1-inch purple flowers followed by conspicuous fuzzy seed pods; central and southern United States; Zones 5-8.

Growing conditions and maintenance: *C. crispa* requires a moist, rich soil and is best propagated from cuttings in summer. *C. texensis* and *C. viorna* prefer a rocky, alkaline soil and can be grown from cuttings or seeds or by layering. All require some shade.

Cleome
(klee-O-me)
BEE PLANT

Cleome serrulata

Hardiness: *hardy annual*

Flowering season: *summer*

Height: *2 to 5 feet*

Flower color: *pink, lavender, white*

Soil: *well-drained, sandy*

Light: *full sun to partial shade*

This western native is an annual that inhabits prairies and open woodlands. It attracts numerous species of small birds that feed on the seeds that follow the showy flowers.

Selected species: *C. serrulata* (Rocky Mountain bee plant)—erect 2- to 5-foot stems with compound leaves composed of three canoe-shaped leaflets 1 to 3 inches long; showy, elongated clusters of pink, lavender, or white flowers from mid- to late summer; individual flowers are ½ inch long with four petals and six long, thin stamens.

Growing conditions and maintenance: Rocky Mountain bee plant is easy to grow in any poor, dry soil in full sun or partial shade. It self-sows freely. Propagate by seed, but sow heavily because germination is poor.

Clintonia
(klin-TOH-nee-a)
BEAD LILY

Clintonia andrewsiana

Hardiness: *Zones 2-9*

Flowering season: *spring to summer*

Height: *4 to 20 inches*

Flower color: *white, rose, yellow*

Soil: *moist, rich*

Light: *shade*

Different species of these low-growing perennials are found in woodlands of the West and the East. All have broad, glossy leaves, delicate flowers, and marble-sized berries.

Selected species: *C. andrewsiana* (bead lily)—10- to 20-inch stalks of deep rose bell-shaped flowers followed by steel blue berries; native to California and Oregon; Zones 8-9. *C. borealis* (blue bead lily)—greenish yellow flowers on 8- to 15-inch stalks followed by bright blue berries; eastern Canada and United States; Zones 2-7. *C. umbellulata* (speckled wood lily, white bead lily)—white flowers with green and purple specks on 6- to 20-inch stalks followed by black berries. *C. uniflora* (bride's bonnet)—4 to 8 inches tall with white flowers and amethyst-blue berries; grows wild from California to Alaska; Zones 4-8.

Growing conditions and maintenance: Clintonias require cool, damp, shady locations, where they make excellent ground covers. Mulch in winter. Propagate by division in fall or early spring, or by seed.

Collinsia
(ko-LIN-see-a)
COLLINSIA

Collinsia heterophylla

Hardiness: *annual*

Flowering season: *spring*

Height: *8 to 24 inches*

Flower color: *purple, white, blue, rose*

Soil: *moist, well-drained to dry*

Light: *full sun to full shade*

Found in the western United States, collinsias are annuals with flowers resembling snapdragons. They are suited to rock gardens, woodland gardens, meadows, and borders.

Selected species: *C. grandiflora* (blue lips)—8 to 15 inches tall; ¾-inch two-lipped flowers singly or in clusters in the leaf axils from mid- to late spring; the upper lip is white or purple and the lower lip is blue or violet. *C. heterophylla* (Chinese houses)—2 feet tall with blossoms arranged in tiers and bright green foliage; the upper lip of the flower is lilac or white and the lower lip is rose-purple or violet.

Growing conditions and maintenance: Grow *C. grandiflora* in full sun to partial shade. It does not tolerate high temperatures and requires cool nights. *C. heterophylla* thrives in partial to full shade. To extend flowering, remove faded blooms before seed can set. Propagate collinsias by seed; they often self-sow.

Coreopsis
(ko-ree-OP-sis)
TICKSEED

Coreopsis verticillata

Hardiness: *Zones 3-9*

Flowering season: *spring, summer*

Height: *1 to 2½ feet*

Flower color: *yellow*

Soil: *sandy, dry to moist, well-drained*

Light: *full sun to partial shade*

The bright daisylike flowers of annual and perennial species of coreopsis decorate roadsides, prairies, and woodlands throughout much of the United States.

Selected species: *C. lanceolata* (lance-leaf coreopsis)—perennial 1½ to 2 feet tall with single yellow 2½-inch flowers in late spring and summer; Zones 4-9. *C. tinctoria* (plains coreopsis, calliopsis)—annual with slender 1- to 2-foot branching stems and small yellow flowers with red-maroon centers all summer. *C. verticillata* (threadleaf coreopsis)—1- to 2½-foot perennial with finely divided, threadlike dark green leaves and yellow 2-inch flowers in early summer; Zones 3-9.

Growing conditions and maintenance: These wildflowers thrive in full sun or partial shade in sandy, well-drained soil. *C. lanceolata* is particularly drought tolerant and will bloom all summer if old flowers are removed. Propagate by seed. Perennial species can also be divided.

Delphinium
(del-FIN-ee-um)
LARKSPUR

Delphinium tricorne

Hardiness: *Zones 4-9*

Flowering season: *spring to summer*

Height: *6 inches to 5 feet*

Flower color: *blue, purple, white*

Soil: *rich, moist to dry*

Light: *full sun to partial shade*

The loosely clustered spikes of spurred flowers make delphiniums attractive additions to dry borders or woodland gardens. The following species are perennials with a wide range of native habitats.

Selected species: *D. nuttallianum* (Nuttall's larkspur)—6 to 15 inches tall with white, blue, or purple flowers; native to sagebrush deserts and dry foothills in the West; Zones 3-9. *D. tricorne* (dwarf larkspur)—12 to 30 inches tall with blue or white flowers; found in moist woodlands from Pennsylvania south to Georgia and west to Oklahoma; Zones 5-9. *D. virescens* (prairie larkspur)—1 to 5 feet tall with terminal spikes of white flowers tinged with purple; native to prairies and open woods of the central United States; Zones 4-9.

Growing conditions and maintenance: Grow *D. tricorne* in partial shade in rich soil with ample moisture during flowering. *D. nuttallianum* and *D. virescens* prefer full sun and dry, well-drained sites. Propagate by seed or division.

Dentaria
(den-TAR-ee-a)
TOOTHWORT

Dentaria diphylla

Hardiness: *Zones 4-9*

Flowering season: *spring*

Height: *6 to 16 inches*

Flower color: *white, pink*

Soil: *moist, rich*

Light: *partial to full shade*

Toothworts are low-growing perennials native to rich woods and bottom lands in the eastern and central United States. They grow from rhizomes, producing loose clusters of small bell-shaped flowers in the spring. After flowering, the plant disappears.

Selected species: *D. diphylla* (toothwort, crinkleroot)—8 to 16 inches tall with deeply dissected leaves and loose clusters of white or pale pink four-petaled flowers from early to late spring; Zones 4-7. *D. laciniata* (cut-leaved toothwort)—6 to 12 inches tall with a whorl of deeply divided and coarsely toothed leaves halfway up each stem; clusters of pink or white flowers above the foliage in spring; Zones 4-9.

Growing conditions and maintenance: Toothworts do not tolerate direct sun. Mulch lightly with leaves in winter. Propagate by seed sown immediately after collection or by division when the plant is dormant.

Dicentra
(dy-SEN-tra)
BLEEDING HEART

Dicentra eximia

Hardiness: *Zones 3-9*

Flowering season: *spring, summer*

Height: *6 to 24 inches*

Flower color: *pink, lavender, white*

Soil: *moist, well-drained, rich*

Light: *partial to full shade*

Dicentras are perennials with finely divided fernlike foliage and dainty sprays of flowers. These woodland natives are ideal for shade gardens.

Selected species: *D. canadensis* (squirrel corn)—6 to 10 inches tall with blue-gray leaves and fragrant, heart-shaped white flowers in late spring; disappears after flowering; widespread in eastern woodlands; Zones 4-7. *D. cucullaria* (Dutchman's-breeches)—up to 10 inches tall with double-spurred white blossoms resembling pantaloons; native to eastern North America and the Northwest; Zones 3-7. *D. eximia* (wild bleeding heart)—1- to 2-foot mound of light green foliage and magenta-pink flowers in spring and summer; native to Appalachian Mountains; Zones 5-8. *D. formosa* (western bleeding heart)—up to 18 inches tall with pink flowers in spring and early summer. There is also a white variety. California to British Columbia; Zones 5-9.

Growing conditions and maintenance: Grow dicentras in humus-rich soil with a constant supply of moisture. Do not overcrowd plants. Propagate by seed or by division.

Dodecatheon
(doh-de-KATH-ee-on)
SHOOTING STAR

Dodecatheon meadia

Hardiness: *Zones 4-8*

Flowering season: *spring, summer*

Height: *4 to 20 inches*

Flower color: *white, pink, red*

Soil: *moist to dry*

Light: *partial shade to full sun*

Shooting stars grow in moist, open woods, on prairies, and on rocky slopes. These perennials have a basal rosette of leaves and leafless stalks bearing showy flowers with sharply backswept petals.

Selected species: *D. amethystinum* [also called *D. pulchellum*] (amethyst shooting star)—rose-crimson flowers on 8- to 16-inch stalks in late spring; Alaska to California; Zones 4-7. *D. dentatum* (dwarf shooting star)—white flowers with a purple spot at the base of the petals on 4- to 14-inch stalks above crinkled, toothed leaves; northwestern United States; Zones 4-8. *D. meadia* (shooting star)—white to deep pink flowers on stalks up to 20 inches; east Texas to western Pennsylvania; Zones 5-8.

Growing conditions and maintenance: Give *D. dentatum* a moist, shaded site. *D. meadia* prefers light, sandy soil with abundant moisture while blooming and drier conditions in fall and winter. Grow *D. pulchellum* in moist, well-drained, alkaline soil in partial shade to sun. Propagate by seed or division.

Echinacea
(ek-i-NAY-see-a)
PURPLE CONEFLOWER

Echinacea purpurea

Hardiness: *Zones 3-9*

Flowering season: *spring, summer*

Height: *1½ to 5 feet*

Flower color: *pink, lavender, yellow, white*

Soil: *dry, well-drained*

Light: *full sun to partial shade*

These upright, bushy perennials inhabit prairies and open woodlands throughout the central and southeastern United States. Neither heat nor drought halts their prolific display of daisylike blooms.

Selected species: *E. angustifolia* (narrow-leaved purple coneflower)—stiff 18- to 30-inch stems topped in summer with lavender-pink flowers with drooping petals and a dark, spiny, cone-shaped center; Zones 3-8. *E. paradoxa* (coneflower)—2 to 3 feet tall with white or rose flowers with a dark brown center in late spring. There is also a yellow variety. *E. purpurea* (purple coneflower)—2 to 4 feet tall; long-lasting lavender flowers up to 4 inches in diameter with purplish brown centers in summer; Zones 5-8.

Growing conditions and maintenance: Purple coneflowers thrive in full sun or partial shade and well-drained soil. They tolerate heat and drought. Propagate by seed or division.

Epilobium
(ep-i-LO-bee-um)
FIREWEED

Epilobium angustifolium

Hardiness: *Zones 2-9*

Flowering season: *summer*

Height: *4 inches to 5 feet*

Flower color: *rose, purple, white*

Soil: *dry to moist, well-drained*

Light: *full sun*

These summer-blooming perennials are native to mountain slopes, dry clearings, and stream banks. They are named for their ability to rapidly colonize an area that has been swept by fire.

Selected species: *E. angustifolium* (fireweed, willow herb) produces clumps of reddish stems 3 to 5 feet tall with elongated, willowlike leaves 3 to 8 inches long. Spikes of lilac-purple, rose, or occasionally white flowers appear atop the stems throughout summer over much of Canada and the United States; Zones 2-9. *E. latifolium* (dwarf fireweed) is found from Alaska south through the mountain states. It grows 4 to 16 inches tall with clusters of large magenta-pink flowers and bluish green leaves.

Growing conditions and maintenance: Epilobiums require full sun but tolerate moist or dry soils provided they are well drained. Given favorable conditions, the plants spread quickly and may become invasive. Propagate by seed or division.

Erigeron
(e-RIJ-er-on)
FLEABANE

Erigeron speciosus

Eriogonum
(er-ee-OG-o-num)
WILD BUCKWHEAT

Eriogonum compositum

Eryngium
(e-RIN-jee-um)
RATTLESNAKE MASTER

Eryngium yuccifolium

Hardiness: *Zones 3-10*

Flowering season: *spring to summer*

Height: *6 to 36 inches*

Flower color: *blue, lavender, violet, pink, white*

Soil: *sandy, dry to moist*

Light: *full sun to partial shade*

Fleabanes inhabit open woods, alpine meadows, roadsides, and coastal bluffs throughout the United States. The following perennial species produce numerous daisylike flowers with bright yellow centers.

Selected species: *E. glaucus* (seaside daisy, beach aster)—compact, bushy plant 6 to 16 inches tall with violet flowers. White and pink varieties are also available. West Coast native; Zones 8-10. *E. philadelphicus* (common fleabane)—up to 3 feet in height with 1-inch white or pink flowers; native to eastern North America; Zones 3-10. *E. speciosus* (showy fleabane)—6 to 30 inches tall with 2-inch white or lavender rays and yellow disk; widespread in western United States; Zones 3-10.

Growing conditions and maintenance: Fleabanes can be grown in either full sun or partial shade in sandy, well-drained soil. Propagate by seed, or by division after flowering.

Hardiness: *Zones 3-10*

Flowering season: *spring, summer, fall*

Height: *3 inches to 3 feet*

Flower color: *white, yellow, orange, red*

Soil: *dry, rocky*

Light: *full sun*

The following wild buckwheat species are drought-tolerant perennials native to open rocky slopes and plains in the western United States.

Selected species: *E. compositum* (northern buckwheat)—1- to 4-inch clusters of white or yellow flowers on 8- to 18-inch stalks in late spring to summer; forms a cushiony mat of oval to heart-shaped leaves that are green above and white and fuzzy below; Zones 4-7. *E. umbellatum* (sulfur buckwheat)—2- to 4-inch rounded clusters of sulfur yellow to cream summer flowers that fade to orange or red; height varies from 3 inches to 3 feet; Zones 3-8. *E. wrightii* (Wright buckwheat)—shrubby, 2 to 3 feet tall with gray leaves; clusters of white flowers in summer and fall that turn reddish orange in cool weather; Zones 6-10.

Growing conditions and maintenance: Grow wild buckwheat species in poor to average well-drained soil in full sun. Propagate by seed.

Hardiness: *Zones 4-9*

Flowering season: *summer*

Height: *2 to 4 feet*

Flower color: *greenish white*

Soil: *well-drained, moist to dry*

Light: *full sun*

The genus *Eryngium* is a perennial native to the central and eastern United States and can be found growing on prairies and in open woodlands. Its stiff, spiny leaves and thistlelike flowers add interesting texture to sunny borders and meadow gardens.

Selected species: *E. yuccifolium* (rattlesnake master, button snakeroot)—¾- to 1-inch globular clusters of tiny, tightly packed greenish white flowers appear at the tops of upright stems 2 to 4 feet tall in mid- to late summer. The stiff, narrow, blue-green sharp-toothed leaves look like small versions of yucca foliage.

Growing conditions and maintenance: Eryngium is easy to grow in full sun and a well-drained soil. It tolerates poor, dry soils and can withstand short periods of flooding. This species self-sows heavily but can be kept in check if the fading flower clusters are removed before seed matures. Propagate by seed or division.

Erythronium
(er-i-THRO-nee-um)
TROUT LILY

Erythronium grandiflorum

Hardiness: *Zones 3-9*

Flowering season: *spring, early summer*

Height: *4 to 18 inches*

Flower color: *white, yellow*

Soil: *moist, well-drained, rich*

Light: *partial shade*

Trout lilies are perennials of moist woodlands and meadows. Their delicate bell-shaped flowers consist of three petals and three sepals, all of them curving sharply backward.

Selected species: *E. albidum* var. *albidum* (white trout lily, dogtooth violet)—a solitary white bell-shaped flower on a 6- to 12-inch stalk in early spring; southern Canada to Arkansas; Zones 4-9. *E. americanum* (yellow trout lily)—handsome 3- to 6-inch leaves mottled with maroon and solitary yellow flowers on 4- to 10-inch stalks in midspring; southern Canada and central states; Zones 3-7. *E. grandiflorum* (yellow fawn lily, trout lily, glacier lily)—up to five bright yellow flowers on each 12- to 18-inch stalk in late spring and early summer above mottled fleshy 14-inch leaves; British Columbia to Colorado; Zones 3-6.

Growing conditions and maintenance: Trout lilies thrive in partial shade in soil that is moist, rich in humus, and well drained. Propagate by seed or by the offsets of the corms.

Eschscholzia
(es-SHOL-zee-a)
CALIFORNIA POPPY

Eschscholzia californica

Hardiness: *Zones 8-10*

Flowering season: *spring, summer, fall*

Height: *4 to 24 inches*

Flower color: *yellow, orange*

Soil: *dry*

Light: *full sun*

This genus includes both annuals and perennials native to grasslands in California and the Southwest. Their flowers open during the day and close at night and in cloudy weather.

Selected species: *E. caespitosa* (tufted California poppy, pastel poppy)—annual with pale yellow flowers on 4- to 12-inch stalks above finely cut basal foliage. *E. californica* (California poppy)—2-foot perennial with 1- to 3-inch yellow or orange flowers from spring to fall and feathery blue-green foliage; grow as an annual north of Zone 8. *E. mexicana* (Mexican gold poppy)—annual 6 to 16 inches in height with 2- to 3-inch yellow-orange flowers in spring and pale, feathery bluish green foliage.

Growing conditions and maintenance: Eschscholzias thrive in full sun and well-drained soils. The bloom period of *E. californica* can be extended with supplemental watering. These species self-sow freely. Propagate from seed.

Eupatorium
(yew-pa-TOR-ee-um)
BONESET

Eupatorium coelestinum

Hardiness: *Zones 3-9*

Flowering season: *summer to fall*

Height: *1 to 8 feet*

Flower color: *pink, purple, blue, white*

Soil: *moist or dry*

Light: *full sun to partial shade*

The bonesets described here are easy-to-grow perennials, most of them native to moist prairies and stream banks, and marshes. All of them have showy mounded or flat-topped clusters of tiny flowers that are valued for the late-season color they lend to a mixed herbaceous border or meadow.

Selected species: *E. coelestinum* (hardy ageratum, mist flower)—1 to 2 feet tall with ½-inch lavender-blue flowers in dense, misty-looking clusters; Zones 6-9. *E. fistulosum* (queen-of-the-meadow)—2 to 7 feet tall or more when the soil is continuously moist with huge domed pink to purple flower clusters persisting well into fall; Zones 5-8. *E. maculatum* (Joe-Pye weed)—to 8 feet or more with large flat terminal clusters of mauve-pink flowers. *E. occidentale* (western thoroughweed)—rarely taller than 2 feet with profuse clusters of reddish purple flowers and aromatic leaves; Zones 5-8. *E. perfoliatum* (common boneset)—2 to 6 feet in height with fuzzy terminal clusters of tiny white flowers beginning in midsummer; Zones 3-9. *E. purpureum* (sweet Joe-Pye weed)—3 to 6 feet tall with large terminal clusters of mauve-pink flowers that are similar to those of *E. maculatum;* Zones 4-7. *E. rugosum* (white snakeroot)—2 to 4 feet tall with brilliant pure white flowers in flattened terminal clusters beginning in late summer; Zones 5-9.

Growing conditions and maintenance: With the exception of *E. occidentale,* which prefers a rocky soil, these bonesets thrive in moist to wet soils. *E. occidentale* needs full sun; *E. rugosum* grows in partial to full shade; and the other species grow in full sun to partial

Eupatorium perfoliatum

shade. Divide every few years to prevent overcrowding. Propagate by division or by seed sown outside in fall or in spring after moist stratification.

Euphorbia
(yew-FOR-bee-a)
SPURGE

Euphorbia marginata

Hardiness: *Zones 3-10*

Flowering season: *summer to fall*

Height: *1 to 5 feet*

Flower color: *white, green*

Soil: *dry to wet*

Light: *full sun*

Euphorbias are annuals or perennials native to rocky prairies and open woodlands. The tiny flowers are often surrounded by showy bracts.

Selected species: *E. corollata* (flowering spurge)—perennial 1 to 3 feet tall with airy sprays of pure white flowers atop slender stems that bear smooth, slender 2-inch leaves; a good cut flower. Native to eastern Canada and United States. *E. marginata* (snow-on-the-mountain)—annual grown as much for its variegated green-and-white foliage as for its tiny green flowers surrounded by white bracts. Usually grows 1 to 3 feet tall but may reach 5 feet. Native to the Plains states.

Growing conditions and maintenance: *E. corollata* thrives in dry soils, while *E. marginata* tolerates wet or dry conditions. Pinch *E. marginata* to keep it bushy. Propagate by seed.

Filipendula
(fil-i-PEN-dew-la)
MEADOWSWEET

Filipendula rubra

Hardiness: *Zones 4-7*

Flowering season: *summer*

Height: *3 to 8 feet*

Flower color: *pink, white*

Soil: *moist, rich*

Light: *full sun to partial shade*

Filipendula is a perennial that grows in the wet woodlands and prairies of the eastern and central United States. Its feathery, long-lasting clusters of pink flowers held above mounds of fine-textured foliage provide a lovely show in the summer border.

Selected species: *F. rubra*—sturdy stems up to 8 feet tall with large, attractive, pinnately compound leaves that are deeply lobed. The flowers are borne in branched clusters at the tops of stems. They have a fuzzy appearance and resemble astilbes. The leaves of the variety 'Venusta Magnifica' emerge mahogany and gradually turn green. The variety 'Venusta Alba' bears white flowers.

Growing conditions and maintenance: Filipendula thrives in full sun or partial shade but requires constant moisture. Mulch in spring. Divide every 3 years. Propagate by seed, cuttings, or division.

Fritillaria
(fri-ti-LAH-ree-a)
FRITILLARY

Fritillaria lanceolata

Hardiness: *Zones 5-10*

Flowering season: *spring to summer*

Height: *2 to 4 feet*

Flower color: *brown, purple, green*

Soil: *well-drained, rocky*

Light: *full sun to partial shade*

Fritillaries are bulb-forming perennials native to grasslands, coniferous forests, and mountain slopes in the Northwest and California. Because individual plants may skip a year or two between blooms, they are best planted in colonies to assure a good flower display every year.

Selected species: *F. lanceolata* (checker lily, mission bells)—cup-shaped flowers borne singly or in clusters are checkered purplish brown and green on the outside and are purple or yellow-green on the inside. Usually grows to 2 to 3 feet but may reach 4 feet. Flowering begins in late spring and continues through early summer.

Growing conditions and maintenance: Grow checker lily in full sun or partial shade in a well-drained soil. Provide supplemental watering during dry periods in summer. Propagate by seed or bulblets.

Gaillardia
(gay-LAR-dee-a)
BLANKET-FLOWER

Gaillardia aristata

Hardiness: *Zones 3-8*

Flowering season: *spring, summer, fall*

Height: *1 to 3 feet*

Flower color: *yellow, red*

Soil: *well-drained, sandy*

Light: *full sun*

Annual, biennial, and perennial gaillardias grow wild in prairies, meadows, and plains in the central and western United States. Their colorful flowers make cheerful additions to borders and meadows.

Selected species: *G. aristata* (blanket-flower)—perennial 1½ to 3 feet tall with showy 2- to 4-inch yellow flowers with yellow or purple centers appearing from mid- to late summer; Zones 3-8. *G. pulchella* (Indian blanket)—annual 1 to 2 feet tall. Flowers are 1 to 2 inches across, with yellow or yellow and red centers and petals that are solid yellow, solid red, or red at the base and yellow at the tips.

Growing conditions and maintenance: Gaillardias are easy to grow in full sun in almost any well-drained soil. Add a generous amount of sand to clayey soil to assure good drainage. Remove faded blossoms to prolong flowering. Propagate by seed or division.

Gaura
(GAW-ra)
GAURA

Gaura lindheimeri

Hardiness: *Zones 3-9*

Flowering season: *spring, summer, fall*

Height: *1 to 5 feet*

Flower color: *white, pink, red*

Soil: *dry, sandy to well-drained*

Light: *full sun to partial shade*

Native to prairies, roadsides, and pond edges in the central and western United States, these perennials have an extended bloom season and a tolerance for summer heat that make them valuable in herbaceous borders and meadow gardens.

Selected species: *G. coccinea* (scarlet gaura)—branched stems 1 to 2 feet tall with narrow, oblong leaves. Fragrant flowers that resemble honeysuckle are clustered on a spikelike inflorescence from late spring and through summer. The flowers open white, fade to pink, and finally turn red; Zones 3-9. *G. lindheimeri* (white gaura)—2 to 5 feet with a vase-shaped open habit. Flowering begins in early summer and lasts until frost; the delicate four-petaled flowers open white and fade to pink as they age; Zones 6-9.

Growing conditions and maintenance: Gaura thrives in dry to well-drained soil and tolerates both heat and drought. Propagate by seed. *G. coccinea* can also be divided.

Gentiana
(jen-shee-AH-na)
GENTIAN

Gentiana saponaria

Hardiness: *Zones 3-8*

Flowering season: *summer to fall*

Height: *6 to 30 inches*

Flower color: *blue, purple, violet*

Soil: *moist, well-drained, rich*

Light: *full sun to partial shade*

Several perennial gentians inhabit low woodlands, alpine meadows, and damp prairies over much of eastern North America. Their flowers are generally shades of blue or purple, providing contrast to the predominately yellow flowers of late summer and fall.

Selected species: *G. andrewsii* (bottle gentian, closed gentian)—2 feet tall with clusters of deep blue 1½-inch bottle-shaped flowers with vertical white bands; petals remain closed; Zones 3-7. *G. puberulenta* (downy gentian)—clusters of funnel-shaped purplish blue blossoms atop a single upright 6- to 24-inch flower stalk; Zones 3-8. *G. saponaria* (soapwort gentian)—to 2½ feet tall with clusters of blue-violet flowers whose petals open partially; Zones 4-7.

Growing conditions and maintenance: Gentians require cool temperatures and rich, well-drained soil with ample moisture throughout the growing season. Propagate by seed or division.

Geranium
(jer-AY-nee-um)
CRANESBILL

Geranium maculatum

Hardiness: *Zones 3-10*

Flowering season: *spring, summer*

Height: *8 to 32 inches*

Flower color: *pink, purple, blue, white*

Soil: *moist, well-drained*

Light: *full sun to partial shade*

Annual and perennial geraniums are found in parts of Canada and throughout the United States, generally in open woodlands and meadows. In the garden they are valued both for their delicate five-petaled flowers and for their lush mounds of foliage.

Selected species: *G. californicum* (mountain geranium)—8- to 24-inch-tall perennial from the West. Palmately lobed leaves and pink to lavender flowers finely veined with purple in early summer; Zones 8-10. *G. carolinianum* (Carolina cranesbill)—annual native to dry, rocky woods and fields over much of the United States. Grows to 22 inches tall with palmately lobed leaves and pale pink or white ¼-inch flowers in late spring. *G. erianthum* (northern cranesbill)—vigorous perennial up to 32 inches in height. Deeply lobed foliage and violet or white flowers with dark veins; Zones 3-7. *G. maculatum* (wild geranium)—perennial to 2 feet. Leaves rise from the plant's base on 1- to 2-foot petioles, or leaf stems. Each leaf is deeply cut into five to seven segments with notched margins. Pinkish lavender to white flow-

ers appear over a 2- or 3-week period in late spring; Zones 3-7. *G. viscosissimum* (sticky wild geranium)—perennial from the West with a large clump of downy bright green leaves. Each leaf has five to seven deeply cut lobes and coarsely toothed margins. Pinkish lavender flowers appear from late spring through summer on sturdy branched stalks that reach 1 to 2 feet in height; Zones 3-7.

Growing conditions and maintenance: *G. carolinianum* tolerates a wide range of soil and light conditions and can become weedy even in poor soils. *G. maculatum, G. californicum,* and *G. erianthum* perform best in moist, rich soil. Water during dry spells. *G. maculatum*

Geranium viscosissimum

and *G. erianthum* require partial shade. *G. californicum* adapts to partial shade or full sun. *G. viscosissimum* prefers full sun but tolerates a variety of soils. Propagate by seed. Rhizomes of perennial species can also be divided.

121

Gilia
(GIL-ee-a)
BIRD'S-EYES

Gilia tricolor

Hardiness: *annual*

Flowering season: *spring to summer*

Height: *1 to 2½ feet*

Flower color: *blue, purple*

Soil: *loose, well-drained*

Light: *full sun*

The following gilias are annuals native to coastal areas of California and the nearby mountain ranges. They are vigorous plants well suited to a sunny meadow garden.

Selected species: *G. achilleifolia* (showy gilia, yarrow gilia)—erect stems 1 to 1½ feet tall with doubly compound leaves. In late spring, deep blue funnel-shaped flowers appear in dense, terminal clusters. *G. capitata* (globe gilia)—1 to 2½ feet tall with finely divided leaves on slender stems. Powder blue globe-shaped flower heads appear in late spring and early summer. *G. tricolor* (bird's-eyes)—1 foot tall with multiple branches and dissected leaves. Flowers are blue with a yellow throat and a dark purple ring at the top.

Growing conditions and maintenance: Gilias are adaptable to most well-drained soils. They are strong self-seeders, but they do not transplant easily. Sow seed where it is to grow.

Helenium
(he-LEE-nee-um)
COMMON SNEEZEWEED

Helenium autumnale

Hardiness: *Zones 3-8*

Flowering season: *summer to fall*

Height: *2 to 6 feet*

Flower color: *yellow, red*

Soil: *moist*

Light: *full sun*

Heleniums can be found growing along roadsides and streams and in meadows throughout much of the United States. Their daisylike flowers are borne in clusters from summer until frost, and they make an effective display when they are planted in groups.

Selected species: *H. autumnale* (common sneezeweed)—stoutly branched upright perennial to 6 feet tall with 3- to 5-inch leaves. Its flowers are 2 inches across with a raised yellow central disk and fan-shaped, toothed yellow petals that point downward. The variety 'Moorheim Beauty' grows to 32 inches and bears copper-red flowers with dark red centers; 'Bruno' grows to 4 feet with mahogany flowers.

Growing conditions and maintenance: Common sneezeweed requires a moist site in full sun. Do not apply nitrogen fertilizer. Early pinching helps promote bushier plants; taller plants may need staking. Divide every 3 to 4 years to prevent overcrowding. Propagate by seed or by division.

Helianthus
(hee-lee-AN-thus)
SUNFLOWER

Helianthus annuus

Hardiness: *Zones 3-9*

Flowering season: *summer, fall*

Height: *1 to 10 feet*

Flower color: *yellow*

Soil: *moist to dry*

Light: *full sun to partial shade*

The annual and perennial sunflowers described here are widely distributed east of the Rocky Mountains. They are generally large, coarse-textured plants with abundant daisylike flowers borne in summer and fall, and are well suited to the back of a mixed border or meadow garden. The seeds are a favorite food of many wild birds.

Selected species: *H. annuus* (common sunflower, mirasol)—sturdy annual to 8 feet or more. Yellow flowers with brown centers are up to 5 inches in diameter in summer and fall. 'Sunspot' is an 18- to 24-inch dwarf variety, and 'Sunset' has mahogany petals tipped with yellow; Zones 3-9. *H. giganteus* (giant sunflower)—perennial species to 10 feet in height with 3-inch yellow flowers at the tops of stems in mid- to late summer; Zones 3-7. *H. maximiliani* (Maximilian's sunflower)—perennial 3 to 10 feet tall with bright yellow 3-inch flowers in leaf axils all along the stems from midsummer through fall; Zones 3-8. *H. rigidus* (stiff sunflower)—showy yellow flowers up to 4 inches across in summer with stiff 3- to 6-foot stems and dark green foliage;

Zones 4-8. *H. simulans* (narrow-leaved sunflower)—perennial with branching stems to 8 feet in height and attractive, narrow gray-green leaves and 2-inch yellow flowers with reddish purple centers borne at stem tips in late summer and fall; Zones 3-9. *H. strumosus* (woodland sunflower)—perennial with stout, erect stems that may reach 7 feet and terminal clusters of 2- to 4-inch yellow flowers from mid- to late summer; Zones 4-8.

Growing conditions and maintenance: *H. annuus* and *H. rigidus* thrive in dry soils and full sun. *H. strumosus* prefers a dry soil and performs best in partial shade. *H. maximiliani* adapts to a variety of well-drained soils; prefers full sun. Grow *H. simulans* and *H. giganteus* in moist locations. Both do well in full sun; *H. simulans* also adapts to partial shade. To promote compact growth and more

Helianthus giganteus

flowers, cut *H. simulans* back by a third in early summer. Sunflowers are easily propagated by seed. Perennial species can also be propagated by division in early spring or by stem cuttings taken prior to flowering.

Heuchera
(HEW-ker-a)
ALUMROOT

Heuchera villosa

Hardiness: *Zones 4-9*

Flowering season: *spring to summer*

Height: *6 to 36 inches*

Flower color: *white, pink, green*

Soil: *moist, well-drained*

Light: *full sun to partial shade*

There are several lovely heucheras native to open woods and mountain slopes of the United States. Attractive foliage that is evergreen except in harsh winters forms low clumps from which slender stalks arise bearing delicate sprays of small, long-lasting, bell-shaped flowers.

Selected species: *H. americana* (alumroot)—eastern species with fuzzy oval 4-inch leaves and sprays of greenish flowers on 18- to 36-inch stalks. In a sunny spot, leaves often turn bronze; Zones 4-9. *H. micrantha* (common alumroot)—1- to 2-foot clump of scalloped reddish leaves and 18- to 24-inch stalks bearing white flowers; native to California and the Northwest; Zones 4-8. *H. villosa* (hairy alumroot)—eastern species with fuzzy pale green maplelike leaves and white to pink flowers on 10- to 18-inch stalks; Zones 6-9.

Growing conditions and maintenance: Heucheras thrive in rich soil with good drainage and partial shade. *H. americana* also tolerates full sun and poor, somewhat drier soil. Propagate by seed or by division.

Hibiscus
(hy-BIS-kus)
MALLOW

Hibiscus coccineus

Hardiness: *Zones 5-9*

Flowering season: *summer*

Height: *3 to 8 feet*

Flower color: *pink, white, red*

Soil: *moist to wet*

Light: *full sun to partial shade*

Native to low meadows, swamps, and marshes, all of these perennial species bear very large bell-shaped flowers.

Selected species: *H. coccineus* (wild red mallow)—4 to 7 feet tall with blue-green leaves and scarlet flowers 6 inches across; Zones 7-9. *H. grandiflorus* (great rose mallow)—grows up to 6 feet tall and bears pale pink to purplish rose flowers, sometimes with crimson centers; Zones 7-9. *H. lasiocarpus* (woolly mallow)—3 to 5 feet tall with terminal clusters of 5- to 8-inch pink or white flowers that sometimes have purple centers; Zones 5-9. *H. moscheutos* (swamp rose mallow, wild cotton)—3 to 8 feet tall with a shrubby habit; gray-green leaves and white, pink, or rose flowers 8 inches across, often with red or purple centers; Zones 7-9.

Growing conditions and maintenance: Plant mallows in a moist spot where they will receive at least half a day's sun. Allow plenty of room between plants, which may spread to 5 feet in width. Propagate by seed or early summer cuttings.

Hymenocallis
(by-men-o-KAL-is)
SPIDER LILY

Hymenocallis occidentalis

Hardiness: *Zones 6-10*

Flowering season: *spring to summer*

Height: *18 to 30 inches*

Flower color: *white*

Soil: *sandy, wet*

Light: *full sun to partial shade*

Spider lilies grow from bulbs and are found in low woodlands, swamps, and moist fields. Their large, fragrant flowers are composed of six straplike petals surrounding a funnel-shaped cup. They are excellent additions to a bog garden.

Selected species: *H. occidentalis* [also listed as *H. caroliniana*] (spider lily)—native to southeastern and south-central United States. It grows 1½ to 2½ feet tall with a basal clump of shiny, light green strap-shaped leaves up to 17 inches long. White flowers 7 inches across are borne atop leafless stalks in clusters of up to six. Flowers appear in spring in the South and in summer in cooler regions.

Growing conditions and maintenance: Plant *H. occidentalis* bulbs in full sun to partial shade in fall, setting them 5 inches deep in a location where they will receive abundant moisture. North of Zone 6, where spider lilies are not hardy, the bulbs can be planted in spring and lifted and brought indoors for winter. Propagate by seed or division of bulb offsets.

Iris
(EYE-ris)
IRIS

Iris douglasiana

Hardiness: *Zones 2-10*

Flowering season: *spring, summer*

Height: *4 inches to 3 feet*

Flower color: *many*

Soil: *wet to dry*

Light: *full sun to partial shade*

There are many native species of iris, all of them noted for their distinctive flowers composed of three drooping petal-like sepals, or falls, and three inner petals, or standards. Irises have attractive grasslike or sword-shaped leaves and grow from either bulbs or rhizomes.

Selected species: *I. brevicaulis* [also called *I. foliosa*] (zigzag stemmed iris)—showy blue, lavender, or white dark-veined flowers in late spring and glossy foliage on 1- to 2-foot stems growing in zigzag fashion. The falls bear a yellow patch near their base. Native to bottom lands, swamps, and marshes throughout much of the central United States; Zones 5-8. *I. cristata* (dwarf crested iris)—6 to 9 inches tall with blue-violet flowers with yellow or white crested ridges called beards in spring. The variety 'Alba' is white with yellow beards; eastern to central United States; Zones 3-9. *I. douglasiana* (Douglas' iris)—flowers throughout spring on short branched stalks in colors varying from red-purple and blue-purple to yellow, cream, and white; dense clumps of dark evergreen leaves up to 2 feet long; open woods and

grassy slopes of the Pacific coast; Zones 8-10. *I. fulva* (copper iris, red iris)—bright copper-red or orange flowers on 3-foot stems from early to midspring and bright green narrow foliage; stream banks and fresh water marshes of south-central United States; Zones 6-8. *I. hartwegii* (Sierra iris)—18 inches tall with cream, yellow, or lavender flowers in late spring; coniferous forests of the Northwest; Zones 7-8. *I. longipetala* (long-petaled iris)—clusters of three to six pale violet and white flowers with purple veins on 20-inch stems in midspring and dark green leaves up to 28 inches long; coastal California; Zones 9-10. *I. prismatica*

Iris fulva

(slender blue flag)—beardless blue-violet flowers in terminal clusters in late spring and early summer and grasslike leaves 1 to 3 feet tall; swampy areas of the East Coast; Zones 5-9. *I. tenax* (Oregon iris)—white, cream, yellow, lavender, blue, or purple flowers in late spring, singly or in pairs, on thin 14-inch stems amid narrow, grasslike leaves up to 20 inches in length; forests of the Northwest; Zones 8-9. *I. versicolor* (blue flag)—flowers usually blue-violet, sometimes with darker purple streaks or splashes of yellow, and 3-foot sword-shaped leaves; marshes and swamps in the Northeast; Zones 2-7. *I. virginica* (southern blue flag)—flowers and foliage very similar to *I. versicolor;* marshes and swamps of the Southeast; Zones 6-10.

Growing conditions and maintenance: Most species of iris thrive in full sun to partial shade. Species vary significantly, however, in their soil requirements. *I. hartwegii* and *I. tenax* prefer a relatively dry, well-drained location. *I. doug-*

lasiana grows in moist or dry soils and tolerates both drought and shade. *I. cristata* prefers a moist, well-drained, acid soil and grows particularly well on slopes, where it provides an attractive ground cover. *I. brevicaulis, I. fulva, I. prismatica,* and *I. longipetala* require constantly moist to wet soils. *I. versico-*

Iris tenax

lor and *I. virginica* prefer to grow with their roots submerged in water. They are well suited to the edges of ponds or garden pools. Propagate irises by division or seed.

Lewisia
(loo-ISS-ee-a)
BITTERROOT, LEWISIA

Lewisia cotyledon

Hardiness: *Zones 3-8*

Flowering season: *spring, summer*

Height: *4 to 12 inches*

Flower color: *white, pink*

Soil: *dry, rocky*

Light: *partial shade*

Lewisias are low-growing perennials that inhabit rocky slopes and open woods of the western United States. They are excellent choices for rock gardens.

Selected species: *L. columbiana* (bitterroot)—evergreen rosette of flat, dark green leaves with branched clusters of pink-veined white or pink flowers on 4- to 12-inch stalks in spring; Zones 4-8. *L. cotyledon* (broadleaf lewisia)—neat rosettes of spoon-shaped leaves and loose clusters of white or pink striped flowers on 12-inch stalks in early summer; Zones 6-8. *L. rediviva* (bitterroot)—rosette of cylindrical leaves appears in late summer and remains green over winter. In early spring showy rose-colored flowers up to 2 inches across are borne on short stems. After flowering the plant goes dormant; Zones 4-8.

Growing conditions and maintenance: Lewisias prefer partial shade and must have excellent drainage. A 1- to 2-inch mulch of gravel or stone chips is beneficial. Propagate by seed.

Liatris
(ly-AY-tris)
BLAZING STAR

Liatris aspera

Hardiness: *Zones 3-9*

Flowering season: *summer to fall*

Height: *8 inches to 6 feet*

Flower color: *purple, lavender, magenta*

Soil: *dry, sandy to moist, well-drained*

Light: *full sun*

Blazing stars are perennials found in prairies and dry, rocky areas from western New York to South Dakota and south to Texas, depending on the species. Their flower spikes provide a vertical accent in herbaceous borders and meadow plantings and attract butterflies.

Selected species: *L. aspera* (rough blazing star)—to 6 feet tall with frilly magenta flowers in 18- to 32-inch spikes. A good cut flower; Zones 3-8. *L. cylindracea* (dwarf blazing star)—8 to 24 inches tall with bright purple flowers; Zones 3-6. *L. punctata* (dotted blazing star)—lavender flowers on stems ranging from 1 to 2 feet tall; Zones 3-9. *L. pycnostachya* (prairie blazing star)—to 5 feet with showy purple flowers in dense cylindrical spikes up to 18 inches long; Zones 3-9.

Growing conditions and maintenance: Blazing stars require full sun and well-drained soil; good winter drainage is essential. They tolerate drought. Propagate by seed or division in spring.

Lilium
(*LIL-ee-um*)
LILY

Lilium columbianum

Hardiness: *Zones 3-10*

Flowering season: *summer*

Height: *1 to 9 feet*

Flower color: *yellow, orange, red*

Soil: *moist to dry*

Light: *full sun to shade*

These perennials bear spectacular trumpet-shaped flowers in every shade of yellow, orange, and red, often with dark brown or purple spots. Native species are found in the wild in prairies, open woodlands, and meadows. All lilies grow from bulbs.

Selected species: *L. canadense* (Canada lily, wild yellow lily)—as many as twenty 3-inch-long yellow to orange-red flowers that droop gracefully from the tops of 3- to 8-foot stems in early summer; whorled, dark green lance-shaped leaves; eastern United States and Canada; Zones 4-7. *L. catesbaei* (pine lily)—2 feet tall with 5- to 6-inch-long flowers that shade from yellow with purple spots near the base to red toward the tip in mid- to late summer; southeastern coastal plains; Zones 7-8. *L. columbianum* (Columbia lily, Oregon lily)—nodding clusters of 2-inch yellow to gold to deep red flowers with maroon spots in summer; usually to 3 feet but may reach 6 feet in ideal conditions. Northwest United States and British Columbia; Zones 6-9. *L. humboldtii* (Humboldt lily)—4 to 8 feet tall with dozens of nodding yellow-orange flowers, usually with brown or maroon spots above bright green to greenish purple foliage in early summer; West Coast; Zones 5-9. *L. michauxii* (Carolina lily, Turk's-cap lily)—1 to 4 feet tall with up to six fragrant, nodding orange-red flowers spotted with purple per stalk; the petals curve sharply backward almost to the flower's base; southeastern U.S. coastal plain to mountains; Zones 7-9. *L. pardalinum* (leopard lily, tiger lily)—3 to 8 feet tall with sharply backswept orange petals flecked with maroon and dark, prominent stamens in early summer; spreads

Lilium canadense

rapidly to form colonies; West Coast; Zones 5-9. *L. parvum* (fairy lily)—2 to 6 feet tall with small bell-shaped orange flowers with maroon spots in late summer; West Coast; Zones 4-9. *L. philadelphicum* (wood lily, orange-cup lily)—1 to 4 feet with reddish orange flowers spotted with purple or brown singly or in clusters of up to four in midsummer; woodlands of southern Canada, New England through the east-central United States and Rockies; Zones 4-7. *L. superbum* (Turk's-cap lily, swamp lily)—3 to 9 feet tall with a loosely branched cluster of up to 50 flowers in midsummer. Each blossom has sharply backswept petals that are green at the base, yellow with brown speckles through the middle, and reddish orange at the apex; wet meadows and woodlands of eastern United States; Zones 4-9.

Growing conditions and maintenance: Lily species vary greatly in their cultural requirements. *L. canadense, L. superbum, L. pardalinum, L. parvum,* and *L. philadelphicum* prefer a moist, well-drained, humus-rich soil. The first two thrive in sun or partial shade, while the latter three species require some shade. *L. catesbaei* prefers a constantly wet, acid soil, and full sun or partial shade. *Lilium columbianum, L. humboldtii,* and *L. michauxii* thrive in drier sites. *L. columbianum* and *L. michauxii* require

Lilium superbum

at least partial shade, while *L. humboldtii* tolerates full sun or partial shade. Do not allow lily bulbs to dry out prior to planting. Lilies can be propagated by separating offsets, by planting individual scales, or from seed. Seed-grown lilies generally reach flowering size in 2 or 3 years.

Linum
(LY-num)
FLAX

Linum perenne var. lewisii

Hardiness: *Zones 5-9*

Flowering season: *spring to summer*

Height: *1 to 2½ feet*

Flower color: *blue, white*

Soil: *well-drained, sandy to rocky*

Light: *full sun to partial shade*

Only one subspecies of perennial flax is native to North America. Although the individual flowers drop the day after they open, plants blossom continuously for several months.

Selected species: *L. perenne* var. *lewisii* (blue flax, prairie flax)—loose branching clusters of sky blue flowers 1 inch wide on the upper portion of gracefully arching stems 1 to 2½ feet tall from late spring through summer. The variety 'Alba' has white flowers.

Growing conditions and maintenance: Grow prairie flax in full sun to partial shade in a well-drained, moderately dry soil. Excess moisture in winter reduces hardiness. This subspecies is drought tolerant. Though short-lived, it self-sows readily. Propagate by seed planted in fall.

Lobelia
(lo-BEE-lee-a)
LOBELIA

Lobelia cardinalis

Hardiness: *Zones 3-10*

Flowering season: *spring, summer, fall*

Height: *1 to 6 feet*

Flower color: *red, blue*

Soil: *moist to wet*

Light: *partial shade to full sun*

Found in wet meadows and damp woodlands and along stream banks, these moisture-loving perennials bear colorful tubular flowers that are frequented by hummingbirds.

Selected species: *L. cardinalis* (cardinal flower)—brilliant red flowers on 8-inch spikes; usually grows 2 to 4 feet tall but may reach 6 feet; blooms in spring, summer, and fall in the southern parts of its range and in late summer and early fall in cool climates; Zones 3-9. *L. glandulosa* (glades lobelia)—blue flowers with white eyes in loose terminal racemes on slender stems 1½ to 5 feet tall in late summer and fall; Zones 7-10. *L. siphilitica* (great blue lobelia, blue cardinal flower)—blue flowers in the leaf axils on erect 2- to 3-foot stems from summer into fall; Zones 4-7.

Growing conditions and maintenance: Lobelias thrive in moist locations in partial shade. *L. cardinalis* will adapt to full sun as long as moisture is abundant. Propagate by seed or stem layering or by division in early spring.

Lupinus
(loo-PY-nus)
LUPINE

Lupinus densiflorus var. aureus

Hardiness: *Zones 3-10*

Flowering season: *spring, summer*

Height: *4 inches to 3 feet*

Flower color: *blue, purple, yellow, white, pink*

Soil: *moist to dry*

Light: *full sun to partial shade*

Annual and perennial lupines inhabit prairies, open woodlands, and dry mountain slopes and bear dense, showy terminal clusters of flowers in spring or summer. They have attractive palmately compound leaves.

Selected species: *L. densiflorus* var. *aureus* (golden lupine)—annual 8 to 16 inches tall with short spikes of yellow flowers in late spring; California Coast Range. *L. nanus* (sky blue lupine)—annual 4 to 20 inches with spikes of sky blue flowers with a white or yellowish spot in late spring; California Coast Range. *L. palmeri* (Palmer's lupine)—perennial 1 to 2 feet in height with blue flowers in late spring; southwestern mountains; Zones 6-9. *L. perennis* (wild lupine)—perennial species up to 2 feet tall with elongated clusters of late-spring to early-summer flowers that are usually purplish blue but occasionally white or pink; Maine to Florida; Zones 4-8. *L. sericeus* (silky lupine)—perennial 1 to 2 feet tall with blue flowers throughout the summer and velvety leaves; California to British Columbia and northern Rockies; Zones 4-7. *L. succulentus* (arroyo lupine)—annual up to 3 feet in height with fragrant deep purple to rusty red flowers from early to late spring. *L. texensis* (Texas bluebonnet)—annual 6 to 18 inches tall with clusters of up to 50 blue flowers with conspicuous white tips and light green velvety leaves. Native to Texas.

Growing conditions and maintenance: Most lupines need full sun and dry soils with excellent drainage. *L. sericeus* also thrives in partial shade and is tolerant of

Lupinus texensis

both moist and dry soils. Lupines benefit from soil or seed inoculants containing nitrogen-fixing bacteria. Propagate both annual and perennial lupines from seed sown in fall; perennial seed can also be sown in spring. Scarifying the seed with sandpaper or by nicking the seed coat will aid germination.

Lysimachia
(ly-sim-MAK-ee-a)
LOOSESTRIFE

Lysimachia quadrifolia

Hardiness: *Zones 4-10*

Flowering season: *summer*

Height: *1 to 3 feet*

Flower color: *yellow*

Soil: *moist, organic, rich*

Light: *full sun to partial shade*

Perennial loosestrifes are native to moist prairies and stream banks throughout the eastern and central United States. Their yellow summer flowers create an attractive display on the banks of a pond or in a moist border.

Selected species: *L. ciliata* (fringed loosestrife)—1 to 3 feet tall with bright yellow 1-inch, five-petaled flowers on slender stalks arising from the leaf axils. The willowlike leaves are pale green. The foliage of *L. ciliata* var. *purpurea* is purple in spring and greenish purple in summer. *L. quadrifolia* (prairie loosestrife)—1 to 3 feet tall with whorls of yellow flowers marked with red and very narrow, stiff leaves.

Growing conditions and maintenance: Loosestrifes thrive in rich soil with ample moisture. *L. ciliata* does well in full sun or partial shade, while *L. quadrifolia* prefers full sun. Under favorable conditions, both species can become invasive. Propagate by division in spring or fall.

Machaeranthera
(mak-e-RAN-ther-a)
TAHOKA DAISY

Machaeranthera tanacetifolia

Hardiness: *annual*

Flowering season: *spring through summer*

Height: *6 to 12 inches*

Flower color: *lavender*

Soil: *well-drained, sandy to rocky*

Light: *full sun*

Native to the sunny, open spaces from southern Canada through the Great Plains to the southwestern United States, this low-spreading annual blooms profusely over a long period.

Selected species: *M. tanacetifolia* (Tahoka daisy)—clusters of 2-inch asterlike lavender flowers with yellow centers and dense mounds of deeply cut, sharply pointed foliage 6 to 12 inches tall. Plants readily seed themselves and will make a pretty and colorful ground cover on a favorable site.

Growing conditions and maintenance: Tahoka daisy requires full sun and is tolerant of most soils as long as it has excellent drainage. Propagate by seed. Plants may begin to flower 6 weeks after sowing, and a succession of sowings can extend the blooming period to 6 months.

Marshallia
(mar-SHAL-ee-a)
MARSHALLIA

Marshallia grandiflora

Hardiness: *Zones 5-9*

Flowering season: *spring to summer*

Height: *8 to 24 inches*

Flower color: *white, pink*

Soil: *moist, well-drained to dry, sandy*

Light: *full sun to partial shade*

These clump-forming perennials grow wild in the eastern and central United States. Their buttonlike flowers and tidy form suit them to planting at the front of a mixed border, along a garden walk, or among stones in a rock garden or terrace.

Selected species: *M. caespitosa* var. *caespitosa* (Barbara's buttons)—ball-shaped clusters of dainty, fragrant white flowers on leafless stalks 8 to 18 inches tall above a rosette of narrow leaves. *M. grandiflora* (large-flowered marshallia)—large, densely packed balls of rose pink flowers with purple stamens on 1- to 2-foot stalks above a dense rosette of glossy, oval, dark green leaves.

Growing conditions and maintenance: Marshallias will grow well in either moist or dry soils as long as drainage is excellent. Propagate by seed or division.

Melampodium
(mel-am-PO-dee-um)
BLACKFOOT DAISY

Melampodium leucanthum

Hardiness: *Zones 4-9*

Flowering season: *spring into fall*

Height: *6 to 12 inches*

Flower color: *white*

Soil: *dry, rocky, well-drained*

Light: *full sun*

Blackfoot daisy inhabits the dry slopes, mesas, and high plains of the Southwest. A deep taproot ensures excellent tolerance for drought. This low-growing evergreen perennial is a good selection for rock gardens and can be massed on a sunny bank to help control erosion.

Selected species: *M. leucanthum* (blackfoot daisy)—1-inch white daisylike flowers with yellow centers borne profusely on slender stalks throughout spring and summer. Gray-green leaves form a neat evergreen mound 6 to 12 inches tall and up to 16 inches wide.

Growing conditions and maintenance: Given full sun and a very well-drained soil, blackfoot daisy is extremely easy to grow. Its naturally mounded form requires no shaping. Propagate by seed sown in warm soil.

Mertensia
(mer-TEN-see-a)
BLUEBELLS

Mertensia virginica

Hardiness: *Zones 3-8*

Flowering season: *spring to summer*

Height: *1 to 3 feet*

Flower color: *blue*

Soil: *moist, acid, rich*

Light: *full sun to full shade*

Mertensias are perennials native to stream banks, moist woods, and damp meadows. Their bell-shaped blue flowers hang in clusters from the ends of leafy stems.

Selected species: *M. ciliata* (mountain bluebells)—1 to 3 feet tall with loose clusters of pink buds opening to sky blue, lightly fragrant flowers from late spring through summer; produces a clump of stems with smooth, succulent 2- to 6-inch leaves; native to western mountains; Zones 3-8. *M. virginica* (Virginia bluebells)—up to 2 feet tall with clusters of lavender-blue flowers in spring and attractive gray-green oval leaves 2 to 5 inches long. The plant disappears after flowering; Zones 3-7.

Growing conditions and maintenance: Mertensias thrive in acid soil with abundant moisture. Add organic matter to the soil before planting. *M. ciliata* adapts to full sun to partial shade, and *M. virginica* requires partial to full shade. Propagate by seed or division.

Mimulus
(MIM-yew-lus)
MONKEY FLOWER

Mimulus lewisii

Hardiness: *Zones 3-10*

Flowering season: *spring, summer, fall*

Height: *1 to 4 feet*

Flower color: *red, yellow, pink*

Soil: *moist*

Light: *full sun to partial shade*

Among the monkey flowers are several perennials that grow along stream banks and in moist meadows in the West. Their brightly colored funnel-shaped flowers have a two-lobed upper lip and a three-lobed lower lip.

Selected species: *M. cardinalis* (scarlet monkey flower)—2 to 4 feet tall with brilliant orange-red flowers from spring through fall. The lower lip of the flower is swept backward and has a patch of yellow; Zones 7-10. *M. guttatus* (golden monkey flower)—2 to 3 feet tall with yellow snapdragon-like flowers spotted with purple on the lower lip in spring and summer; Zones 6-10. *M. lewisii* (Lewis monkey flower)—1 to 2½ feet tall with pink to rose red flowers often marked with darker lines or maroon blotches in the throat; Zones 3-9.

Growing conditions and maintenance: Monkey flowers thrive in partial shade in moist soil. Golden monkey flower also grows in full sun, though its flowers last longer with afternoon shade. It can be grown as an annual in cooler climates. Propagate by seed or by division of clumps.

Mirabilis
(my-RAB-i-lis)
WILD FOUR-O'CLOCK

Mirabilis multiflora

Hardiness: *Zones 5-10*

Flowering season: *spring to summer*

Height: *1½ to 3 feet*

Flower color: *pink, purple, magenta*

Soil: *dry, rocky*

Light: *full sun*

Among the four-o'clocks are several perennials native to dry areas of the western United States. The tubular flowers open in the afternoon and close the following morning. They are lovely massed as a ground cover or trailing over a wall.

Selected species: *M. froebelii* (wild four-o'clock, wishbone plant)—numerous clusters of 1½- to 2¼-inch-long deep rose pink to reddish purple flowers at the ends of much-branched stems up to 3 feet; Zones 7-10. *M. multiflora* (wild four-o'clock)—up to 18 inches with magenta tubular flowers about 2 inches long and dark green leaves; Zones 5-10.

Growing conditions and maintenance: Four-o'clocks are easily grown, long-lived drought-tolerant perennials. Supplemental watering during dry periods will extend the flowering season. Propagate by seed or divide roots in the fall.

Mitchella
(mi-CHEL-a)
PARTRIDGEBERRY

Mitchella repens

Hardiness: *Zones 3-9*

Flowering season: *spring*

Height: *2 to 4 inches*

Flower color: *white*

Soil: *moist, acid*

Light: *partial to full shade*

Partridgeberry is a dainty low-growing evergreen native to woodlands and stream banks of the eastern and central United States. It provides a fine-textured year-round ground cover for shaded areas and is a lovely addition to a rock garden.

Selected species: *M. repens* (partridgeberry, twinberry)—pairs of ¾-inch white flowers in late spring and bright red berries in fall. Small, rounded, shiny dark green leaves with white veins on trailing stems up to 1 foot long that root as they creep over.

Growing conditions and maintenance: Partridgeberry thrives in cool, moist, humus-rich soil in partial to full shade. Mulch lightly with leaves in winter. The easiest way to propagate partridgeberry is to take 6-inch stem cuttings in early spring; keep them evenly moist in well-drained soil.

Monarda
(mo-NAR-da)
BEE BALM, BERGAMOT

Monarda didyma

Hardiness: *Zones 3-10*

Flowering season: *spring, summer, fall*

Height: *6 inches to 4 feet*

Flower color: *lavender, pink, red, yellow, white*

Soil: *sandy, dry to moist*

Light: *full sun to partial shade*

These aromatic annuals and perennials grow wild in prairies, meadows, and marshes. Numerous small funnel-shaped flowers are crowded into dense clusters or whorls.

Selected species: *M. citriodora* (horsemint, lemon mint)—annual up to 2 feet tall with whorls of pink to lavender flowers from spring to fall. *M. didyma* (bee balm, Oswego tea)—perennial up to 4 feet tall with 2-inch dense rounded terminal clusters of scarlet red flowers in summer; Zones 5-7. *M. fistulosa* (wild bergamot)—perennial 2 to 4 feet tall with 2- to 4-inch terminal pompomlike clusters of lavender, pink, or white flowers in summer; Zones 3-8. *M. punctata* (spotted bee balm, horsemint)—perennial up to 3 feet tall with whorls of purple-spotted yellow flowers in summer; Zones 4-10.

Growing conditions and maintenance: Grow *M. didyma* and *M. fistulosa* in rich, moist soil and *M. citriodora* and *M. punctata* in dry, sandy soil. Monardas can be very aggressive and may need frequent division. Propagate by seed. Perennials can also be propagated by division.

Monardella
(mo-nar-DEL-a)
COYOTE MINT

Monardella odoratissima

Hardiness: *Zones 6-10*

Flowering season: *summer*

Height: *4 to 16 inches*

Flower color: *blue, purple, red, white*

Soil: *dry, well-drained*

Light: *full sun*

Several of the coyote mints are perennials native to the western states, where they inhabit dry mountain slopes, ridges, and forest openings. Often used in rock gardens, they attract butterflies and hummingbirds.

Selected species: *M. macrantha* (hummingbird mint, scarlet coyote mint)—4 to 16 inches tall with tubular bright red flowers in showy round terminal clusters and glossy green foliage; Zones 8-10. *M. odoratissima* (coyote mint, mountain mint)—flowers ranging from nearly white to bright blue-purple in 2-inch clusters; the stems form large mats about 1 foot tall with fragrant leaves; Zones 6-10.

Growing conditions and maintenance: Plant coyote mints in full sun and sandy, well-drained soil. They are very drought tolerant. Propagate by seed, by cuttings, or by division.

Muhlenbergia
(myoo-len-BUR-jee-a)
MUHLY

Muhlenbergia capillaris

Hardiness: *Zones 6-10*

Flowering season: *fall*

Height: *1½ to 4 feet*

Flower color: *pink, purplish*

Soil: *moist, sandy to dry, rocky*

Light: *full sun to partial shade*

The graceful foliage and airy flowers of these clump-forming perennial grasses make them valuable for mass plantings or as garden accents. The softly colored seed heads that develop in fall remain attractive through winter.

Selected species: *M. capillaris* (pink muhly, hair grass)—1½ to 3 feet with narrow, wiry, nearly evergreen leaves; 8- to 20-inch clusters of soft pink flowers on branching stems in early fall followed by purplish seed heads; native to eastern half of United States. *M. lindheimeri* (Lindheimer muhly)—clumps of narrow blue-green leaves 18 inches long and purplish flower spikes on stalks up to 4 feet tall in fall, followed by silvery seed heads; Texas native; Zones 7-9.

Growing conditions and maintenance: Pink muhly needs full sun. It adapts to moist to dry, sandy to clayey soil and tolerates occasional flooding or drought. Lindheimer muhly prefers full sun and a moist, well-drained rocky soil, but it tolerates both drought and some shade. Cut muhly grasses to the ground in early spring before new growth begins. Propagate by seed.

Nemophila
(nem-OFF-i-la)
BABY-BLUE-EYES

Nemophila maculata

Hardiness: *annual*

Flowering season: *spring to summer*

Height: *6 to 12 inches*

Flower color: *white, purple, blue*

Soil: *moist, well-drained to dry*

Light: *full sun to partial shade*

These low-growing annuals are pretty in mixed herbaceous borders or rock gardens or spilling over the edge of a wall.

Selected species: *N. maculata* (five-spot)—clusters of 1¾-inch white blossoms with a deep purple or blue spot at the tip of each of the five petals on trailing stems up to 12 inches long from midspring to midsummer. Flowers in clusters at branch tips; native to California. *N. menziesii* (baby-blue-eyes)—sky blue flowers 1½ inches across with white centers throughout spring; trailing stems form a mound 6 inches tall and 12 inches wide with deeply cut foliage; native to California and Oregon. *N. phacelioides* (baby-blue-eyes)—1-inch pale blue flowers with white centers in spring on trailing or partially upright 12-inch stems; Arkansas, Oklahoma, and Texas.

Growing conditions and maintenance: *N. menziesii* and *N. phacelioides* like moist locations with relatively cool summer nights. *N. menziesii* adapts to full sun or partial shade; *N. phacelioides* needs partial shade. *N. maculata* prefers a well-drained to dry soil and full sun. It dies in summer. Propagate by seed.

Nymphaea
(nim-FEE-a)
WATER LILY

Nymphaea odorata

Hardiness: *Zones 2-10*

Flowering season: *summer*

Height: *2 to 4 inches above water*

Flower color: *white, pink*

Soil: *shallow water*

Light: *full sun*

The sweetly scented flowers of these aquatic perennials grace ponds, lakes, and ditches over much of the eastern and central United States. The flowers, each of which lasts for about 3 days, float on the surface of the water. They close at night and on cloudy days.

Selected species: *N. odorata* (water lily, pond lily)—white or pink flowers 3 to 5 inches across with numerous gold stamens from mid- to late summer. Flat 4- to 12-inch leaves are green on the upper surface and reddish below, and float on the surface of the water.

Growing conditions and maintenance: Plant rhizomes 3 to 4 inches deep in pots containing clayey soil and cover the soil surface with 2 inches of fine gravel. Submerge the pots in up to 4 feet of water. In a cold climate in which the water may freeze solid in winter, store the pots indoors in a cool location over the winter. Propagate by dividing the rhizomes.

Oenothera
(ee-no-THEE-ra)
OENOTHERA

Oenothera speciosa

Hardiness: *Zones 3-10*

Flowering season: *spring to summer*

Height: *2 to 24 inches*

Flower color: *white, yellow, pink*

Soil: *infertile, dry to well-drained*

Light: *full sun*

The perennials and annuals in this genus are subdivided into sundrops, whose flowers are open by day, and the evening primroses, whose flowers open in the late afternoon or evening and close up in the morning.

Selected species: *O. caespitosa* (gumbo evening primrose)—perennial with fragrant 3-inch flowers held 4 to 6 inches above a basal clump of downy 5-inch leaves, opening white and fading to pink before they close the following day from spring to summer. Spreads by lateral roots, making it a good ground cover where its evening flowers will be visible; Zones 4-9. *O. deltoides* (desert evening primrose)—annual desert native with fragrant 3-inch flowers in spring opening white in the evening, then fading to pink. Two to 10 inches tall with trailing stems up to 36 inches long and woolly 1- to 3-inch leaves; Zones 5-10. *O. fruticosa* (sundrops)—day-flowering perennial up to 2 feet in height with loose clusters of 1- to 2-inch yellow blossoms; native to edge of woodlands throughout eastern United States; Zones 3-8. *O. macrocarpa* [also called *O. missourensis*] (Missouri evening primrose)—perennial 8 to 10 inches tall from rocky prairies of the central United States with 2- to 3-inch yellow flowers in summer and narrow, thick gray-green leaves; Zones 4-8. *O. speciosa* (pink evening primrose)—perennial up to 18 inches tall with large dark pink to white cup-shaped flowers over a long period in spring and summer; native to rocky prairies and open woods from Kansas to Texas, where it quickly colonizes poor dry soil, making it a good ground cover for hot exposed sites; Zones 5-9.

Growing conditions and maintenance: Oenotheras thrive in full sun; *O. fruticosa* will tolerate light shade. All prefer

Oenothera missourensis

dry, infertile soil. Propagate by seed sown outside in fall. Most perennial species can also be propagated by dividing in fall or from cuttings taken in early summer.

Panicum
(PAN-i-kum)
PANIC GRASS

Panicum virgatum

Hardiness: *Zones 5-9*

Flowering season: *summer*

Height: *3 to 6 feet*

Flower color: *reddish purple*

Soil: *dry to moist*

Light: *full sun*

Panic grass is widely used in meadows and other naturalistic plantings, and its height makes it useful for screening or as a vertical accent when planted singly. Its seeds are eaten by many species of birds.

Selected species: *P. virgatum* (switch grass, panic grass)—erect clump-forming perennial 3 to 6 feet tall with long, narrow leaves that are bluish green in summer and yellow in fall. Airy panicles of reddish purple summer flowers followed by seed heads that are grayish white or brown in winter. There are a number of cultivars, including 'Haense Herms', with reddish foliage from midsummer to frost. Native from Nova Scotia to Arizona.

Growing conditions and maintenance: Switch grass is easy to grow, thriving in both moist and dry soils and tolerating poor drainage and drought. Cut old foliage to the ground before new growth emerges in spring. Propagate by seed or by division.

Passiflora
(pas-i-FLOR-a)
PASSIONFLOWER

Passiflora incarnata

Hardiness: *Zones 6-10*

Flowering season: *summer*

Height: *to 15 to 25 feet with support*

Flower color: *white, lavender, yellow*

Soil: *well-drained*

Light: *full sun to partial shade*

The perennial passionflowers are herbaceous vines native to the eastern United States with showy flowers, lush, tropical-looking foliage, and edible fruit.

Selected species: *P. incarnata* (passionflower, maypop)—to 25 feet with white to lavender flowers 2 to 3 inches across followed by large apricot-colored fruit. The 4- to 6-inch leaves have three lobes and are dark green above and whitish below. *P. lutea* (passionflower)—to 15 feet with greenish yellow flowers and purple-black fruit. Its leaves turn yellow in fall.

Growing conditions and maintenance: Grow passionflowers in well-drained soil. *P. incarnata* adapts to either sun or partial shade, while *P. lutea* prefers partial shade. Their abundant growth requires sturdy support. Pinch vines their first growing season to increase bushiness. Propagate by seed or cuttings, or separate suckers from the base of established plants.

Penstemon
(pen-STEE-mon)
BEARDTONGUE

Penstemon digitalis

Hardiness: *Zones 3-10*

Flowering season: *spring, summer, fall*

Height: *1 to 5 feet*

Flower color: *white, pink, lavender, blue, purple*

Soil: *well-drained, sandy*

Light: *full sun to partial shade*

Penstemons are perennials with showy terminal clusters of brightly colored two-lipped flowers. Most species are natives of the sunny plains and prairies of the Midwest. Good drainage is essential for all penstemons.

Selected species: *P. ambiguus* (sand penstemon)—1-inch white to pink flowers on a symmetrical mounded plant 1 to 4 feet tall and up to 3 feet wide. Blooms most heavily in late spring, with sporadic flowers through fall; Zones 5-9. *P. canescens* (gray beardtongue)—pale lavender to white flowers in early summer on erect stems to 2 feet tall; Zones 5-7. *P. cobaea* (cobaea penstemon, giant foxglove)—flowers 2 to 3 inches long on 1- to 2-foot stems rising from a rosette of leaves. Flower color ranges from white to pale pink, lavender, and purple, with dark purple markings in the throats; Zones 5-8. *P. digitalis* (beardtongue, white penstemon)—3 to 5 feet tall with white or pinkish flowers on erect purplish stems in early summer; eastern to central United States; Zones 3-8. *P. grandiflorus* (large-flowered penstemon)—pink to lavender flowers on stout un-branched 2- to 4-foot stems with waxy blue-green leaves in late spring and summer; Zones 3-9. *P. heterophyllus* (foothill penstemon)—a profusion of 1-inch blue or violet flowers in late spring and early summer on a neat, shrubby plant to 1½ feet in height that is evergreen in mild climates and tolerates drought and heat; California; Zones 8-10. *P. smallii* (Small's beardtongue)—rose to dark pink white-throated flowers in spring on branching stems 1½ to 2½ feet tall above a rosette of shiny dark-veined leaves that turn red-

Penstemon smallii

dish in fall; southern Appalachian Mountains; Zones 7-9. *P. strictus* (Rocky Mountain penstemon)—deep blue to purple flowers from late spring to early summer on 1- to 3-foot stems above a mat of evergreen foliage; Zones 4-5.

Growing conditions and maintenance: Plant these species in sandy, well-drained soil. All are adapted to full sun, and *P. smallii* also thrives in partial shade. Since penstemons are usually short-lived, leave some fading flowers in place to produce seed so the plants can self-sow. Propagate from seed after moist-stratification.

Phacelia
(fa-SEEL-ee-a)
DESERT BELLS

Phacelia sericea

Hardiness: *Zones 5-10*

Flowering season: *spring, summer*

Height: *4 to 48 inches*

Flower color: *blue, lavender, purple*

Soil: *well-drained to dry, sandy*

Light: *full sun*

Phacelias are annuals and perennials native to the deserts, dry rocky slopes, and open flats of the West. Their bell-shaped flowers bloom in clusters along one side of curved stems.

Selected species: *P. campanularia* (California bluebell)—annual to 16 inches in height with deep blue flowers in early to midspring. *P. minor* (wild Canterbury bell, whitlavia)—annual to 2 feet in height with purple flowers from mid- to late spring. *P. sericea* (silky phacelia)—4- to 16-inch perennial with dark blue, lavender, or purple flowers in summer and silvery stems and foliage covered with silky hairs. *P. tanacetifolia* (lacy phacelia, fiddleneck)—perennial 1 to 4 feet tall with blue or lavender flowers in spring and finely divided leaves covered with stiff hairs.

Growing conditions and maintenance: Phacelias thrive in full sun and well-drained to dry soil. Propagate by seed sown in late summer or early fall.

Phlox
(flox)
PHLOX

Phlox paniculata

Hardiness: *Zones 3-9*

Flowering season: *spring, summer, fall*

Height: *6 inches to 4 feet*

Flower color: *pink, red, blue, purple, white*

Soil: *dry, sandy to moist, acid, fertile*

Light: *full sun to partial shade*

With one exception, all phloxes are North American natives. Among them are a number of very popular garden plants with many cultivars and some lovely but lesser-known species. Phloxes have a great range of cultural requirements and growth habits. Some are annuals, others perennial; some are low and spreading, suitable for a rock garden or a sunny bank, while others grow tall and erect and contribute color and fragrance to the middle or rear of a perennial border.

Selected species: *P. carolina* (Carolina phlox)—perennial to 24 to 30 inches tall with lavender, pink, and (rarely) white flowers in late spring and early summer, often continuing to bloom sporadically until frost; native to woodland edgings and openings in southeast United States; Zones 6-8. *P. divaricata* ssp. *laphamii* (blue phlox, wild sweet William)—perennial with loose clusters of fragrant purple flowers, each with a dark eye, in spring and early summer on 12- to 30-inch flower stalks rising from semitrailing stems; moist woodlands throughout much of the eastern United States; Zones 4-9. *P. drummondii* (Drum-

mond's phlox, annual phlox)—annual 6 to 20 inches tall with 1-inch flowers that may be pink, red, white, lavender, or purple. Seeds are available in both single and mixed colors. Compact varieties make excellent container plants; native to Texas. *P. glaberrima* ssp. *interior* (marsh phlox)—perennial 20 to 30 inches tall with pink, lavender, or white flowers throughout the summer; native wet woodlands in central United States; Zones 5-6. *P. paniculata* (summer phlox)—3- to 4-foot perennial with pink, lavender, or white flowers in summer in clusters from 4 to 8 inches wide. Dozens of cultivars are available. Native to open

Phlox pilosa

woods and meadows throughout much of the eastern and central United States; Zones 4-8. *P. pilosa* (prairie phlox)—perennial 1 to 2 feet tall with extremely fragrant pale pink or lavender flowers in spring or early summer. Prairies, sand hills, and dry open woods of United States from Plains states to East Coast; Zones 3-9. *P. subulata* (moss pink, moss phlox)—perennial with masses of pink, white, or purple flowers on a dense mat of needlelike evergreen leaves that makes a fine ground cover for dry areas; eastern United States; Zones 5-8.

Growing conditions and maintenance: Phloxes generally prefer an acid soil, but here their cultural similarities end. *P. drummondii, P. pilosa,* and *P. subulata* thrive in dry, sandy soils and full sun. If fading flowers are removed, *P. drummondii* usually blooms all summer, and *P. pilosa* often reblooms if cut back after flowering. *P. carolina* tolerates soils from moist to dry, as long as they are well drained. It prefers partial

shade, is resistant to powdery mildew, and often self-sows. *P. divaricata* ssp. *laphamii, P. glaberrima* ssp. *interior,* and *P. paniculata* require a moist, fertile soil. *P. glaberrima* ssp. *interior* requires partial shade, while the other

Phlox divaricata ssp. laphamii

two moisture-loving species adapt to full sun or partial shade.

Start annual phlox from seed. Perennial phlox can be propagated by cuttings, division, or seed. Germination is enhanced by moist-stratification.

Podophyllum
(po-doh-FIL-um)
MAY APPLE

Podophyllum peltatum

Hardiness: *Zones 3-9*

Flowering season: *spring*

Height: *12 to 18 inches*

Flower color: *white*

Soil: *moist, rich*

Light: *partial to full shade*

May apple, a perennial, grows in moist woodlands in the eastern half of the United States. It grows from rhizomes, spreading to form a dense ground cover. Its bold leaves are especially attractive in combination with ferns or other fine-textured plants.

Selected species: *P. peltatum* (May apple, mandrake, raccoon berry)—rounded leaves up to 10 inches across on sturdy, erect leaf stems 12 to 18 inches tall. Leaves are folded when they first appear in spring, then open like an umbrella. A solitary 2-inch white flower forms beneath the leaves and is followed by an edible yellow 2-inch fruit. The flowers are seen to their best advantage when May apples are planted on a slope above a path.

Growing conditions and maintenance: May apple needs at least partial shade and abundant moisture. To keep this vigorous spreader under control in a small garden, plant it in a large pot sunk in the ground. Propagate by seed or root division.

Polemonium
(po-le-MO-nee-um)
JACOB'S-LADDER

Polemonium viscosum

Hardiness: *Zones 2-9*

Flowering season: *spring, summer*

Height: *4 to 36 inches*

Flower color: *pink, purple, blue, white*

Soil: *moist to rocky, well-drained, rich*

Light: *full sun to partial shade*

The polemoniums are natives of meadows, open woodlands, and stream banks. Their dark green compound leaves provide an attractive foil for their upward-facing, cup-shaped flowers.

Selected species: *P. carneum* (royal polemonium)—1 to 2 feet tall with clusters of purple, pink, or salmon flowers 1½ inches across from spring through summer; California and Oregon; Zones 7-9. *P. occidentale* [also called *P. caeruleum* ssp. *amygdalinum*] (western polemonium)—to 3 feet with clusters of pale blue summer flowers; Alaska to Colorado; Zones 3-9. *P. reptans* (creeping polemonium)—to 2 feet with large clusters of blue or pink flowers from spring to summer; eastern United States; Zones 2-9. *P. viscosum* (sky pilot)— 4 to 20 inches tall with light blue or white flower clusters in spring and summer; western mountains; Zones 3-7.

Growing conditions and maintenance: *P. viscosum* grows in full sun and well-drained rocky soil. The other species prefer partial shade and moist soil; for *P. reptans,* provide ample organic matter. Propagate by seed or division.

Polygonatum
(po-lig-o-NAY-tum)
SOLOMON'S-SEAL

Polygonatum biflorum

Hardiness: *Zones 3-9*

Flowering season: *late spring*

Height: *1 to 6 feet*

Flower color: *greenish white*

Soil: *moist, acid, rich*

Light: *partial to full shade*

These woodland perennials native to the eastern half of the United States bear drooping greenish white flowers suspended from the undersides of gracefully arching stems in late spring. Blue berries follow the flowers.

Selected species: *P. biflorum* (small Solomon's-seal)—small, ½- to 1-inch bell-shaped greenish white flowers in pairs on zigzag stems 1 to 3 feet long. The prominently veined leaves are 2 to 6 inches long. Blue berries follow the flowers. *P. commutatum* (great Solomon's-seal)—grows to 6 feet with flowers similar to those of *P. biflorum* in clusters of two to 10 and leaves to 7 inches long.

Growing conditions and maintenance: Solomon's-seals are easily grown in light to dense shade and a rich, moist, acid soil, where they will spread to form dense colonies. They benefit from organic matter added to the soil before planting. Propagate by seed or by division of rhizomes.

Pontederia
(pon-te-DEER-ee-a)
PICKERELWEED

Pontederia cordata

Hardiness: *Zones 4-9*

Flowering season: *summer to fall*

Height: *1 to 4 feet*

Flower color: *blue-purple*

Soil: *shallow water to wet soil*

Light: *full sun*

Pickerelweed is an aquatic perennial that grows wild in shallow fresh water in the eastern half of the United States. Its vivid flowers, long blooming season, and attractive foliage make it a good choice for bog and water gardens.

Selected species: *P. cordata*—spikes of blue-purple funnel-shaped flowers held 1 to 2 feet above the water's surface on sturdy stems from early summer through fall. Dark green heart-shaped leaves up to 10 inches long and 6 inches wide rise 2 to 4 feet above the surface on long stems.

Growing conditions and maintenance: Pickerelweed will grow in wet boggy soil, but it performs best when its roots are covered by several inches of water. When setting out new plants, use stones or pebbles to hold them in place until their roots are established. In the case of a small garden pool, plant pickerelweed in a large container. Propagate by division in summer.

Pycnanthemum
(pik-NAN-thee-mum)
MOUNTAIN MINT

Pycnanthemum tenuifolium

Hardiness: *Zones 4-8*

Flowering season: *summer*

Height: *20 inches to 6 feet*

Flower color: *white, lavender*

Soil: *moist to dry, well-drained*

Light: *full sun to partial shade*

Mountain mints grow wild over much of the eastern and central United States. Their dainty clusters of summer flowers and crisp, mint-scented foliage are nice additions to a naturalistic garden.

Selected species: *P. incanum* (mountain mint)—erect stems 3 to 6 feet tall with terminal clusters of many small, two-lipped white to lavender flowers with purple spots; the leaves just below the flowers are whitish, while the rest of the foliage is dark green; Zones 5-8. *P. tenuifolium* (slender mountain mint) —closely resembles *P. incanum* but is smaller, growing up to 30 inches in height; Zones 4-8. *P. virginianum* (mountain mint)—2 to 3 feet tall with many small, dense clusters of white flowers spotted with purple. The leaves are covered with a white bloom; Zones 3-8.

Growing conditions and maintenance: Plant *P. incanum* in a rich, acid, moist to dry soil. Plant *P. tenuifolium* in a moist to dry soil. *P. virginianum* needs a moist soil. All three species adapt to full sun or partial shade. Water during dry periods. Propagate by seed, division, or cuttings.

Ratibida
(ra-ti-BID-a)
PRAIRIE CONEFLOWER

Ratibida columnifera

Hardiness: *Zones 3-9*

Flowering season: *spring, summer, fall*

Height: *1½ to 5 feet*

Flower color: *yellow, red, bicolored*

Soil: *well-drained to dry*

Light: *full sun to partial shade*

Prairie coneflowers are sturdy perennials with brightly colored daisylike flowers that bloom in summer in the northern parts of their ranges and from late spring through fall in the milder zones.

Selected species: *R. columnifera* (Mexican hat)—branching stems 1½ to 3 feet tall bearing daisylike flowers with drooping yellow, red, or bicolored notched petals surrounding an elongated purplish brown cylindrical cone that rises as much as 2 inches above the petals; native to prairies and waste areas from the central United States to British Columbia; Zones 3-9. *R. pinnata* (gray-headed coneflower)—3 to 5 feet tall with long-stalked flowers composed of yellow petals surrounding a grayish brown cone; prairies and woodland edges in the central and southern United States; Zones 3-8.

Growing conditions and maintenance: Prairie coneflowers thrive in well-drained soil and full sun. Gray-headed coneflower also grows in partial shade, and both species tolerate drought. They can be aggressive, so plant them among other competitive plants. Propagate by seed.

Rhexia
(REEK-see-a)
MEADOW BEAUTY

Rhexia mariana

Hardiness: *Zones 4-9*

Flowering season: *summer*

Height: *1 to 2 feet*

Flower color: *rose, red, pink, white*

Soil: *moist, acid, sandy to wet boggy*

Light: *full sun to partial shade*

Meadow beauties are perennials that bloom all summer in their native wetlands and moist meadows in the eastern United States. The individual blossoms last less than a day.

Selected species: *R. mariana* (Maryland meadow beauty)—grows to 2 feet with loose clusters of white, pink, or pale rose flowers 2 inches across with bright yellow stamens. Plants spread by rhizomes to form colonies; Zones 4-9. *R. virginica* (Virginia meadow beauty)—1 to 2 feet in height with purplish red petaled flowers 1½ inches across with bright yellow stamens. Foliage is bright green. *R. virginica* also spreads by rhizomes to form colonies; Zones 5-9.

Growing conditions and maintenance: Rhexias thrive in boggy soil or in rich, sandy garden soil as long as moisture is abundant. They prefer full sun but tolerate light shade. Propagate by seed or by dividing the rhizomes.

Rudbeckia
(rood-BEK-ee-a)
CONEFLOWER

Rudbeckia hirta

Hardiness: *Zones 3-9*

Flowering season: *summer*

Height: *1 to 4 feet*

Flower color: *yellow*

Soil: *moist to dry*

Light: *full sun to partial shade*

Rudbeckias are annuals, biennials, and perennials from open woodlands and meadows throughout most of the United States. Their gay yellow daisylike flowers are favorites among wildflower gardeners.

Selected species: *R. grandiflora* (large coneflower)—perennial 1½ to 3 feet tall. Flowers up to 6 inches or more across have drooping petals and a brown cone-shaped center; Zones 5-9. *R. hirta* (black-eyed Susan)—may be an annual, a biennial, or a short-lived perennial 1 to 3 feet tall with 2- to 3-inch flowers with dark centers; Zones 3-9. *R. subtomentosa* (sweet coneflower)—perennial 1 to 4 feet tall with 3-inch flowers with dark centers; Zones 5-9.

Growing conditions and maintenance: *R. grandiflora* thrives in dry soils, *R. subtomentosa* prefers moist conditions, and *R. hirta* adapts to either. Propagate by seed. Perennials can also be divided.

Ruellia
(roo-EL-ee-a)
RUELLIA

Ruellia caroliniensis

Hardiness: *Zones 4-9*

Flowering season: *summer, fall*

Height: *1 to 3 feet*

Flower color: *lavender, purple*

Soil: *dry, sandy*

Light: *full sun to partial shade*

Ruellias are perennials found growing wild in open woods and prairies in the eastern United States. Their loose clusters of funnel-shaped flowers add a delicate touch to wildflower meadows, herbaceous borders, and woodland edges.

Selected species: *R. caroliniensis* (ruellia)—clusters of two to four light purple flowers near the tops of unbranched stems 2 to 3 feet tall throughout summer; Zones 6-9. *R. humilis* (wild petunia)—showy lavender to purple 2-inch flowers on compact bushy plants 1 to 2 feet tall throughout summer and fall; Zones 4-9.

Growing conditions and maintenance: Ruellias prefer dry soils that are sandy or rocky but will adapt to other types of soil as long as they are not too moist. Propagate by seed or cuttings taken in summer.

Sagittaria
(sa-ji-TAY-ree-a)
ARROWHEAD

Sagittaria latifolia

Hardiness: *Zones 3-10*

Flowering season: *summer*

Height: *to 4 feet*

Flower color: *white*

Soil: *shallow water to wet soil*

Light: *partial shade*

Arrowhead, a perennial found throughout the United States and southern Canada in wet meadows, marshes, and ponds, has whorled clusters of showy flowers set off by large, leathery leaves. Arrowhead produces edible tubers relished by ducks.

Selected species: *S. latifolia* (wapatoo, duck potato)—up to 4 feet tall with white flowers on leafless 12- to 36-inch stems from mid- to late summer. The arrow-shaped leaves are up to 16 inches long.

Growing conditions and maintenance: Arrowhead grows best when its roots are submerged in shallow water, but it can also be grown in the wet soil of a bog garden. For a garden pool, plant arrowhead in containers, cover the soil with 2 inches of gravel, and submerge the containers. Propagate by seed or division in fall.

Salvia
(SAL-vee-a)
SALVIA, SAGE

Salvia dorrii

Hardiness: *Zones 3-10*

Flowering season: *spring, summer, fall*

Height: *4 inches to 3 feet*

Flower color: *blue, violet, white, pink*

Soil: *sandy, dry to well-drained*

Light: *full sun to partial shade*

Salvias are sun-loving annuals and perennials that have beautiful flowers in whorled clusters and thick foliage that is woolly in many species and, because these plants belong to the mint family, frequently aromatic.

Selected species: *S. columbariae* (chia) —annual 4 to 20 inches tall with globelike clusters of tiny blue flowers throughout spring. The velvety leaves are up to 4 inches long and irregularly lobed. Native to dry, open sites in the Southwest. *S. dorrii* (grayball sage)— shrublike perennial 2 to 3 feet in height and as wide or wider with long showy spikes of deep violet-blue flowers in late spring. Leaves are stiff and silvery gray. Western native from dry open areas; Zones 6-9. *S. farinacea* (mealy blue sage, mealy-cup sage)—2- to 3-foot perennial from the Southwest grown as an annual in cooler areas. Dark blue, blue-purple, or white flowers on a dense spike up to 9 inches long from midspring through fall; Zones 8-10. *S. lyrata* (lyre-leaf sage) perennial found in open woods and meadows throughout much of the eastern United States with pale blue to violet

flowers on 1- to 2-foot stems in spring above a basal clump of large lyre-shaped evergreen leaves. The foliage may turn purplish in winter; Zones 5-8. *S. spathacea* (hummingbird sage)—perennial 2 to 3 feet in height from the Coastal Range of California. The magenta-pink flowers, which are a favorite of hummingbirds, bloom in spring on stems rising well above the broad light green quilted leaves; Zones 9-10.

Salvia spathacea

Growing conditions and maintenance: Most salvias require full sun and dry soils with excellent drainage. *S. spathacea* can also be grown in slightly moist soil, and *S. lyrata* grows in dry to moist soil; these two species also tolerate some shade. *S. lyrata* is a good ground cover for a lightly shaded dry site and self-sows freely. Propagate annual salvias by seed. *S. dorrii* and *S. farinacea* can be grown from seed or cuttings. Propagate *S. spathacea* and *S. lyrata* by seed or division.

Sanguinaria
(sang-gwi-NAR-ee-a)
BLOODROOT

Sanguinaria canadensis

Hardiness: *Zones 3-9*

Flowering season: *spring*

Height: *6 to 14 inches*

Flower color: *white*

Soil: *moist, well-drained, rich*

Light: *partial shade*

Bloodroot is one of the loveliest spring-blooming woodland wildflowers native to eastern North America, and its large round blue-green leaves make an attractive ground cover. The plant is named for its red sap.

Selected species: *S. canadensis* (bloodroot, red puccoon)—solitary white flower to 1½ inches across with gold stamens on a 6- to 10-inch stalk. Each flower bud is surrounded by a furled leaf when it emerges. When fully expanded, the leaves are up to 1 foot across and have five or more lobes whose edges curl slightly upward.

Growing conditions and maintenance: Bloodroot thrives in rich, moist soil and benefits from added organic matter. It does best when planted beneath deciduous trees, where it receives bright sunshine before the trees leaf out and partial shade for the rest of the growing season. Mulch lightly with deciduous leaves in winter. Propagate by seed planted immediately after collection, or by dividing rhizomes in fall or early spring.

Sarracenia
(sar-a-SEE-nee-a)
PITCHER PLANT

Sarracenia leucophylla

Hardiness: *Zones 2-10*

Flowering season: *spring to summer*

Height: *8 inches to 4 feet*

Flower color: *yellow, purple, red*

Soil: *wet, acid*

Light: *full sun to partial shade*

Pitcher plants are valued in bog gardens for the striking upright trumpets formed by their furled leaves as well as for their handsome flowers borne on tall leafless stems. Insects trapped in the water-filled trumpets furnish nutrients for the plants.

Selected species: *S. flava* (yellow pitcher plant, trumpet pitcher plant)—trumpet of yellowish green red-veined leaves up to 4 feet tall ; drooping yellow flowers up to 4 inches across; Zones 6-7. *S. leucophylla* (crimson pitcher plant)—red-veined trumpet 2 to 4 feet tall and dark red flowers 3 to 4 inches across; Zones 8-10. *S. purpurea* (northern pitcher plant)—bronze-green trumpet 8 to 18 inches tall; solitary 2-inch maroon-purple flowers; Zones 2-9.

Growing conditions and maintenance: Pitcher plants thrive in wet sandy soil or peat bogs. They require constant moisture. Propagate by seed sown immediately after collection or by division.

Saxifraga
(Saks-IF-ra-ga)
SAXIFRAGE, ROCKFOIL

Saxifraga pensylvanica

Hardiness: *Zones 2-8*

Flowering season: *spring to summer*

Height: *4 inches to 3 feet*

Flower color: *white, purple, yellow, greenish*

Soil: *dry, rocky to moist, well-drained*

Light: *full sun to shade*

The saxifrages described here include two western perennials well suited to rock gardens and containers and an eastern perennial for boggy or moist gardens.

Selected species: *S. californica* (California saxifrage)—clusters of white flowers on 4- to 12-inch stalks in spring and low rosettes of broad fuzzy leaves; mountains from California to Oregon; Zones 6-8. *S. oppositifolia* (purple saxifrage)—showy flowers with crimped purple petals and brownish orange anthers in summer above a dense 2-inch mat of narrow pointed leaves; Canada, Alaska, and western mountains; Zones 2-6. *S. pensylvanica* (swamp saxifrage)—clusters of greenish, yellow, or purple flowers on stems 1 to 3 feet tall in spring above a rosette of 1-foot leaves; Maine to Missouri; Zones 5-8.

Growing conditions and maintenance: Grow *S. oppositifolia* in dry, rocky soil in full sun to partial shade. *S. californica* requires a moist, well-drained location and partial to full shade. *S. pensylvanica* grows in wet to moist soils in full sun to partial shade. Propagate by seed.

Schizachyrium
(ski-ZAK-e-ree-um)
LITTLE BLUESTEM

Schizachyrium scoparium

Hardiness: *Zones 3-10*

Flowering season: *summer to fall*

Height: *2 to 5 feet*

Flower color: *white*

Soil: *well-drained to dry*

Light: *full sun*

This clump-forming perennial grass is native to prairies, rocky slopes, and open woodlands from Canada to the Gulf of Mexico and west to Idaho. Little bluestem can be massed as a ground cover, used in a meadow garden, or planted singly in a perennial border. Its flowers and seed heads are attractive in arrangements.

Selected species: *S. scoparium* (little bluestem, prairie beard grass)—narrow blue-green foliage in an upright clump, most often about 3 feet tall and to 8 inches in diameter. In fall the foliage turns mahogany brown. Loose clusters of tiny flowers on 2½-inch spikes open from late summer to fall and are followed by shiny white seed heads.

Growing conditions and maintenance: Little bluestem is adaptable and easy to grow, thriving in most dry or well-drained soils, including those of low fertility. It does not, however, tolerate wet conditions. Mow in early spring before new growth begins. Propagate by seed. Young plants can also be propagated by division.

Sedum
(SEE-dum)
SEDUM, STONECROP

Sedum spathulifolium

Hardiness: *Zones 3-10*

Flowering season: *spring, summer*

Height: *2 to 8 inches*

Flower color: *red-purple, yellow, white*

Soil: *well-drained*

Light: *partial to full shade*

Sedums are succulent plants commonly found growing on rocky outcrops or in woodlands. The following perennial species make attractive specimens for rock gardens or ground covers.

Selected species: *S. rosea* ssp. *integrifolium* (roseroot)—to 6 inches high with bright green rounded leaves topped by clusters of star-shaped red-purple flowers from spring to summer and showy red-purple seed pods; Alaska to California and Colorado; Zones 3-9. *S. spathulifolium* (common stonecrop)—2- to 8-inch stems bearing clusters of yellow flowers in spring and summer above rosettes of green, blue-green, or white leaves; California to British Columbia; Zones 7-10. *S. ternatum* (wild stonecrop)—white flowers on 4- to 8-inch stalks above creeping stems with light green foliage; New York to Minnesota and south to Tennessee; Zones 5-10.

Growing conditions and maintenance: These sedums grow in well-drained soil in partial shade. *S. ternatum* also adapts to full shade. Propagate by seed, division, or cuttings.

Senecio
(se-NEE-see-o)
GROUNDSEL, SENECIO

Senecio aureus

Hardiness: *Zones 4-10*

Flowering season: *spring, summer, fall*

Height: *1 to 5 feet*

Flower color: *yellow*

Soil: *moist to dry, sandy*

Light: *full sun to partial shade*

The daisylike flowers of the perennial groundsels described here add a golden glow to their native grasslands or wooded areas for several weeks.

Selected species: *S. aureus* (golden groundsel, golden ragwort)—1 to 3 feet tall with clusters of deep golden yellow flowers in late spring and summer above the heart-shaped dark green basal foliage. It spreads rapidly by horizontal offshoots to form an attractive ground cover; eastern North America; Zones 4-8. *S. douglasii* (shrubby senecio)—shrubby perennial up to 5 feet tall with yellow flowers in summer and fall and fuzzy white foliage; California; Zones 6-10.

Growing conditions and maintenance: Grow *S. aureus* in moist, acid soil and full sun to partial shade. *S. douglasii* grows in full sun and prefers a well-drained sandy or rocky soil. Propagate by seed, division, or cuttings.

Sidalcea
(sy-DAL-see-a)
CHECKERMALLOW

Sidalcea malviflora

Hardiness: *Zones 4-10*

Flowering season: *spring to summer*

Height: *2 to 4 feet*

Flower color: *pink, purple, mauve*

Soil: *wet to dry*

Light: *full sun to partial shade*

Perennials from the western United States, the checkermallows have showy flowers resembling hollyhocks and provide a colorful vertical accent in mixed herbaceous borders or meadow plantings.

Selected species: *S. malviflora* (checkermallow, checkerbloom)—up to 4 feet tall with pink or purple flowers on erect stems in spring and summer and dark green lobed leaves. The flowers open in the morning and close up in the evening; Zones 5-10. *S. neomexicana* (prairie mallow)—up to 3 feet tall with mauve flowers in spring and early summer; Zones 4-10.

Growing conditions and maintenance: *S. malviflora* prefers soil that is moist in winter and well drained to dry in summer and grows in full sun to partial shade. *S. neomexicana* grows in moist, well-drained to wet soils in full sun. Remove faded flowers or cut back spent flower stems to prolong blooming. Propagate by seed or division.

Silene
(sy-LEE-ne)
CAMPION, PINK

Silene virginica

Hardiness: *Zones 4-10*

Flowering season: *spring, summer*

Height: *3 to 30 inches*

Flower color: *white, pink, red*

Soil: *well-drained, rocky*

Light: *partial shade*

Campions grow in open woods and on rocky slopes and have flared tubular flowers with five petals. The following perennial species are easy to grow and will provide weeks of reliable color in a perennial border or rock garden.

Selected species: *S. caroliniana* (wild pink)—dense clusters of white to dark pink flowers held just above a compact 3- to 8-inch-tall mound of narrow bluish green leaves in spring; eastern United States; Zones 5-8. *S. laciniata* (Mexican campion)—up to 2½ feet tall with bright red flowers from spring to late summer; Texas to California; Zones 7-10. *S. virginica* (fire pink)—1 to 2 feet tall with loose terminal clusters of bright red flowers in spring and summer; southern Canada and eastern and southern United States; Zones 4-9.

Growing conditions and maintenance: Grow campions in well-drained rocky soil and partial shade. Propagate by seed, cuttings, or division.

Sisyrinchium
(sis-i-RINK-ee-um)
BLUE-EYED GRASS

Sisyrinchium bellum

Hardiness: *Zones 3-10*

Flowering season: *spring, summer*

Height: *3 to 18 inches*

Flower color: *blue, white, purple*

Soil: *moist to seasonally dry*

Light: *full sun to partial shade*

Sisyrinchiums are dainty-looking perennials with starry six-petaled flowers and clumps of grasslike leaves. They are especially pretty planted in naturalistic drifts in the dappled shade of deciduous trees.

Selected species: *S. angustifolium* (narrow-leaved blue-eyed grass)—light blue flowers on twisted stalks that rise just above the 12- to 18-inch clump of foliage from spring to summer; eastern Canada and United States; Zones 3-10. *S. bellum* (California blue-eyed grass)—3 to 18 inches high with great numbers of blue, violet, or white flowers in spring. The foliage may be evergreen; Zones 8-10. *S. douglasii* (Douglas blue-eyed grass)—6 to 12 inches high with reddish purple flowers up to an inch across in spring; British Columbia to California and Nevada; Zones 4-9.

Growing conditions and maintenance: Sisyrinchiums thrive in full sun or light shade. *S. angustifolium* needs a poor to average, evenly moist soil. *S. bellum* and *S. douglasii* need soil that is moist in spring and dry in summer. Propagate by seed or division.

Smilacina
(smy-la-SEE-na)
FALSE SOLOMON'S-SEAL

Smilacina racemosa

Hardiness: *Zones 2-8*

Flowering season: *spring*

Height: *1 to 3 feet*

Flower color: *white*

Soil: *moist, deep, rich*

Light: *partial to full shade*

These perennial woodland natives are found throughout much of the United States and Canada. Their graceful arching stems, spring flowers, and fall berries make them an outstanding choice for a shady garden.

Selected species: *S. racemosa* (false Solomon's-seal, false spikenard)—stems up to 3 feet tall with conical flower clusters at the tips and 3- to 6-inch elliptical leaves. The berries that follow the flowers are green in summer, turning pinkish red in fall; Zones 4-8. *S. stellata* (starry false Solomon's-seal)—arching zigzag stems 1 to 2 feet tall with terminal clusters of star-shaped flowers and dark green leaves. The berries are dark red in fall; Zones 2-7.

Growing conditions and maintenance: Smilacinas grow best in moist, deep, humus-rich soil in shade. *S. stellata* tolerates somewhat drier soil and more sun, but its growth will be stunted. Propagate by seed or division.

Solidago
(sol-i-DAY-go)
GOLDENROD

Solidago canadensis

Hardiness: *Zones 3-10*

Flowering season: *summer, fall*

Height: *1 to 10 feet*

Flower color: *yellow*

Soil: *moist, well-drained to dry*

Light: *full sun to partial shade*

The upright stems of goldenrods are tipped with eye-catching clusters of yellow flowers in summer and fall. These tough, dependable perennials are native to meadows and prairies in Canada and throughout most of the United States. They make excellent cut flowers, and butterflies feed on their nectar.

Selected species: *S. caesia* (blue-stemmed goldenrod, wreath goldenrod)—slender blue- or purple-tinged stems 1 to 3 feet with small arching sprays of yellow flowers in late summer and fall; Zones 4-8. *S. canadensis* (Canada goldenrod)—2 to 4 feet tall with branching flower clusters in late summer; Zones 3-10. *S. juncea* (early goldenrod)—up to 6 feet or more in height with arching clusters of flowers from mid- to late summer; Zones 3-7. *S. missouriensis* (Missouri goldenrod)—an early-blooming goldenrod with nodding flower clusters on reddish stems 1 to 2 feet tall from mid- to late summer; Zones 4-8. *S. nemoralis* (gray goldenrod)—up to 2 feet high with plume-shaped flower clusters in late summer and fall; Zones 3-9. *S. odora* (sweet goldenrod)—2 to 5 feet tall with large flower clusters from midsummer through fall and neat, bright green foliage that smells like anise when crushed; Zones 3-9. *S. rugosa* (rough-leaved goldenrod)—2 to 5 feet tall with flower sprays composed of thin, arching stems for 3 to 4 weeks in fall; Zones 3-8. *S. sempervirens* (seaside goldenrod)—large branching clusters of flowers on stems to 8 feet tall

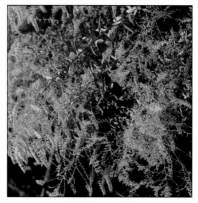

Solidago odora

in late summer and fall above a clump of narrow evergreen leaves up to 16 inches long; Zones 4-8.

Growing conditions and maintenance: Goldenrods thrive in full sun in soils of average fertility. *S. caesia* also tolerates partial shade. *S. sempervirens* tolerates salt spray and can be pinched in early summer to encourage compact growth. Most goldenrods are aggressive growers and may need dividing every 2 to 3 years. *S. caesia, S. odora,* and *S. sempervirens* are less vigorous growers than the others and easier to keep within bounds. Propagate goldenrods by division or seed.

Sphaeralcea
(sfee-RAL-see-a)
GLOBE MALLOW

Sphaeralcea coccinea

Hardiness: *Zones 3-10*

Flowering season: *spring, summer, fall*

Height: *2 to 3 feet*

Flower color: *orange, pink, red*

Soil: *dry, rocky*

Light: *full sun*

Globe mallows are drought-resistant perennials native to dry, rocky slopes and desert plains of the western United States. They bear brightly colored cupped flowers and are pretty choices for sunny rock gardens.

Selected species: *S. ambigua* (desert mallow)—3-foot stems bearing wandlike clusters of apricot-orange flowers up to 2 inches across in spring; Zones 6-10. *S. coccinea* (prairie mallow, scarlet globe mallow)—3 feet tall with orange-pink flowers surrounded by red bracts in spring, summer, or fall and hairy gray-green leaves; Zones 3-10. *S. munroana* (Munro's globe mallow)—2 to 3 feet tall with spikes of numerous bright pink to deep apricot flowers and gray-green foliage; Zones 4-10. *S. parvifolia* (globe mallow)—2 to 3 feet tall with clusters of orange-red flowers and whitish gray leaves from spring to summer; Zones 5-10.

Growing conditions and maintenance: Plant sphaeralceas in full sun and dry, rocky soil. They tolerate drought. Though individual plants are often short-lived, they usually self-sow. Propagate by seed or cuttings.

Sporobolus
(spor-OB-o-lus)
DROPSEED

Sporobolus heterolepis

Hardiness: *Zones 3-8*

Flowering season: *summer to fall*

Height: *2 feet*

Flower color: *green*

Soil: *dry, sandy*

Light: *full sun*

Native to the prairies of the central United States and Canada, this perennial grass forms a fountainlike clump of fine-textured, gracefully arching leaves. It is ideal for small and large meadow gardens, herbaceous borders, and as a ground cover in dry, sunny sites.

Selected species: *S. heterolepis* (northern prairie dropseed)—narrow rich green leaves 20 inches long in a clump 2 feet tall and 3 feet wide. Loose clusters of dark green flowers bloom in summer and fall. The entire plant, including the seed heads, turns an attractive tan-bronze in fall.

Growing conditions and maintenance: Northern prairie dropseed prefers dry, sandy soil and full sun, but it will tolerate a little shade. Plants require about 3 years to reach their mature size. Propagate by seed sown in fall or spring. The dense root system makes division difficult.

Tephrosia
(te-FROH-zee-a)
TEPHROSIA

Tephrosia virginiana

Hardiness: *Zones 5-10*

Flowering season: *spring to summer*

Height: *1 to 2 feet*

Flower color: *pink and yellow*

Soil: *dry, sandy*

Light: *full sun*

Tephrosia is a perennial member of the pea family native to open woods and sandy fields of the eastern and central United States. Its pretty two-toned flowers resemble sweet peas, and the finely cut foliage is appealing all season long. The seed attracts ground birds such as quail.

Selected species: *T. virginiana* (goat's-rue)—1 to 2 feet tall with compact clusters of ¾-inch flowers composed of yellowish upper petals and purplish pink lower petals from late spring to early summer above a mound of attractive silvery foliage. The pinnately compound leaves have eight to 15 pairs of small leaflets covered with silky white hairs.

Growing conditions and maintenance: Plant *T. virginiana* in a sunny location with dry, sandy soil. Inoculating the soil with nitrogen-fixing bacteria will enhance growth. Propagate by seed.

Thalictrum
(thal-IK-trum)
MEADOW RUE

Thalictrum dasycarpum

Hardiness: *Zones 3-10*

Flowering season: *spring to summer*

Height: *8 inches to 8 feet*

Flower color: *green, purple, cream*

Soil: *moist, rich*

Light: *full sun to full shade*

Meadow rues, native to the woodlands, meadows, and prairies in southern Canada, on the West Coast, and in much of the eastern United States, are prized for their finely cut leaves and delicate flowers.

Selected species: *T. dasycarpum* (purple meadow rue)—to 6 feet tall with purplish stems and green flowers in loose terminal clusters; Zones 3-6. *T. dioicum* (early meadow rue)—8 to 28 inches tall with beautiful long-stalked foliage divided into many rounded segments. Female flowers have purple petals. Male flowers lack petals but produce a tassel of yellow stamens; Zones 4-9. *T. polycarpum* (meadow rue)—2 feet tall; grown mainly for its attractive foliage divided into rounded segments. Tiny green flowers bloom in spring; Zones 6-10. *T. polygamum* (tall meadow rue)—to 8 feet tall with showy cream-colored flowers in summer and feathery blue-green foliage; Zones 4-7.

Growing conditions and maintenance: *T. dasycarpum, T. dioicum,* and *T. polycarpum* grow in partial to full shade. *T. polygamum* grows in full sun to partial shade. Mulch in spring to keep soil moist. Propagate by seed.

Thermopsis
(ther-MOP-sis)
FALSE LUPINE

Thermopsis montana

Hardiness: *Zones 3-9*

Flowering season: *spring, summer*

Height: *1½ to 5 feet*

Flower color: *yellow*

Soil: *dry, rocky to moist, rich*

Light: *full sun to partial shade*

The false lupines, which inhabit open woodlands, meadows, and stony flats, are perennials with dense clusters of yellow lupinelike flowers that combine handsomely with ornamental grasses in a sunny perennial border.

Selected species: *T. montana* (golden pea)—western native with slender branched stems to 32 inches tall bearing dense 4- to 12-inch clusters of bright yellow flowers in spring, followed by velvety pods; Zones 3-8. *T. villosa* (bush pea)—native of Appalachian Mountains 3 to 5 feet with dark green foliage and deep yellow flowers in dense clusters up to a foot long from spring to summer, followed by hairy pods; Zones 4-9.

Growing conditions and maintenance: Grow *T. montana* in full sun in a well-drained, sandy soil. *T. villosa* adapts to full sun or light shade and prefers a humus-rich soil and supplemental watering during dry periods. Propagate *T. montana* by seed and *T. villosa* by seed or division.

Tiarella
(ty-a-REL-a)
FOAMFLOWER

Tiarella cordifolia

Hardiness: *Zones 3-9*

Flowering season: *spring to summer*

Height: *6 to 12 inches*

Flower color: *white*

Soil: *moist, well-drained, rich*

Light: *partial shade to shade*

Foamflowers are low-growing perennials found in cool, moist woodlands and on the banks of streams. They are ideal ground covers or edgings along a woodland garden path and are also effective in a shady rock garden.

Selected species: *T. cordifolia* (foamflower)—eastern native with compact clusters of tiny star-shaped white flowers on 6- to 12-inch stalks above neat mounds of lobed leaves from midspring to early summer. Mature plants spread by runners; Zones 3-8. *T. unifoliata* (western foamflower, sugar scoop)—western native white bell-shaped flowers on 6- to 8-inch stalks from midspring to summer above rounded evergreen leaves. Flowers are followed by fruits shaped like sugar scoops; Zones 5-9.

Growing conditions and maintenance: Foamflowers thrive in full or partial shade and moist, rich, slightly acid soil with a high organic content. Water during dry spells. Propagate by seed or division.

Tradescantia
(trad-e-SKAN-shee-a)
SPIDERWORT

Tradescantia ohiensis

Hardiness: *Zones 3-10*

Flowering season: *spring, summer*

Height: *10 to 36 inches*

Flower color: *blue-violet, blue*

Soil: *well-drained, humus-rich*

Light: *full sun to partial shade*

Found in open woods and on prairies, spiderworts are upright or trailing perennials whose flowers have three wide petals and showy stamens.

Selected species: *T. bracteata* (bracted spiderwort)—clusters of blue-violet flowers surrounded by leaflike bracts on erect 10- to 16-inch stems with grasslike foliage in late spring to early summer; Zones 3-8. *T. ohiensis* (Ohio spiderwort)—blue flowers clustered at the tops of erect, branching stems 2 to 3 feet tall from spring to summer in warm climates and summer in cooler zones; Zones 4-10. *T. virginiana* (Virginia spiderwort)—blue to blue-violet flowers 1½ to 3 inches wide from spring to summer on a dense clump of branching stems up to 3 feet tall with narrow bright green leaves 12 inches long; Zones 4-10.

Growing conditions and maintenance: Plant spiderworts in full sun or partial shade in well-drained, humus-rich soil. Propagate by seed, stem cuttings taken at any time, or division.

Trillium
(TRIL-ee-um)
TRILLIUM, WAKE-ROBIN

Trillium grandiflorum

Hardiness: *Zones 2-9*

Flowering season: *late spring*

Height: *6 to 18 inches*

Flower color: *white, pink, maroon*

Soil: *moist, acid, rich*

Light: *partial shade to shade*

Trilliums are woodland perennials whose solitary flowers consist of three broad petals and three greenish sepals. Below each flower is a whorl of three leaves.

Selected species: *T. cernuum* (nodding trillium)—12 to 18 inches tall with nodding white flowers 1½ inches across with deep rose anthers; Zones 3-7. *T. erectum* (purple trillium, squawroot)—to 18 inches tall with upward-facing maroon flowers 2½ inches across that have an unpleasant scent detectable at close range; Zones 2-6. *T. grandiflorum* (large-flowered trillium, white wake-robin)—up to 15 inches tall with upward-facing, long-lasting white flowers 3 to 4 inches across that turn pink with age; Zones 3-8. *T. sessile* (red trillium, toadshade)—to 12 inches tall with maroon flowers whose petals point upward; Zones 4-9.

Growing conditions and maintenance: Trilliums require at least partial shade and moist, humus-rich soil. Propagate using the technique illustrated on page 81, by seed, or by dividing rhizomes in fall. It may take 5 years for seed-grown trilliums to bloom.

Uvularia
(yew-vew-LAR-ee-a)
MERRY-BELLS

Uvularia grandiflora

Hardiness: *Zones 3-8*

Flowering season: *spring*

Height: *10 to 24 inches*

Flower color: *yellow, cream*

Soil: *moist, humus-rich*

Light: *partial to full shade*

Merry-bells are dainty woodland perennials found in the eastern half of North America. Named for the bell-shaped flowers gracefully suspended from their stems, they are most effective when planted in large numbers.

Selected species: *U. grandiflora* (big merry-bells)—arching stems 18 to 24 inches tall with lemon yellow flowers 1½ inches long. The petals are slightly twisted; Zones 3-8. *U. sessilifolia* (little merry-bells, wild oats)—10 to 15 inches tall with cream-colored inch-long flowers; Zones 4-8.

Growing conditions and maintenance: Grow merry-bells in moist, shaded locations and incorporate organic matter into soil prior to planting. Mulch with leaves in winter. Propagate by seed sown immediately after ripening or by division in the fall.

Verbena *(ver-BEE-na)* **VERVAIN, VERBENA**	*Vernonia* *(ver-NON-ee-a)* **IRONWEED**	*Veronicastrum* *(ve-ron-i-KAS-trum)* **CULVER'S ROOT**

Verbena stricta

Vernonia noveboracensis

Veronicastrum virginicum

Hardiness: *Zones 3-10*

Flowering season: *spring, summer, fall*

Height: *8 inches to 5 feet*

Flower color: *pink, purple, blue, violet*

Soil: *dry, sandy to moist, well-drained*

Light: *full sun*

Hardiness: *Zones 4-9*

Flowering season: *summer, fall*

Height: *4 to 8 feet*

Flower color: *purple*

Soil: *moist to wet*

Light: *full sun to partial shade*

Hardiness: *Zones 3-8*

Flowering season: *summer*

Height: *2 to 6 feet*

Flower color: *white, pale blue, pale pink*

Soil: *moist, well-drained, rich*

Light: *full sun to partial shade*

The perennial verbenas described below are native to meadows, prairies, and open woods.

Selected species: *V. canadensis* (rose verbena)—fragrant ¾-inch pink flowers in rounded clusters in summer and fall on a mat of creeping stems 8 to 12 inches tall and 3 feet across. Native from the Southeast west to Colorado; Zones 6-10. *V. gooddingii* (pink verbena)—18-inch-tall mat of purplish stems and deeply divided leaves with bright purple flowers in rounded clusters in spring. Southwest to California; Zones 5-10. *V. hastata* (blue verbena)—2 to 5 feet with spikes of blue-purple flowers in late spring and summer; widely found in moist sites in the United States and Canada; Zones 4-10. *V. stricta* (woolly verbena, hoary vervain)—1 to 4 feet tall with dense 12-inch spikes of blue to violet flowers in summer and fall; large woolly leaves. Ontario south to Texas and west to Idaho; Zones 3-10.

Growing conditions and maintenance: Full sun is best, though *V. canadensis* and *V. hastata* adapt to partial shade. *V. hastata* prefers moist soil; the other three dry, sandy soil. Propagate by seed.

Ironweeds are tall perennials native to moist meadows and prairies in the eastern half of the United States. Their loosely branched terminal clusters of purple flowers are effective in the back of a wildflower border or in a meadow garden.

Selected species: *V. altissima* (tall ironweed)—5 to 8 feet with ½-inch reddish purple flower heads in clusters of 30 to 40 from late summer through midautumn. The lance-shaped dark green leaves are up to 12 inches long. Native from New York south to Louisiana and west to Nebraska; Zones 4-9. *V. noveboracensis* (New York ironweed)—4 to 6 feet tall with clusters of as many as 50 frilly purple flower heads in late summer. Native to southern New England, mid-Atlantic states, and the Southeast; Zones 5-8.

Growing conditions and maintenance: Ironweeds thrive in full sun and in rich to average moist soil. *V. altissima* grows equally well in marshes and other wet sites. *V. noveboracensis* will tolerate wet soil, and both species will tolerate partial shade. Ironweeds have sturdy stems that rarely require staking. Propagate by seed, cuttings, or division.

Veronicastrum is a perennial found on stream banks and moist prairies of the eastern United States. It produces showy, erect clusters of narrow flower spikes atop tall stems from mid- to late summer, making it a valuable performer at the back of a herbaceous border.

Selected species: *V. virginicum* [also listed as *Veronica virginica*] (Culver's root, bowman's root)—strong, unbranched stems up to 6 feet tall with white or pale blue flowers in spikes up to 9 inches long arranged in candelabra-like clusters at the top of stems. The sharply toothed 6-inch leaves fan out horizontally from the stem in symmetrical whorls. The variety 'Roseum' has pale pink blossoms.

Growing conditions and maintenance: *V. virginicum* is easy to grow in full sun or light shade in moist, well-drained soil. The stems require no staking. Propagate by seed, cuttings, or root division.

Viola
(vy-O-la)
VIOLET

Viola pedata

Hardiness: *Zones 3-8*

Flowering season: *spring*

Height: *3 to 16 inches*

Flower color: *blue, violet, purple, white*

Soil: *moist to dry, well-drained*

Light: *full sun to full shade*

Violets produce dainty five-petaled flowers in white and shades from blue to purple and often have dark purple or yellow markings. The following species are perennials native to the eastern or central United States and bloom in late spring. They are useful as ground covers in woodland gardens, under shrubs, or at the front of shaded borders.

Selected species: *V. affinis* (Le Conte's violet)—6 to 10 inches tall bearing violet flowers with a white throat in late spring and glossy heart-shaped leaves. Each of the three lower petals has a tuft of hairs, or beard; Zones 3-8. *V. canadensis* (Canada violet)—8 to 16 inches tall bearing fragrant white flowers with yellow centers and purple veins in mid- and late spring. The erect clump has dark green heart-shaped leaves; Zones 3-8. *V. conspersa* (American dog violet)—4 to 6 inches tall with pale blue to deep purple flowers in late spring and small heart-shaped leaves with rounded teeth; Zones 3-7. *V. papilionacea* [also called *V. sororia*] (common blue violet, woolly blue violet)—3 to 8 inches tall with dark blue or purple flowers with white centers from mid- to late spring. The two lateral petals have beards; Zones 3-8. *V. pedata* (birdfoot violet)—4- to 10-inch-tall clump of deeply divided leaves. Its large pansylike flowers, up to 1½ inches across, range from dark lavender to white and are sometimes bicolored; Zones 3-8. *V. rostrata* (beaked violet, long-spurred violet)—leafy stems 4 to 16 inches tall and lilac-purple flowers from mid- to late spring. The lowest petal extends backward in a prominent ½-inch-long spur that curves upward; Zones 4-7.

Viola canadensis

Growing conditions and maintenance: *V. affinis, V. canadensis,* and *V. rostrata* require rich, moist soils and are partial to full shade. They benefit from the incorporation of leaf mold or other organic matter into the soil prior to planting and do best with a winter mulch. *V. conspersa* and *V. papilionacea* also need partial to full shade but tolerate a wider range of soil moisture, from damp to dry. *V. pedata* thrives in full sun and sandy soil; good drainage is essential. Propagate by seed. *V. pedata* can also be propagated by root cuttings and the other five species by division.

Yucca
(YUK-a)
YUCCA

Yucca filamentosa

Hardiness: *Zones 4-10*

Flowering season: *summer*

Height: *4½ to 12 feet*

Flower color: *white, greenish white*

Soil: *dry, well-drained*

Light: *full sun*

Yuccas have bold, stiff, sword-shaped basal leaves with a sharply pointed tip. Their flowers are borne on a stalk that rises high above the leaves. These drought-tolerant perennials are native to dry plains, sand hills, and prairies.

Selected species: *Y. filamentosa* (Adam's-needle)—native of southeastern United States with a rosette of blue-green leaves 2 to 3 feet long. The leaf margins have long curly threads. The 2-inch white flowers bloom on a stalk as much as 12 feet high and are followed by tan seed pods; Zones 5-10. *Y. glauca* (soapweed)—western native with a 3-foot clump of slender pale green leaves edged with white and threads along the margins. Fragrant greenish white flowers bloom on a 4½-foot stalk and are followed by cream-colored pods; Zones 4-8.

Growing conditions and maintenance: Grow yuccas in full sun in light, well-drained soil. They tolerate drought exceptionally well. Propagate by seed, offsets, or rhizome cuttings.

Zauschneria
(zawsh-NEER-ee-a)
CALIFORNIA FUCHSIA

Zauschneria californica

Hardiness: *Zones 8-10*

Flowering season: *summer to fall*

Height: *12 to 36 inches*

Flower color: *red*

Soil: *moist, well-drained to dry*

Light: *full sun*

Zauschnerias are shrubby perennials native to the western United States, where they are found in rocky slopes and canyons. They spread rapidly by rhizomes to form broad mats that make fine ground covers. Their large fuchsialike flowers attract hummingbirds.

Selected species: *Z. californica* (California fuchsia)—broad shrubby perennial with much-branched stems 12 to 36 inches in height and woolly gray-green foliage. Trumpet-shaped, brilliant scarlet flowers 2½ inches long bloom from late summer through fall. *Z. latifolia* [also called *Epilobium canum* ssp. *latifolium*] (California fuchsia, hummingbird trumpet)—compact shrubby plant up to 2 feet tall with trumpet-shaped scarlet flowers from early summer through fall.

Growing conditions and maintenance: Grow *Z. californica* in well-drained soil. It tolerates drought. *Z. latifolia* prefers a moist soil. Both species require full sun. Mulch for winter protection and pinch back stems to promote bushiness. Propagate by seed, fall cuttings, or root divisions in early spring.

Zephyranthes
(ze-fi-RANTH-eez)
RAIN LILY

Zephyranthes atamasco

Hardiness: *Zones 7-10*

Flowering season: *spring*

Height: *8 to 15 inches*

Flower color: *white, pink*

Soil: *moist, rich*

Light: *partial shade*

This small bulbous perennial is found growing in colonies in damp woods and bottom lands in the southeastern United States, where it flowers profusely in spring. Rain lilies can be naturalized in the dappled shade of a woodland garden or planted near the front of a partially shaded border.

Selected species: *Z. atamasco* (atamasco lily, rain lily)—showy funnel-shaped white flowers 3 inches long on leafless stalks about 1 foot tall in mid- to late spring. The flowers are sometimes tinged with purple and turn pink as they age. The thick, shiny, grasslike leaves form a clump 8 to 15 inches tall.

Growing conditions and maintenance: *Z. atamasco* grows best where it will receive a few hours of direct sun each day and is shaded for the rest of the day. It prefers a moist, acid loam or sandy soil. In colder climates, dig the bulbs in fall and store them indoors in a cool location over winter. Propagate by seed, basal offsets, or division of mature clumps.

Zinnia
(ZIN-ee-a)
ZINNIA

Zinnia grandiflora

Hardiness: *Zones 4-10*

Flowering season: *spring through fall*

Height: *6 to 8 inches*

Flower color: *yellow, white*

Soil: *well-drained to dry*

Light: *full sun to partial shade*

Most gardeners are familiar only with annual zinnias. The two perennial species described here are native to the central and southwestern United States, where they are commonly found along roadsides and on dry slopes. Both of these wildflowers bloom profusely for months and are attractive in rock gardens and on dry banks, where they help control erosion.

Selected species: *Z. acerosa* (dwarf white zinnia)—much-branched, shrubby plant 6 inches tall with ¾-inch white flowers with yellow centers. The narrow, silvery leaves are less than an inch long; Zones 8-10. *Z. grandiflora* (little golden zinnia, prairie zinnia, Rocky Mountain zinnia)—1½-inch yellow flowers with red or green centers on an 8-inch mound of needlelike, nearly evergreen, foliage; Zones 4-10.

Growing conditions and maintenance: Both species require well-drained to dry average soil and are very tolerant of drought and heat. Propagate by seed sown in spring or fall. Young plants can also be divided in spring.

Acknowledgments and Picture Credits

The editors wish to thank the following individuals and institutions for their valuable assistance in the preparation of this volume:
Scott Aker, U.S. National Arboretum, Washington, D.C.; Ethel Dutky, Department of Botany, University of Maryland, College Park; Cheryl Lowe, New England Wildflower Society, Framingham, Massachusetts.

Bibliography

Books:

Aiken, George D. *Pioneering with Wildflowers.* Brattleboro, Vt.: Alan C. Hood, 1978.

The American Horticultural Society Encyclopedia of Gardening. New York: Dorling Kindersley, 1993.

Art, Henry W.:

A Garden of Wildflowers. Pownal, Vt.: Storey Communications, 1986.

The Wildflower Gardener's Guide: California, Desert Southwest, and Northern Mexico Edition (Garden Way Publishing). Pownal, Vt.: Storey Communications, 1990.

The Wildflower Gardener's Guide: Midwest, Great Plains, and Canadian Prairies Edition (Garden Way Publishing). Pownal, Vt.: Storey Communications, 1991.

The Wildflower Gardener's Guide: Northeast, Mid-Atlantic, Great Lakes, and Eastern Canada Edition (Garden Way Publishing). Pownal, Vt.: Storey Communications, 1987.

The Wildflower Gardener's Guide: Pacific Northwest, Rocky Mountain, and Western Canada Edition (Garden Way Publishing). Pownal, Vt.: Storey Communications, 1990.

The Audubon Society Field Guide to North American Wildflowers: Eastern Region. New York: Alfred A. Knopf, 1983.

Austin, Richard L. *Wild Gardening.* New York: Simon and Schuster, 1986.

Borror, Donald J., Charles A. Triplehorn, and Norman F. Johnson. *Study of Insects* (6th ed.). Fort Worth, Tex.: Harcourt Brace College Publishers, 1992.

Bubel, Nancy. *52 Weekend Garden Projects.* Emmaus, Pa.: Rodale Press, 1992.

Buczacki, Stefan. *The Plant Care Manual.* New York: Crown Publishers, 1993.

Burn, Barbara. *North American Wildflowers* (The National Audubon Society Collection Nature series). New York: Crown Publishers, 1984.

Clausen, Ruth Rogers, and Nicolas H. Ekstrom. *Perennials for American Gardens.* New York: Random House, 1989.

Darke, Rick. *For Your Garden: Ornamental Grasses.* New York: Michael Friedman Publishing Group, 1994.

Diekelmann, John, and Robert Schuster. *Natural Landscaping.* New York: McGraw-Hill, 1982.

Emery, Dara E. *Seed Propagation of Native California Plants.* Santa Barbara, Calif.: Santa Barbara Botanic Garden, 1988.

Ferreniea, Viki. *Wildflowers in Your Garden.* New York: Random House, 1993.

Fichter, George S. *Insect Pests.* Racine, Wis.: Western Publishing, 1966.

Garden Pests and Diseases. Menlo Park, Calif.: Sunset Publishing, 1993.

Giles, F. A., Rebecca McIntosh Keith, and Donald C. Saupe. *Herbaceous Perennials.* Reston, Va.: Reston Publishing, 1980.

Greenlee, John. *The Encyclopedia of Ornamental Grasses.* Emmaus, Pa.: Rodale Press, 1992.

Holmes, Roger (Ed.). *Taylor's Guide to Natural Gardening.* New York: Houghton Mifflin, 1993.

House, Homer D. *Wildflowers of the United States* (Vol. 1, *Northeastern States).* New York: McGraw-Hill, 1965.

Imes, Rick. *Wildflowers.* Emmaus, Pa.: Rodale Press, 1992.

Johnson, Eric A., and Scott Millard. *How to Grow the Wildflowers.* Tucson, Ariz.: Ironwood Press, 1993.

Johnson, Lady Bird, and Carlton B. Lees. *Wildflowers across America.* New York: Abbeville Press, 1993.

Jones, Samuel B., Jr., and Leonard E. Foote. *Gardening with Native Wild Flowers.* Portland, Ore.: Timber Press, 1990.

Kruckeberg, Arthur R. *Gardening with Native Plants of the Pacific Northwest.* Seattle: University of Seattle Press, 1989.

Landscaping with Wildflowers and Native Plants. San Ramon, Calif.: Ortho Books, 1984.

Liberty Hyde Bailey Hortorium. *Hortus Third: A Concise Dictionary of Plants Cultivated in the United States and Canada.* New York: Macmillan, 1977.

Loewer, Peter. *The Wild Gardener.* Harrisburg, Pa.: Stackpole Books, 1991.

Martin, Laura C. *The Wildflower Meadow Book.* Charlotte, N.C.: Fast & McMillan Publishers, 1986.

Michalak, Patricia S. *Controlling Pests and Diseases* (Rodale's Successful Organic Gardening series). Emmaus, Pa.: Rodale Press, 1994.

Mickel, John T. *Ferns for American Gardens.* New York: Macmillan, 1994.

Miles, Bebe. *Wildflower Perennials for Your Garden.* New York: Hawthorn Books, 1976.

National Council of State Garden Clubs. *Resources on Wildflower Propagation.* John S. Swift, 1981.

The National Wildflower Research Center's Wildflowers Handbook (2d ed.). Stillwater, Minn.: Voyageur Press, 1992.

Nokes, Jill. *How to Grow Native Plants of Texas and the Southwest.* Austin, Tex.: Texas Monthly Press, 1986.

The Ortho Book of Gardening Basics. San Ramon, Calif.: Ortho Books, 1991.

Ottesen, Carole. *The Native Plant Primer.* New York: Harmony Books, 1995.

Perennials: 1001 Gardening Questions Answered. Written by Maggie Oster and the Editors of Garden Way Publishing. Pownal, Vt.: Storey Communications, 1989.

Pfadt, Robert E. (Ed.). *Fundamentals of Applied Entomology* (3d ed.). New York: Macmillan, 1978.

Phillips, Harry R. *Growing and Propagating Wild Flowers.* Chapel Hill: University of North Carolina Press, 1985.

Phillips, Judith. *Southwestern Landscaping with Native Plants.* Santa Fe: Museum of New Mexico Press, 1987.

Pirone, Pascal P. *Diseases and Pests of Ornamental Plants.* New York: John Wiley & Sons, 1978.

Plant Care (The Best of *Fine Gardening* series). Newtown, Conn.: Taunton Press, 1994.

Reilly, Ann. *Park's Success with Seeds.* Greenwood, S.C.: Geo. W. Park Seed Co., 1978.

Rickett, Harold William. *Wildflowers of the United States* (6 vols.). New York: McGraw-Hill, 1965-1973.

Scott, Jane. *Field and Forest.* New York: Walker, 1992.

Smith, J. Robert, and Beatrice S. Smith. *Prairie Gardens: 70 Native Plants You Can Grow in Town or Country.* Madison: University of Wisconsin Press, 1980.

Smith, Miranda, and Anna Carr. *Garden Insect, Disease, and Weed Identification Guide.* Emmaus, Pa.: Rodale Press, 1988.

Sperka, Marie. *Growing Wildflowers.* New York: Harper & Row, 1973.

Springer, Lauren. *The Undaunt-*

ed Garden. Golden, Colo.: Fulcrum Publishing, 1994.

Stokes, Donald, and Lillian Stokes. *The Wildflower Book: From the Rockies West.* Boston: Little, Brown, 1993.

Tarling, Thomasina. *The Container Garden* (The Wayside Gardens Collection). New York: Sterling Publishing, 1994.

Taylor, Kathryn S., and Stephen F. Hamblin. *Handbook of Wild Flower Cultivation.* New York: Macmillan, 1963.

Taylor's Guide to Natural Gardening. Boston: Houghton Mifflin, 1993.

Tenenbaum, Frances. *Gardening with Wildflowers.* New York: Ballantine Books, 1986.

Toop, Edgar W., and Sara Williams. *Perennials for the Prairies.* Edmonton, Alberta: University of Alberta, 1991.

Turcotte, Patricia L. *Perennials for the Backyard Gardener.* Woodstock, Vt.: Countryman Press, 1993.

Wasowski, Sally, with Andy Wasowski:
Gardening with Native Plants of the South. Dallas, Tex.: Taylor Publishing, 1994.
Requiem for a Lawnmower. Dallas, Tex.: Taylor Publishing, 1992.

Westcott, Cynthia:
The Gardener's Bug Book (3d ed.). Garden City, N.Y.: Doubleday, 1964.
Plant Disease Handbook (3d ed.). New York: Van Nostrand Reinhold, 1971.

Western Garden Book. Menlo Park, Calif.: Sunset Publishing, 1995.

Wilson, Jim:
Landscaping with Container Plants. Boston: Houghton Mifflin, 1990.
Landscaping with Wildflowers. Boston: Houghton Mifflin, 1992.

Wilson, William H. W. *Landscaping with Wildflowers and Native Plants.* San Ramon, Calif.: Ortho Books, 1984.

Woods, Christopher. *Encyclopedia of Perennials.* New York: Facts on File, 1992.

Wyman, Donald. *Wyman's Gardening Encyclopedia* (2d ed.). New York: Macmillan, 1986.

Yepsen, Roger B., Jr. (Ed.). *The Encyclopedia of Natural Insect and Disease Control.* Emmaus, Pa.: Rodale Press, 1984.

Young, James A., and Cheryl G. Young. *Collecting, Processing, and Germinating Seeds of Wildland Plants.* Portland, Ore.: Timber Press, 1986.

Periodicals:

Bender, Steve:
"Beauty in the Bog." *Southern Living,* 1990.
"Fringed Campion—Back from the Brink." *Southern Living,* June 1994.

Bir, Richard E. "Woodies from the Wetlands." *American Horticulturist,* April 1994.

Borland, Jim. "Soils for Troughs and Other Containers." *Bulletin of the American Rock Garden Society,* Spring 1994.

Brune, Rick. "Maintenance for a Prairie Garden." *Rocky Mountain Gardener,* Spring 1994.

Collins, Leo. "New to the Garden?" *Native Notes,* Fall 1994.

"Container Basics." *Southern California Gardener,* January/February 1995.

Cox, Jeff. "Something Wild." *Organic Gardening,* September/October 1990.

Curless, Chris. "Renovating a Perennial Bed." *Fine Gardening,* May/June 1994.

Delaney, Denise D. "Containerize Native Summer Color." *Wildflower,* July/August 1994.

Gardner, Rob. "Return of the Natives." *Carolina Gardener,* March/April 1995.

Kane, Mark. "Soil Amendments: How Lime, Sulfur, and Organic Matter Improve Soil." *Fine Gardening,* July/August 1991.

Lovejoy, Ann. "Gardening Where We Live." *American Horticulturist,* June 1990.

Mastalerz, John W. "A Mulch Primer." *Fine Gardening,* January/February 1993.

Oxley, F. M. "Wildflower Focus" (editorial). *Wildflower,* Fall/Winter 1993.

Potter, Charles H. "Drainage in Solid-Bottom Plant Containers." *Flower and Garden,* December/January 1993.

Rouse, Wesley. "Three-Season Container Plantings." *Fine Gardening,* May/June 1994.

Taylor, Patricia A. "Spring Woodland Perennials." *Flower and Garden,* February/March 1991.

Wilson, Jim. "Quick Color from Annual Wildflowers." *Carolina Gardener,* January/February 1995.

Other Sources:

Art, Henry W. "Creating a Wildflower Meadow." Bulletin A-102. Pownal, Vt.: Storey Communications, 1988.

Beal, Ernest O. "A Manual of Marsh and Aquatic Vascular Plants of North Carolina." North Carolina Agricultural Experiment Station, 1977.

"Creating a Wildlife Garden." Pamphlet. Austin, Tex.: National Wildflower Research Center.

"Gardening and Landscaping with Native Plants." Pamphlet. Austin, Tex.: National Wildflower Research Center.

"Gardening with Wildflowers and Native Plants." *Plants and Gardens, Brooklyn Botanic Garden Record,* 1990.

"North Carolina Native Plant Propagation Handbook." North Carolina Wild Flower Preservation Society, Spring 1977.

Slater, Michael. "Trough Construction." Bulletin. Denver: American Rock Garden Society, Spring 1994.

Weigel, C. A., and L. G. Baumhofer. "Handbook on Insect Enemies of Flowers and Shrubs." Miscellaneous Publication No. 626. Washington, D.C.: U.S. Government Printing Office, 1948.

"Wildflower Meadow Gardening." Pamphlet. Austin, Tex.: National Wildflower Research Center, n.d.